D0271792

Total War

Also by Michael Jones

The King's Mother
Bosworth 1485 – Psychology of a Battle
Agincourt 1415 – A Battlefield Guide
Stalingrad: How the Red Army Triumphed
Leningrad: State of Siege
The Retreat: Hitler's First Defeat

Total War

From Stalingrad to Berlin

MICHAEL JONES

JOHN MURRAY

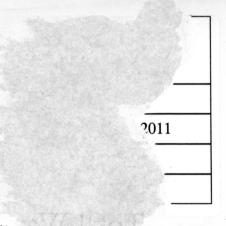

First published in Gre.. ... ..., jOhn Murray (Publishers)
An Hachette UK Company

I

Maps drawn by Rodney Paull

A CIP catalogue record for this title is available from the British Library

Hardback ISBN 978-1-84854-229-7
Trade paperback ISBN 978-1-84854-230-3
Ebook ISBN 978-1-84854-246-4

Typeset in 12.5/15 Monotype Bembo by Servis Filmsetting Ltd, Stockport, Cheshire

Printed and bound by Clays Ltd, St Ives plc

John Murray policy is to use papers that are natural, renewable and recyclable products and
made from wood grown in sustainable forests. The logging and manufacturing processes are
expected to conform to the environmental regulations of the country of origin.

John Murray (Publishers)
338 Euston Road
London NW1 3BH

www.johnmurray.co.uk

I Saw the Battle

Believe me, I saw fighting I could not have imagined – even
   in my dreams,
As shell after shell shrouded the mound of bodies in smoke
And jagged metal traced our fates with its claw –
Ripping all asunder,
Carving black mushroom clouds in the sky.

Believe me, I saw the fighting, and felt its chill
As death marched alongside us
And I will remember that fighting for ever –
As it closes its hands around my throat
And I wake at night, helpless,
A boat caught in a whirlpool, unable to break free of its swirl.

But I am no longer afraid.
I survived at the gates of hell –
I saw the battle.

Mikhail Borisov

Contents

List of Illustrations

29. Fighting for Poznan, early February 1945
30. Soviet troops in Königsberg, 9 April 1945
31. Lieutenant General Vasily Chuikov of the Eighth Guards Army at his command post. The heroic commander at Stalingrad was now closing in on Berlin
32. A Red Army mortar company fights its way through Berlin's suburbs, 22 April 1945
33. A street in central Berlin after its occupation by the Red Army. Food wagons have been brought up to feed the civilian population
34. Red Army lieutenant Alexei Kovalev holds the Red flag aloft over the Reichstag. His identity was subsequently suppressed for nearly fifty years

Acknowledgements: 1–2, kindly provided by Andrei Toom, from the Antokolsky family archive; 3–5, 8–10, 13–16, 18–24, 29–33 from the RIA Novosti Picture Collection; 6–7, from the private collection of Mikhail Borisov; 11–12, 17 and 25–26 from the collection of the Blavatnik Archive Foundation; 27, courtesy of the Yad Vashem Archive, Jerusalem; 28, from private collection of Mark Slavin; 34 Yevgeny Khaldei/Getty Images.

List of Maps

Preface

Combat on the Second World War's eastern front was on a scale unparalleled in modern warfare. More than eight million Red Army soldiers died in four years of vicious fighting between Nazi Germany and the Soviet Union, and the total number of casualties among Russia's soldiers and civilians has been estimated at 27 million. Those who survived were permanently marked by what they had endured. In this book I seek to pay tribute to the remarkable courage of these Russian fighters. I draw on a wide variety of sources – letters, diaries and personal interviews – and tell the human story of the Red Army as it turned the tables on the Germans at Stalingrad and then fought its way to Berlin, the capital of Hitler's Reich.

This book has grown out of my earlier works on Stalingrad, Leningrad and the battle for Moscow but is far broader in scope. It is not intended as a conventional military narrative – rather, its focus is on the Red Army's psychological experience: the human cost of fighting this terrible war. It takes the reader on a journey of unfolding horror, as Soviet soldiers witnessed genocide in the Ukraine and Belorussia and uncovered the truth about the Holocaust. The focal point of the book is the Red Army's liberation of Auschwitz on 27 January 1945. Russian veterans can never forget what they found there. But the response of some Soviet troops when they reached German soil – committing a series of atrocities against the civilian population – was equally appalling. In this book, Russian fighters are candid about the rapes, murders and looting committed by their own side. These actions besmirched the heroism of the Red Army.

But the achievement remains a heroic one nonetheless. Between brittle Soviet propaganda – never able to acknowledge that victory against the Nazis was a flawed triumph – and Western cynicism, which denigrates the unflinching courage of the vast majority of Red Army fighters, lies a remarkable human story, one of astonishing bravery, brutalizing depravity and a deeply moving struggle against the corrosive cruelty of the war. For while some Russian soldiers succumbed to this cruelty, revelling in atrocities they themselves committed against the weak and the unprotected, many others pulled back from the brink. 'Our army was battling for its very soul,' one veteran said. It was a battle never fully won. But the very fact it was fought at all makes the story powerfully redemptive.

It is a pleasure to acknowledge the help I have received in enabling these human voices to come alive again. Julie Chervinsky, the director of the Blavatnik Foundation Archive in New York, has kindly given me full access to this valuable collection of Jewish Red Army letters, diaries and testimonies. Artem Drabkin, editor and compiler of the 'I Remember' section of www.russianbattlefield.com, has been an unfailing source of encouragement, as has the Russian Council of War Veterans in Moscow, which facilitated many of my interviews. I have acted as a consultant to the RIA Novosti History Project and the Russia Today TV series on the eastern front, and both these organizations have allowed me to draw upon their own research material. Veterans Anatoly Mereshko, Mark Slavin and Mikhail Borisov have given up weeks of their time in support of this project, and Mikhail Borisov has generously given me unlimited access to his collection of war poetry.

Colonel David Glantz, Professors Oleg Budnitskii and Maxim Shrayer have generously shared their expertise on Red Army war experience. My Moscow-based researcher and translator Lena Yakovleva has helped me in countless meetings with veterans and also provided valuable additional material from her own interview transcripts. Caroline Walton has assisted with translations of Red Army letters, memoirs and poetry. Further acknowledgements are to be found in the Endnotes, but I would particularly like to thank Andrei Toom, grandson of Soviet war correspondent and poet Pavel Antokolsky, for making his entire family archive available to me.

Antokolsky's poem 'Son' commemorated the loss of his own son's life in battle. It also spoke for a generation mutilated by war – facing a level of hardship and suffering hard to imagine in the West. In *Total War* I want to evoke the story of this loss, on the hard road from Stalingrad from Berlin. Without this sacrifice, Nazi Germany would never have been vanquished.

The Soviet Vistula-Oder Offensive
January 1945

Front line January 1945
Kreigsmarine activities

SWEDEN

BALTIC SEA

ARMY GROUP NORTH

Courland Pocket

2nd Baltic Front

Memel Pocket

Memel

1st Baltic Front

Samland Peninsula

Pillau

Königsberg

Danzig

ARMY GROUP CENTRE

3rd Belorussian Front

Elbing

EAST PRUSSIA

Kolberg

POMERANIA

Narew

ARMY GROUP VISTULA

WARTHELAND

Thorn

ARMY GROUP A

2nd Belorussian Front

Stettin

Vistula

Bug

Berlin

Kustrin

Poznan

Warthe

Warsaw

1st Belorussian Front

Frankfurt an der Oder

LOWER SILESIA

Magnuszew Bridgehead

Oder

Lodz

Pilica

Pulawy Bridgehead

Lublin

Breslau

POLAND

Kielce

UPPER SILESIA

ARMY GROUP HEINRICI

Sandomierz Bridgehead

Sudeten Mountains

Oder

Auschwitz

Krakow

1st Ukrainian Front

Prague

0   150 kms

0   200 miles

SLOVAKIA

West Beskid Mountains

4th Ukrainian Front

Timeline

1941

22 June: Hitler launches Operation Barbarossa – German invasion of the Soviet Union. The Führer's allies, Italy and Romania, declare war on Russia.

26–27 June: Finland and Hungary also declare war on Soviet Union.

28 June: Germans capture Minsk, capital of Belorussia.

8 July: 290,000 Red Army soldiers surrounded south-west of Minsk.

28 August: Tallinn, capital of Estonia, falls to Wehrmacht.

8 September: Leningrad cut off from rest of Soviet Union.

16 September: Germans encircle 665,000 Soviet troops near Kiev.

17 September: Compulsory military training introduced for all males in Soviet Union between ages of 16 and 50.

2 October: Germans launch Operation Typhoon – assault on Moscow.

13 October: Twin encirclement battles of Bryansk and Vyazma – Wehrmacht captures another 750,000 prisoners.

19 October: State of siege proclaimed in Moscow.

13–15 November: After delays caused by autumn rainy season, German offensive against Soviet capital resumes.

27 November: Advance units of Wehrmacht less than 30 km from Moscow.

5–6 December: German advance is halted and Soviet counter-offensive begins.

19 December: Hitler appoints himself commander-in-chief of the Wehrmacht.

1942

8 January: Red Army launches general offensive along entire front.

3 February: Germans encircle Soviet Twenty-Ninth Army near Rzhev.

8 February: Soviet Thirty-Third Army surrounded at Yukhnov.

19 March: Russian Second Shock Army encircled in Volkhov pocket.

20 April: End of Soviet general offensive. Germans pushed back up to 320 km from Moscow, but front stays intact.

16 May: Collapse of Red Army forces in Crimea – 176,000 casualties.

29 May: Battle of Kharkov ends with 230,000 Soviet casualties.

28 June: German Army Group South begins Operation Blue.

2 July: Soviet Second Shock Army destroyed at Volkhov – 33,000 casualties.

28 July: Stalin issues Order 227 – 'Not a Step Back!' order.

23 August: German Sixth Army reaches Volga north of Stalingrad. Richthofen's Eighth Air Fleet bombs city.

26 August: General Georgi Zhukov appointed Deputy Supreme Commander of Red Army.

14 September: Germans reach centre of Stalingrad.

30 September: Wehrmacht resumes advance in Caucasus.

14 October: German offensive at Stalingrad splits Soviet Sixty-Second Army in two.

6 November: Failure of last Wehrmacht attempt to reach Caucasus oilfields.

11 November: Final German assault at Stalingrad – Soviet 138th Rifle Division is cut off on Volga embankment.

19 November: Soviet South-Western and Don Fronts launch northern pincer of Stalingrad counter-offensive, Operation Uranus.

20 November: Soviet Stalingrad Front launches southern pincer of counter-offensive.

23 November: Red Army troops meet at Kalach surrounding German and Romanian forces at Stalingrad.

12 December: Field Marshal Erich von Manstein launches attempt to relieve Stalingrad.

24 December: German relief effort fails.

1943

10 January: Soviet forces launch Operation Saturn, or Ring, reduction of Stalingrad pocket.

18 January: Red Army breaks German blockade of Leningrad and establishes land route to city.

31 January: Commander of German Sixth Army, newly promoted Field Marshal Friedrich Paulus, surrenders to Red Army.

2 February: All German resistance in Stalingrad ceases.

12–15 March: Manstein recaptures Kharkov.

15 April: Hitler issues directive for 'Citadel' offensive against Kursk salient.

5 July: German Army Groups Centre and South commence Operation Citadel.

10 July: Allied landings in Sicily.

12 July: Great tank battle at Prokhorovka. Result is inconclusive, but following day Hitler abandons Operation Citadel.

5 August: Orel and Belgorod recaptured by Red Army.

23 August: Soviet forces take Kharkov, bringing Kursk counter-offensive to an end.

22 September: Bukrin bridgehead established on River Dnieper.

14 October: Zaporozhye regained by Soviet forces and its giant dam saved from demolition.

6 November: Kiev falls to Red Army.

28 November–1 December: The Tehran Conference – first meeting of the 'big three': Churchill, Roosevelt and Stalin.

1944

27 January: Siege of Leningrad finally ended.

16 February: Fighting at Korsun (Ukraine) culminates with about 50,000 Germans killed, another 18,000 captured.

1 March: German troops pushed back 210 km from Leningrad.

19 March: Soviet Sixty-Fifth Army discovers 'typhoid camps' at Ozarichi.

26 March: Red Army troops reach Romanian border.

10 April: Odessa recaptured.

9 May: Liberation of Sevastopol.

22 June: Operation Bagration launched against German Army Group Centre.

3 July: Minsk recaptured by Red Army.

23 July: Soviet forces liberate extermination camp at Majdanek, near Lublin.

28 July: First Belorussian Front reaches River Vistula near Warsaw.

1 August: Polish Home Army launches Warsaw Uprising.

23 August: Romania renounces alliance with Germany.

5 September: Finland agrees to ceasefire with Soviet Union.

9 October: First Baltic Front cuts Army Group North off in Courland.

16–22 October: Third Belorussian Front enters East Prussia.

7 November: Second Ukrainian Front reaches south-eastern suburbs of Budapest.

1945

12 January: First Belorussian and First Ukrainian Fronts open Vistula–Oder offensive.

27 January: Red Army liberates Auschwitz.

4–11 February: Churchill, Roosevelt and Stalin meet at Yalta Conference.

22 February: German garrison at Poznan surrenders.

6–9 April: Red Army storms Königsberg.

16 April: First Belorussian Front attacks German defence line on Seelow Heights.

21 April: Soviet forces enter suburbs of Berlin.

30 April: Hitler commits suicide. Red Army assault groups fight their way into Reichstag.

2 May: Berlin garrison surrenders.

8 May: German Armed Forces surrender unconditionally at Karlshorst.

9 May: Army Group North surrenders in Courland.

Introduction

I AM STANDING on Poklonnaya Hill, looking at the Museum of the Great Patriotic War in Moscow. Ahead of me is the main victory monument, a granite obelisk depicting scenes from the conflict. Its design has breathtaking boldness. It is 141.8 metres high, symbolizing the 1,418 days and nights of the war. At the 100-metre mark is a flying, winged figure. It is Nika, the goddess of victory. She holds a garland of glory in her right hand; two bronze victory angels sound victory trumpets at her feet. I am struck by its religious theme. The monument and museum were created four years after the collapse of the Soviet Union and the communist state. They honour the fiftieth anniversary of the ending of the Second World War in the west and the victory over Nazi Germany. A terrifying evil was destroyed. At the foot of the monument is a bronze statue of St George, striking at a coiled dragon with his spear.

Inside the museum are a mass of halls and a formidable array of exhibitions. Beautifully painted dioramas illustrate key battles and sieges of the war. But it is the Hall of Memory that I return to. The lighting is subdued and Mozart's *Requiem* plays softly in the background. The walls are reddish-brown – the colour of human blood. A white marble figure is bowed in sorrow and grief. Thousands of crystal pendants hang from the ceiling. They symbolize tears – crying for the dead of the Great Patriotic War. There were 27 million of them, soldiers and civilians. The suffering was unimaginable.

Every year on 22 June, the anniversary of the war's beginning, veterans gather here in a candlelit ceremony to honour the dead. It was a war on a vast scale, and one that made colossal demands on its participants. Vladimir Hotenkov was a country lad who couldn't stand the sight of blood. 'When my mother asked me to kill a hen, I just couldn't do it,' he said. But faced by a terrible invader, the hitherto squeamish Hotenkov found incredible resilience. In 1943, at Kursk, German tanks 'ironed' his trench, rolling over it, then reversing to bury its defenders in the collapsed earth. Hotenkov summoned the will to push his way out of the clay soil. Astounded soldiers in the next trench (about to be 'ironed' themselves) remember him clambering out, clutching two Molotov cocktails, and blowing up their assailant.

Russian soldiers were expected to stand and fight: penalties for unauthorized retreat were severe. With the ending of the communist regime, many veterans are frank about this. Jacob Studenikov manned a lone machine gun against a company of advancing Germans at Ponyri, on Kursk's northern salient. When asked about his heroism, he retorted: 'What was I supposed to do? If I surrendered to the Germans I would die anyway; if I tried to retreat, I would end up before a military tribunal.' Then came a glimpse of something else beneath his cynicism. He added forcefully: 'I was fighting for my own land.'

The 22nd of June 2011 is the seventieth anniversary of the Great Patriotic War's beginning, and the last major anniversary that many of these veterans will see. I follow their story from Stalingrad, where the tide of war turned, to Berlin, where that war ended. Soviet lieutenant Anatoly Mereshko described a vital change of mood at Stalingrad, where slogans such as 'Not a Step Back!' and 'There is no Land for us beyond the Volga!' took on a meaning, both emotional and spiritual, far beyond defence of the communist state: 'We were no longer fighting for a city, but for each little piece of land, every bush and river,' Mereshko said. He fought all the way to the Reichstag, and was present in the room where the surrender of Berlin took place.

Standing in the Hall of Memory, amid its hanging crystal tears, I struggle to comprehend the scale of it all. 'This was a brutalizing war', veteran Mikhail Shinder acknowledged, 'that brought out the very best and the very worst human beings are capable of.' We now know the very worst about the Red Army – its killings, lootings and rapes. We know less about the horror it faced and the bravery of many of its soldiers. The victory over Nazi Germany was a tarnished one. But we did not have to endure what the Red Army endured. On this seventieth anniversary I want to rekindle its human experience through letters, diaries and personal testimonies – 'the dark poetry of the war', as one veteran put it. I want to portray its suffering – what the troops saw and encountered. And above all, I want to honour the bravery of the vast majority of its soldiers. Their struggle and eventual victory over Nazi Germany must never be forgotten.

I

A Year of Living Dangerously

ON 22 JUNE 1942 the war between Germany and the Soviet Union was one year old. For a year, millions of soldiers on either side had fought a series of massive battles. The toll in casualties was on an unimaginable scale. And no end to the war was in sight.

As the first anniversary of the war approached, Pavel Antokolsky said goodbye to his son Vladimir at Moscow's Kiev Station. It was a beautiful June morning. For an hour they had walked together in the square in front of the railway station. They strolled up and down, making small talk. Vladimir was eighteen, had completed his period of military training and was now leaving for the front. As the time for departure approached, Antokolsky felt his son becoming more distant. Both became aware of it at the same time, and Vladimir turned to his father apologetically. 'You know,' he said, 'I seem to have picked up the habit of instantly switching to another time and place.' His comrades were already gathering on the station platform ahead of him. Then his voice changed. 'Father,' he continued, 'let's say goodbye like men'. The two solemnly shook hands, and Vladimir strode forward to join his fellow soldiers. He turned, smiled, and waved his cap – before disappearing into the throng.

Later that day Antokolsky wrote in his diary: 'At seven in the morning I saw my little boy off at Kiev Station. Towards the appointed hour there converged from all sides many like him, young men with identical black collar tabs. All of them seemed splendid lads. They were accompanied by solemn fathers and mothers, hushed and pale. Some of the soldiers, a very few, were seen off by girls with branches of lilac blossom. We went out on to the platform. With a roar, the company descended upon the empty green wagons of a suburban train – like a school party on an excursion.' At the moment of departure Antokolsky had struggled to keep his composure, and somehow his son instinctively sensed it. 'The train began to move, faster and faster,' the father concluded, 'and for one last time I glimpsed the pale, delicate and distraught face of my dear child.'

Antokolsky, a war correspondent, well knew the costs of the terrible struggle with Germany and the danger his son would face. A year earlier, in the summer months of 1941, the German Wehrmacht had carried all before it, winning a series of dazzling victories against demoralized Soviet forces. The enemy's mood was one of heady euphoria as town after town fell to their advance, swathes of territory were annexed and hundreds of thousands of prisoners taken. They had launched a surprise offensive against a country with which they had signed a non-aggression pact. Bewildered Russians, caught by surprise by an attack no one had expected, struggled to contain their opponent's advance.

Hitler's original intention had been to defeat the Soviet Union in one swift military operation. His Barbarossa plan envisaged the destruction of the Red Army close to the frontier, after which fast-moving German motorized formations would strike deep into the country's hinterland. The final objective was 'the attainment of a line sealing off Asiatic Russia, running from the Volga River to Archangel'. Three army groups were deployed: a northern one, which would take Leningrad; a central one, which would capture Moscow – the seizure of the Soviet Union's capital city being regarded as a crucial political and military objective – and a southern one, to occupy the Ukraine. The German High Command had planned a single, unremitting campaign – to be concluded within three to four months.

The first week of the war was devastating for the Soviet Union. Much of their air force was destroyed on the ground. Armies were surrounded or forced into desperate retreat. The chain of command seemed to be dissolving in chaos.

'What do I remember about the first week of the war?' said Red Army artilleryman Alexander Goncharov. 'The dead bodies lying by the side of the road. The burning wheat fields and the rising black smoke, that completely blotted out the sky. As we retreated I saw a soldier hanging out of a vehicle on a blown-up bridge. Near by lay a wounded border guard – face down in a pool of blood. From the bubbles in the pool I could tell that he was still alive. I turned him over on his back so he could breathe more easily. Did the medics come by to pick him up later? Who knows?'

'It was a dismal picture,' said Soviet private Georgi Semenyak. 'Bombing, shooting, artillery fire continued non-stop.' As Semenyak's unit – the 204th Rifle Division – began to pull back from the frontier, German planes strafed the retreating soldiers. A flood of soldiers and civilians streamed eastwards. Officers abandoned their men, hitching rides on departing military vehicles. 'By the time we reached Minsk, we were left virtually leaderless,' said Semenyak. 'There was nothing we could do to defend ourselves against the German onslaught.'

More than 250,000 Red Army troops – more than eleven divisions – were encircled at Minsk. Alarming reports from fleeing refugees and soldiers were creating a mood of panic.

'The retreat is in danger of turning into a rout,' Panteleimon Ponomarenko, the head of the Belorussian Communist Party, warned Stalin. 'The soldiers are exhausted. And the fear of encirclement is so great that some formations collapse under the first enemy bombardment. Troops run off into the forest – or simply drop their weapons and go home.' To assuage these fears, and provide some reassurance, on 3 July Stalin spoke to the Soviet nation by radio. He warned: 'Above all it is essential that our people understand the immensity of the danger that threatens our country. The enemy is cruel and implacable. He is out to seize our lands, our grain and oil . . . The issue is one of life and death for our Soviet state, whether our people shall remain free or fall into slavery.' And the Soviet leader emphasized: 'This cannot be considered an ordinary war. For it is far more than a series of engagements between armies. It is the struggle of our entire people against German Fascism.'

Stalin had every reason to adopt a serious tone. He had promised the Soviet people that they would never have to endure a war on their own territory. The army would guard the frontier vigilantly and any enemy incursion would be swiftly dealt with. The reality was somewhat different. By mid-July German forces had pushed between 650 and 800 kilometres into the Soviet Union. Red Army defences had been breached on all sections of the front. In the north, German troops had occupied Lithuania, Latvia and most of Estonia and had reached the River Luga, only 112 kilometres from Leningrad. In the centre, the Wehrmacht was encircling Smolensk. In the south, the Germans and their allies the Romanians were advancing into the Ukraine and menacing Odessa. Despite these hammer blows, the Russians kept fighting.

After a period of initial shock, Stalin gathered himself, and appointed an able commander – Marshal Semyon Timoshenko – to try to halt the enemy's onslaught. Timoshenko reorganized Red Army defences and stiffened morale and discipline in the central sector of the front, astride the Smolensk–Moscow motor highway. In early August the pace of the German advance briefly slowed. Their armies began experiencing logistical problems, with lines of communication and supply overstretched and their vehicles experiencing wear and tear. But their military strength remained formidable. General Heinz Guderian – one of the Wehrmacht's best commanders and the architect of Blitzkrieg, 'lightning war', swung his Panzers past Smolensk, defeated the Soviet 28th Army and established a bridgehead at Roslavl, in readiness for a full-scale assault on Moscow.

As the Germans pushed deep into Russia, Antokolsky's son Vladimir had been thrust from school graduation into hastily digging anti-tank ditches with other members of the Komsomol, the communist youth league. At the beginning there had been a sense of unreality about it all. The weather was sunny – the youngsters were digging by the Dnieper river north-east of the city of Smolensk. A cheerful camaraderie prevailed. But the Germans captured Smolensk at the end of July. The workforce was pulled back – and fresh defences were constructed further east, at Roslavl. By August, the Germans had breached them. The Komsomol detachment was recalled to Moscow. As the crisis worsened, Vladimir was called up and sent beyond the Ural mountains, to Alma-Ata, to train to be an air force pilot.

A major disagreement now broke out between Hitler and his generals over how to continue the invasion of the Soviet Union. Field Marshal Walther Brauchitsch – head of the German army – and Field Marshal von Bock – commander of Army Group Centre – wanted to launch a full-scale attack on Moscow. Hitler decided against this plan, instead diverting his forces south, into the Ukraine.

On 8 September the German Army Group North took up siege positions around the city of Leningrad. In the centre the situation was now static. To the south, the Germans achieved a huge encirclement of Red Army forces around Kiev. It was the Wehrmacht's greatest encirclement victory of the war – and more than 650,000 Soviet soldiers were killed or captured.

Red Army artilleryman Anatoly Khonyak was one of those taken prisoner by the Germans. 'We were force-marched more than eighty miles in terrible heat to a concentration camp at Kremenchug,' he recalled.

> We received no food or water, and those who were wounded or too weak to carry on were immediately shot. About a third of the prisoners had been killed before we even reached the camp. Our living conditions were squalid and the camp routine cruel and sadistic. Once I heard the sound of shooting, and saw some German officers had ordered a few of our POWs to climb a tree. Then they stood around and shot at them for target practice. On another occasion, a small group of prisoners unsuccessfully attempted to escape. They lined us all up and shot every fourth person. By this time I was in such a state that I just wanted an end to it all – I couldn't stand it any more. But I was only third in line so I missed an execution – I remember feeling really aggrieved about it!

During the first months of the war, with the Red Army in steady retreat, the Germans would capture millions of Soviet soldiers. At one time, the Soviet Union had refused to sign several international conventions on the humane treatment of prisoners of war, but once the war started, Stalin declared his willingness to be bound by them. Stalin's gesture was evidently reluctant, since in August 1941 he also issued his notorious Order No. 270, which forbade Red Army soldiers to surrender voluntarily and was often interpreted as an order never to be captured, regardless of the circumstances. The Germans, however, now ignored Stalin's pronouncement on humane treatment of POWs; instead, Nazi propaganda used the Soviet Union's failure to sign the Third Geneva Convention of 1929 as an excuse to mistreat captured Red Army soldiers. Herded together in concentration camps, they would face a terrible fate: starvation, lack of shelter, filth and abusive guards.

But underneath such German opportunism lay the pitiless Nazi ideology of racial superiority. The war in the east was portrayed as a war against subhumans, the *Untermensch*, in which the Slavs and above all the Jews were singled out for particularly vicious treatment. German private Heinz Postenrieder, advancing into the northern Ukraine with the 134th Infantry Division, noted: 'The Jews have all been finished off here – in the most terrible fashion.' On 19 September, German troops entered the Ukraine's capital, Kiev. Ten days later, all the city's Jews were assembled and marched out to the ravine of Babi Yar. One of Kiev's inhabitants, Irina Khorushunova, wrote in her diary: 'We still don't know what they did to the Jews. There are terrifying rumours . . . but they are impossible to believe. Only one thing seems clear: all their documents, possessions, food have been confiscated. Then they are chased into Babi Yar and there . . . I don't know. I only know one thing: there is something terrible, horrible, going on, something inconceivable – that cannot be understood, grasped or explained.'

At the beginning of October Hitler's forces stood poised to make one last assault, on Moscow – the Russian capital – and it seemed that success here might end the war. Two further encirclement victories at Vyazma and Bryansk killed or cap-

tured nearly three-quarters of a million Soviet soldiers. Red
Army troops were overwhelmed by the scale of the calamity.
'We should simply stop fighting,' said one private in the
Soviet Sixteenth Army after the Vyazma disaster. 'Our generals shouted that we were going to defeat the enemy on his
own soil,' complained another. 'Well – it has turned out
quite the opposite.' 'The road to Moscow was now open,'
said Soviet tank man Alexander Bodnar, 'and we had so little
left to stop the Germans with – it was terrifying. We thought
they could be in the capital in three days.'

Moscow's defence was now entrusted to the Soviet
Union's best commander, General Georgi Zhukov. Zhukov
had to win time, so that fresh reinforcements could be
brought up to the Soviet capital. The Red Army made a
desperate stand at Borodino, on the Smolensk–Moscow
highway, on the site of the great battle against Napoleon's
Grande Armée in 1812.

'We used the Bagration *flêches*, the same arrow-shaped
redoubts that General Bagration had erected against
Napoleon,' Bodnar continued.

> We positioned our tanks behind these earthwork fortifications,
> with their guns pointing through the apertures. On the first days
> fighting we lost six tanks – mine was covered in large dents.
> German infantry nearly stormed our position. I opened up on
> them from close range with my tank's machine gun. Their
> greatcoats were unbuttoned – and as I opened fire shreds from
> their coats, flecked in blood, flew up into the air like sparrows.

Alexander Bodnar's 20th Tank Brigade had been equipped
with some of the new Soviet tanks – the T-34s and KVs –
whose heavy front armour was causing the German Panzers
problems. 'Our smaller tanks burned like candles, but the
enemy struggled against our T-34s and KVs,' Bodnar said.

At the start of Hitler's invasion, the Wehrmacht's intelligence had no knowledge that these tanks even existed. Another surprise was the Soviet multiple rocket launcher – nicknamed by Red Army soldiers the 'Katyusha' – which was again deployed in strength at Borodino. The Germans had little information on the scale of Russia's technological proficiency and industrial capacity.

Yet after four days of terrible fighting, Soviet forces had to retreat. 'The Germans finally brought up reinforcements and infiltrated our position,' Bodnar said. But the retreat did not turn into a rout. Zhukov marshalled his forces with considerable skill, and Russian soldiers – galvanized by the threat against their capital – fought with desperate courage. Now, in mid-October, the weather conditions dramatically deteriorated, and the German offensive suddenly lost its momentum – becoming bogged down in the autumn mud, as torrential rain turned the roads into quagmires. Temperatures dropped rapidly, yet the German High Command had made no provision for winter clothing or equipment. Hitler and his generals had grievously underestimated Russia.

On 7 November Stalin chose to hold the traditional military parade on Moscow's Red Square. It was a signal act of defiance, with some German units only 48 kilometres from the capital. The Soviet leader had now resolved to hold the city at all costs, and Stalin's High Command threw everything it could against the enemy. For those undergoing training further east, conditions were chaotic. On 19 November Vladimir Antokolsky wrote to his father: 'Our instruction course has not yet begun. We are told it will start soon – but the situation is totally confused. It seems I am to be enrolled as an air force pilot; but tomorrow – who knows?' The cadets still had not been assigned a dormitory and were sleeping on the floor, but Vladimir felt uneasy relaying news of such small hardships with his father still in the capital. 'Conditions in Moscow must be incomparably harsher,' he added, 'with the cold and food shortages. At least here I always have something to eat.'

At the beginning of December 1941, some German forces were within 32 kilometres of the Russian capital, and their advance units believed they could see the domes of the Kremlin gleaming in the winter sun. But these men were not to reach the Russian capital. On 3 December Captain Wilhelm Hosenfeld – a Wehrmacht staff officer in German-occupied Warsaw – wrote: 'The battle for Moscow is reaching its climax. Our troops are still inching forward, but I do not believe they will take the city. The supply difficulties have become insuperable.' Hosenfeld – a liaison officer, well informed about military events – was becoming disillusioned by the cost of the war in the east, stating: 'In this war, millions of young lives have now been sacrificed for the supposed good of our nation.'

Hosenfeld was shocked by the brutality underlying Hitler's race propaganda. He found the mistreatment of Soviet POWs abhorrent: 'We leave them to starve to death in their thousands,' he said. 'Our behaviour is cruel and inhumane, and will do untold damage to our cause.'

By early December 1941, with the German army on Moscow's doorstep, occupied territory contained nearly 40 per cent of the Soviet Union's entire population, most of the wheat-producing area of the Ukraine, the coal of the Donetz Basin – and vast supplies of raw materials and food. Millions of Soviet people now lived under German control. But Hitler's Barbarossa plan had not come to fruition. In the north, besieged Leningrad was enduring terrible hardship, with hundreds of thousands of its citizens dying of starvation, yet still held out against the enemy. In the south,

Soviet forces had successfully counter-attacked at Rostov-on-Don.

At Moscow, the Red Army had fought the Germans to a standstill. Its initial retreat had not escalated into mass flight. Time had been won to evacuate vital industries east, beyond the Ural mountains, and to redeploy fresh troops from the Soviet Far East in front of the Russian capital. German hopes for a lightning campaign had been dashed.

On 6 December Hitler's soldiers received their first major blow. In temperatures dropping below −30 degrees Celsius, Soviet armies around Moscow launched a powerful counter-offensive, pushing back the invader. Hitler's forces struggled in hellish winter conditions, jettisoning masses of equipment, which no longer functioned in the extreme cold – and suffering terrible casualties.

For the first time, the Führer's European Blitzkrieg had failed – there would be no easy victory in Russia. And the scope of the war was widening. On 7 December the Japanese attacked the US Pacific Fleet at Pearl Harbor. Four days later Hitler also declared war on America. As he did so, his armies were pulling back from Moscow. It was the Wehrmacht's first defeat.

The Soviet Union's successful defence of its capital was an astonishing achievement but one bought at a terrible price. 'The struggle with Fascist Germany cannot be called an ordinary war', Soviet leader Joseph Stalin had proclaimed, and in the first six months of that war the Red Army lost over 2,760,000 soldiers killed, missing or taken prisoner and a vast array of military equipment. The Germans did not think it possible for a country to sustain such losses and keep fighting. But somehow Russia held on, and now it was counter-attacking the enemy – although that counter-attack drew upon the last of reserves of its strength.

'The German army near Moscow is now in a terrible state,' noted Lieutenant Fyodor Sverdlov, a company commander in the Soviet 19th Rifle Brigade. 'The confidence of the summer and autumn has evaporated. Instead, we find frostbitten soldiers struggling to keep warm, wrapped in woollen kerchiefs stolen from old women in villages. We will push forward, and try to kill as many of them as possible.' An angry and disillusioned Hitler – unable to accept military failure – sacked Field Marshal Walther von Brauchitsch and took command of the German army himself. It made little difference.

In the early new year Vladimir Antokolsky was transferred to a military school at Fergana in northern Uzbekistan. His training as an air force pilot had been jettisoned, followed – a couple of weeks later – by training as an aircraft mechanic. With Russian troops moving forward again, the need was now for artillerymen. Antokolsky would be a gunner in the Red Army. On 16 January 1942 he wrote to his father: 'Everything is OK. Finally – after months of a nomadic existence – I have started regular classes. And I even have my own bed to sleep in!'

The German army was now in full retreat. On 22 January 1942 German captain Wilhelm Hosenfeld wrote: 'Each Wehrmacht bulletin brings fresh reports of heavy fighting all along the front. The Red Army is attacking us continuously, from Petersburg to the Crimea . . . It is incredible that the Soviet forces are launching a major offensive against us in the coldest part of the winter. They are pushing hard, not allowing us any time to recover.'

As the Germans pulled back, and countless towns and villages were liberated, evidence was unearthed of the atrocities committed by the invader against the civilian population. 'I have seen some of the places occupied by the Fascist beasts,'

Soviet artilleryman Mikhail Volkov wrote to his wife in February 1942. 'Whatever they write in the newspapers, the reality is much worse. I have seen burnt-out towns and villages, corpses of women and children, inhabitants whose every belonging has been plundered. These terrible sights have strongly affected me – and all my soldiers.'

Pavel Antokolsky – hearing of one incident during the enemy's retreat – was inspired to compose a patriotic poem about it. In 'The Ballad of an Unknown Boy' a young Russian witnesses the murder of his mother and sister by the SS. The boy escapes, and wanders in a desolate landscape of burnt-out villages. He is assailed by despair, but does not succumb to it. In this cruel war, the boy grows into a man, and takes revenge. As the Germans pull back he lies in wait by the side of the road, and flings a grenade into a passing staff car, killing all its occupants. Although no one knows the boy's identity, his act of heroism inspires countless others.

Stalin now became overambitious, ordering his forces to keep pressing forward, and not allowing Red Army units time to rest and recover. 'After the initial success of our counter-offensive, our High Command believed the Germans would simply run away from Moscow in panic,' commented Soviet platoon commander Georgi Osadchinsky. 'Well – that just didn't happen. The Germans were retreating, but they did not lose their will to resist. And as we outstripped our supply lines we suffered greater and greater losses.' Osadchinsky was disturbed by the needless assaults, the unnecessary casualties and the loss of battle-hardened soldiers and officers who could not easily be replaced.

'Our understanding of modern warfare has been shown up,' Soviet lieutenant Leonid Bobrov wrote honestly from the Leningrad front on 12 February 1942. Hopes of breaking the German siege of Leningrad – with a fresh offensive under

General Mereshkov – had also been dashed. 'The enemy has shown skill and resourcefulness,' Bobrov continued. 'He uses the terrain well, and constructs good defensive positions. When we advance too far, he sets traps for us, encircling our forces. There is no substitute for professional expertise – and we do not have enough. We have to face reality here – not shut our eyes to it.'

In the early spring of 1942, the front stabilized. Both sides were now exhausted. In the aftermath of the titanic battle for Moscow – which saw a ferocious German assault met by an equally fearsome Soviet counter-attack – neither side had won the decisive victory it hoped for. As the war entered its second year, Hitler and Stalin made fresh plans and raised new armies.

Vladimir Antokolsky's training was progressing well. As spring approached, his letters were upbeat. 'The classes are straightforward,' he informed his father, 'and I will not need to do specialist courses in mathematics and optics. A little theory and plenty of practice will be quite sufficient. It won't be long before your son will be commanding his own artillery battery.' On 8 May he relayed good news. 'Today I passed all my exams.' Antokolsky had become an artillery lieutenant in the Red Army, and was strongly motivated to start fighting for his country. 'As you can see,' he told his father, 'a transitional stage in my life has now passed. Soon I will be engaged more responsibly and productively.'

Several weeks later, Antokolsky left Fergana, and on the morning of 8 June was briefly reunited with his father in Moscow before proceeding to the front. It was a moment etched on the father's memory. 'A bright, cloudless, sunny day,' Pavel Antokolsky recorded. 'To my intense pride, I found a grown man standing before me, quiet, dignified and self-assured.' The two chatted together in front of Moscow's

Kiev Station, the son sensitive and considerate towards his father and excited to be joining his fellow Red Army fighters.

After Vladimir boarded the train, they exchanged final glances and the father saw – or found himself believing that he saw – a shadow fall across the face of this optimistic, determined young man. Then the train pulled out of the station.

The troops disembarked at Kaluga, 160 kilometres southwest of Moscow, and then undertook a series of marches. On 13 June Vladimir sent a first postcard: 'I am writing this by the fireside as we heat up some porridge,' he began. 'We are still looking for our forward position, but no one seems to know its whereabouts. Occasionally, gunfire can be heard in the distance, but all is generally calm and peaceful.' On 18 June he wrote at more length.

> Dear Dad, All is well. At last, our gun battery is in position – after 10 days, we have finally reached the front line. Everyone is bustling around. The sound of artillery fire is constant, but it doesn't bother me in the slightest. We have a good defensive position. The troops we are joining are excellent, the dugouts well-constructed and comfortable ... This evening we are cooking a big meal with a whole host of ingredients, potatoes, meat and cabbage, in a large cast-iron pot ... Well that's all for now. Do write as often as possible – mail delivery is running pretty smoothly. I embrace you warmly, Your Son.

German fortunes, however, were once more in the ascendant. On 22 June 1942 Leningrad citizen Nikolai Gorshkov recorded: 'Today is the anniversary of the beginning of the war – ten months from when the enemy first reached our city. He is still firmly entrenched around us.' Alexei Vinokurov added: 'In cinemas, when the movie finishes the police check everyone's papers. Many are stopped in the street and questioned. They are trying to round up anyone dodging conscription. A friend of mine was ordered to join the army yesterday, even though his application had previously been rejected on grounds of poor health.' The Red Army was suffering a serious manpower shortage.

Officially conscription began at the age of eighteen, but in the summer of 1942 seventeen-year-olds were also being called up. Vinokurov recalled a particular episode: 'A little chap came up to me and asked me for a light. I said to him "You're a bit young to be starting smoking". He looked at me, then responded "I'm seventeen today – and I've just been ordered to join the army".' Vinokurov was utterly taken aback. Yet he was struck by the increasingly vague tone of Soviet news reports, as if something important was being held back. 'Oh how little do we really know about what is going on around us,' he lamented. 'Our information bulletins only talk about trivia – they rejoice in small successes of our soldiers or partisans, but do not say anything about the bigger picture – what is really happening in this war.'

There was good reason not to talk about the bigger picture, for in the late spring of 1942 the Soviet Union had suffered a fresh series of defeats. At Lyuban, the Soviet Second Shock Army – which had been attempting to break the siege of Leningrad – was itself surrounded and defeated by the Germans. Further south, a Soviet offensive at Kharkov was encircled and destroyed and some quarter of a million soldiers were killed or taken prisoner. To add to this dismal picture, Red Army forces were also routed in the Crimea. The hapless infantry of the Soviet Fifty-First Army were ordered to attack ceaselessly well-fortified German positions. Here 176,000 Soviet soldiers died in a mere twelve days. 'The land was strewn with corpses,' remembered Russian war journalist Konstantin Simonov. 'The massacre took place on an open, muddy, absolutely barren field.' Then the supply system collapsed. Soviet artilleryman Mikhail Borisov recalled how his unit – without food for two weeks – was reduced to scavenging for scraps of horsemeat. The guns had pitifully few shells – and were only able to fire twice a day.

As it struggled against the might of the Wehrmacht, the Soviet Union received military aid from both Britain and America. American deliveries to Russia under the Lend-Lease agreement used Arctic convoys – which sailed to the Soviet ports of Murmansk and Archangel – the land corridor through Iran and the Pacific route to Vladivostock. Stalin's regime was given tanks, planes, ammunition and explosives – and with 1,523 Soviet factories evacuated beyond the Urals in the first six months of the German invasion, and struggling to recover their output, this help was important. US assistance with army transport was particularly valuable: the American Studebaker truck was superior to anything the Russians could produce and thousands were being delivered. But in the actual fighting, the Red Army still bore a crippling burden. From the beginning of the Moscow counter-offensive in December 1941 to the end of May 1942 more than 1,200,000 of its soldiers were killed or taken prisoner, bringing its total losses from the beginning of the war to around four million. This was a staggering figure, and Stalin and his generals knew that the burden would only lessen when the Western Allies opened up a Second Front, by landing a large force in German-occupied France.

Holding the military initiative once more, Hitler's attention was now fixed firmly on the south. He wanted to capture the Caucasus, win the Soviet Union's vital oil reserves and take the city of Stalingrad – Stalin's namesake city on the River Volga, a major communications centre.

The Soviet High Command had not anticipated this new plan. It believed that the Germans would resume their offensive on Moscow. Southern Russia was seen as a safe haven, and they had begun to evacuate civilians, particularly children, to its major cities. As Alexei Vinokurov bemoaned the plight of Leningrad, twelve-year-old Galina Rusanova was preparing to leave the city. She had longed for such an opportunity, for in the terrible winter of 1941/42 mass starvation had killed hundreds of thousands of her fellow inhabitants. 'People were dying before our eyes,' she remembered. 'The food rations were pitiful – it seemed impossible to survive.' But in the late spring of 1942 Rusanova was chosen for evacuation. Her new destination was far from the war, and seemingly safe – the city of Stalingrad, on the Volga river, 1,530 kilometres south-east of Leningrad.

When Galina arrived in Stalingrad, in June 1942, the horror of war briefly receded, and the contrast with besieged Leningrad could not have been greater. 'At the beginning,' Rusanova said, 'Stalingrad seemed a paradise. There was sunshine, brightly lit streets, lots of brisk trading and plenty of people in the city's parks. I thought that the nightmare we had endured the previous winter, with its blackouts and food shortages, had now been left behind.'

On 25 June Pavel Antokolsky received the first card from his son. He was both relieved and worried by its contents. 'Well, finally, the first message from my boy. It has taken twelve days to arrive. When he wrote it, he was searching for his unit's front-line position. Where will he be now?' On 28 June he received the longer letter, and a mailing address. Vladimir had reached the front line, and his father responded immediately: 'I wait endlessly for your news,' he wrote, 'and try to imagine you in your new surroundings. Each day and each hour I wish you health, strength, courage and happiness. Please try to write often . . . I will read each word over and over again.'

But Antokolsky did not hear anything further. On 12 July he wrote to Vladimir anxiously. 'Dearly beloved . . . Almost two weeks have passed with no message from you . . . You can imagine how hard that is. Mama is worrying like mad about you. We wait impatiently for news . . .' Three days later Antokolsky received a short letter from his son's friend and fellow soldier, Vasily Sevrin. 'It grieves me to tell you such sad news,' he began. 'Your son was killed in a fierce battle with the German bandits. We buried him by the banks of the River Resseta. We will avenge his death.'

Vladimir Antokolsky died on the morning of 6 July 1942. The quiet of his section of the front was abruptly disturbed, for at first light two German Panzer divisions and a supporting infantry force attacked the Russian position, attempting to push across the Resseta river. Vladimir jumped up from his trench and ran towards his gun. But he was spotted by a German sniper and shot in the face. He fell back, clutching at his jaw in a last reflex action. His death was instant.

One death – in a vast and terrible war that had already claimed millions of lives. The same day Antokolsky wrote in his diary:

> My son is no more. His short life ended before it really began. He was not able to accomplish anything. His only achievement was to grow up healthy and handsome, ready for love and happiness. Yet it was not his lot to experience it. Only a brief, terrible initiation into a fearful and bloody conflict. At first he was a baby, then a charming, curly-headed toddler who attracted everybody's attention, then a schoolboy. He grew, became more serious, more handsome and clever; he developed character, will and an outlook on the world . . . All this has ended.

Antokolsky struggled to continue: 'Sensitive, a little shy, a passionately honest and upright person, he was for some reason, by some terrible accident of fate, my son. Why am I writing this?' he concluded bleakly.

Stalin had failed to capitalize on the German failure before Moscow the previous winter. In the north, the remnants of the Soviet Second Shock Army surrendered in early July and their commander – General Andrei Vlasov – defected to the Germans, offering to raise a Russian National Liberation Army to fight against the Bolshevik regime. In the central sector, violent positional battles near Rzhev were killing thousands of Red Army soldiers every day but failing to produce any significant results. In the south, the situation was disastrous. Soviet forces had been unable to forge a coherent defence line and were once more on the retreat. Morale was deteriorating. German assaults became faster and more furious – the enemy now hoped to break through to the Caucasus and the Volga river. Lying directly in his path was the showpiece city named after the leader himself – Stalingrad.

2

Fire on the Volga

I N THE SUMMER of 1942 the Soviet Union's plans for a great assault to drive the Germans out of their country lay in ruins. Once again, it was the Germans who were dictating military affairs. The Black Sea port of Sevastopol had been captured by the Wehrmacht at the beginning of July, and Rostov had fallen soon afterwards. German troops were pushing towards the Caucasus mountains and the Volga river.

Hitler's attention was focused on the Soviet Union's oil-producing areas. His unfolding offensive – codenamed Operation Blue – would be in two stages. Firstly, the Wehrmacht's Army Group B would advance to the city of Stalingrad, to sever Russia's river and rail communications to the south. Once this was achieved, Army Group A would occupy the Caucasus. But with Soviet resistance in southern Russia collapsing, the Führer became even more ambitious. On 23 July 1942 he altered the plan, demanding that his army groups now occupy Stalingrad and the Caucasus simultaneously. 'In a campaign, which has lasted little more than three weeks,' he enjoined, 'the broad objectives set out by me . . . have largely been achieved.' Hitler believed that Russia was close to collapse.

German Army Group A was now instructed to occupy immediately the eastern coastline of the Black Sea. Army Group B – which consisted of the Wehrmacht's Sixth

Army, with support from the Fourth Panzer Army and
troops provided by Germany's ally Romania – was ordered
to 'thrust forward to Stalingrad, smash the enemy forces
concentrated there, occupy the city and block the land communications between the rivers Don and Volga'. Five days
later, on 28 July, Stalin responded with the 'Not a Step Back!'
order. He decreed that the Motherland was in terrible danger,
that the Soviet Union could no longer afford to surrender
territory and natural resources to the enemy, and that the
Red Army must hold its ground, stand and fight.

'It was a desperate situation,' recalled Private Boris
Gorbachevsky of the Soviet Thirtieth Army. 'As the "Not a
Step Back!" order was read out, everyone froze on the spot
and men's faces paled. "Further retreat means ruin for your-
self and ruin for your Motherland" – how could anyone pos-
sibly take these words calmly?'

Stalin's decree appealed to Soviet soldiers' patriotism, but
his order also set up punitive measures. For the first time
since the Russian Civil War penal companies for soldiers and
penal battalions for officers were reintroduced into the army.
The order threatened anyone who retreated without permission to do so, whether he was a top military commander or
an ordinary soldier. That evening, everyone in Gorbachevsky's
platoon was discussing it. Some praised it; others cursed it
thoroughly. All were worried by the situation on the steppe
lands approaching Stalingrad. As Gorbachevsky's battalion
commander said as he finished reading the order: 'The fate of
the Motherland is now being decided in the battles in the
south.'

The Soviet press began to channel this sense of deadly
danger into hate propaganda against the Germans. 'Hatred of
the enemy' was the title of a *Pravda* editorial on 11 July. It
warned: 'Our country is living through serious days. The

Nazi dogs are frantically trying to seize our economic resources . . . May holy hatred become our chief and only feeling.' After the fall of Rostov the tone became even more threatening and insistent. On 24 July the paper published war correspondent Konstantin Simonov's poem 'Kill Him!', a work that exhorted the reader to 'kill a German every time you see one . . .' The rhetoric began to have a powerful impact on Red Army soldiers.

Soviet lieutenant Mikhail Alekseyev of the 29th Artillery Division had been transferred to the Stalingrad front early in July. His exploits in breaking out of enemy encirclement had been publicized in the army newspaper *Red Star*. In an article entitled 'Our Heroes', Alekseyev's style of leadership was praised. 'He always led from the front. His forces were out-numbered, but he turned the tables on the enemy. He did not retreat.' On 9 August Alekseyev wrote: 'The Germans want to destroy our land. I want to live in a country that will not be enslaved. We have to save Russia and kill the Germans.' He continued: 'I want to shout out across the rooftops: "Comrades, friends, if you can hold a weapon – even a spade, pitchfork or shovel – attack the Germans with it! They want to devour us. Kill a German whenever you can, and you will save your Motherland!"'

A language of vengeance had come into being. On 12 August Alexei Surkov published a poem, 'I Hate', in the army's *Red Star*. A day later war correspondent Ilya Ehrenburg returned to the same theme. 'Today there is only one thought,' he wrote. 'Kill the Germans. Kill them all and dig them into the earth.' Colonel General Andrei Yeremenko, commander of the Stalingrad front, received a petition from an eighty-year-old inhabitant whose village had been burned down by the Wehrmacht. It described the suffering of the Russian civilians – killed or taken captive, to work as forced labourers in Germany – and ended with the appeal: 'Red Army soldiers – take revenge on the hated enemy!'

German troops were closing in on Stalin's showpiece city on the Volga. Sixteen-year-old Nikolai Orlov had grown up in Stalingrad. 'It was a beautiful city,' he recalled. 'The centre was studded with fine four- and five-storey houses, and further out were attractive "merchant dwellings" made of brick and wood. And the city was green, really green. I had found everything I wanted there, the chance to study, to enjoy life, even to fish – the Volga was teeming with fish.'

Stalingrad was indeed spacious – the city ran for about fifty kilometres along the Volga river, and had ample parks, trees and grassland. The river itself was about a kilometre and a half wide, and dotted with attractive islands. The city centre was dominated by the Mamaev Kurgan – a 102-metre-high hill with commanding views over Stalingrad and the river; to the north was the factory district, to the south the freight railway station and massive grain elevator. When the war with Germany broke out, the population of Stalingrad was about 450,000. A year later, this figure had almost doubled, rising to over 860,000, for the city had been chosen as a safe haven for a large number of evacuees, including hundreds of thousands of children. Now these refugees were once more in terrible danger.

The Red Army was struggling to contain the new German offensive, and Soviet troops – hurriedly thrown into the breach – were demoralized and dejected. 'I arrived at the military assembly point at 2.00 p.m.,' wrote Nikolai Sokolov, a political officer in the Fifty-Seventh Army, on 27 July. 'The first thing I noticed was a mass of wounded and half-starved soldiers.' Four days later Sokolov continued grimly: 'We are anticipating another German aerial bombardment. Everyone is tired and on edge. We do not get any opportunity to rest.

When will this damned war end? Yesterday the commissar gave a briefing, telling us to try to lift our soldiers' morale. I am supposed to be following these orders, but in our present plight, what I say to the men makes no difference whatsoever.'

The view from Moscow was also grim. These fresh defeats were hard to bear. Soviet war correspondent Pavel Antokolsky, who had lost his son only a month earlier, was now hearing of countless other deaths of young Red Army soldiers – at Rzhev, and on the approaches to Stalingrad. On 6 August he wrote to his wife Natalia – who had been evacuated to Tashkent – still scarcely able to contain his grief: 'That which used to be our most terrible nightmare has assumed an awful reality,' he began. 'The kind of everyday reality with which you fall asleep and awaken, breathe, look into people's eyes, read the newspaper. Reality . . . Our son is gone. Our son is gone!'

The Germans had regained their drive and sense of purpose. 'We were all focused on capturing Stalingrad,' said Panzer lieutenant Hans-Erdmann Schönbeck. 'Its prestige value was enormous. We knew the Red Army would make a stand here. It was Stalin's city – and we felt he would not budge from it.' 'We were very confident,' confirmed Wigand Wüster, an officer in the German 71st Infantry Division. 'We were sure that Stalingrad would be ours – and that we would hold a line against the enemy on the Volga itself.'

But liaison officer Wilhelm Hosenfeld was looking at the bigger strategic picture. On 7 August he wrote: 'After our advance to the Don, we will without doubt strike at Stalingrad. Further south, our troops are pushing on towards the Caucasus mountains. One town after another is captured, the Kuban river has been crossed and the rail links between the Black Sea and Caspian Sea have been cut. All Soviet diversionary attacks have failed, and further German successes are in the offing.'

But then Hosenfeld paused reflectively: 'But we do not hear anything of great encirclement battles, of masses of captured enemy troops or equipment. Is the German army command holding back the full extent of our achievements, or is there nothing else to report as we move forward? Is it really possible to cut the Russians off from their oil supplies in the Caucasus?' Hosenfeld felt a stirring of doubt.

Are the Russians retreating because of some deeper strategic plan, or have they been caught by surprise by our offensive? In the centre of the front, around Rzhev, the Red Army attacks incessantly. We have not captured Leningrad or Moscow, and attempts to cut the road links to Murmansk have also failed. The summer of 1942 will soon be at an end, and we have achieved far less than in the previous year. Our chances of bringing the war to a successful conclusion are not high.

Hosenfeld knew that Hitler was struggling to mount a full offensive. In the summer of 1941 the Wehrmacht had advanced on three fronts. In the summer of 1942 there simply was not the strength to do the same. Although there were 3.25 million German troops in the Soviet Union, the Russians now disposed of around 6 million men, despite the horrific losses of the previous year – and more were being mobilized. Many of these new soldiers were poorly trained and equipped, and junior officers often lacked initiative and skill – but the Red Army was still very much in being. In August Field Marshal Erich von Manstein's Eleventh Army was transferred to Leningrad with orders to capture the city. But Army Group Centre was on the defensive, and the offensive in the south relied on support from the weaker armies of Germany's allies, Romania, Italy and Hungary.

Hosenfeld was also aware that German atrocities were

fuelling the surge of Russian hate propaganda. He said starkly:

> In the meantime, what is happening in the occupied territories will work more and more strongly against us. The starvation, the mass disappearances, all the manifestations of German terror ... One day, if the Red Army goes on to a general offensive, these people will rise up against their persecutors. For all those we attack have been given a moral cause, to fight for the liberation of their country – and this will inspire self-belief and courage. But what are we fighting for? We sleepwalked into this terrible war – and no longer know how to bring it to an end. And we carry too much blood-guilt on our hands to receive a shred of sympathy from our opponent.

Hosenfeld's comments were far sighted and perceptive. But for most Russians, the immediate situation still looked desperate. The ace in the German pack was the professional skill and well-honed coordination of its fighting units. Lieutenant Hans-Erdmann Schönbeck of the 24th Panzer Division said: 'Our great strength was combat flexibility. In 1942 all our tanks had radio communication, and were fitted with special microphones and headphones. We could react quickly to the battle situation, and change our tactics accordingly. Our opponents lacked this equipment.' Soviet lieutenant Anatoly Mereshko added: 'The Germans used artillery and air strikes in unison with infantry and tank attacks; ours operated piecemeal. In the summer of 1942 our military training and organization was definitely inferior to our opponent's.'

On the central front, at Rzhev, 210 kilometres north-west of Moscow, the Red Army was attacking incessantly, in a desperate attempt to tie down German forces that might otherwise be moved south, to further support the attack on

Stalingrad. But these attacks – poorly planned and badly coordinated – achieved little, and Soviet casualties rose alarmingly.

German artilleryman Helmut Pabst commented:

The Russians have been attacking here at Rzhev since the end of July. Their losses must be frightful. Every yard of ground is bitterly contested. Day after day we break up their assembly areas. They seldom manage to deploy their infantry, even within reach of our machine guns. We see the bomb craters, we see them drag in their wounded, their tanks get stopped, their aircraft crash. They run about frightened and helpless when we drop our heavy shells in front of their noses. But then they come on again in open order, and move into the woods where they get plastered by our artillery and Stukas.

Soviet private Boris Gorbachevsky was in one of these assault formations: 'Suddenly Stuka dive-bombers appeared above the battlefield from the direction of Rzhev,' he remembered. 'Confidently, impudently, they headed straight for our tanks. One tank . . . a second . . . a third exploded from their direct attacks, turning into large black-and-crimson bonfires . . . The bloody feast of these vultures was easily seen by our charging soldiers – and caused a commotion. Where were our own planes, why hadn't they arrived to protect the tanks and infantry?'

Panic seized the attackers. 'Shell bursts, shell fragments and bullets swept away our infantry lines,' Gorbachevsky continued,

shredding the living and the dead . . . The remnants of former battalions and companies turned into a senseless mass of onward charging, desperate men . . . Amid the bedlam, we stopped recognizing each other. Faces became pale, lips compressed. Many men were shaking uncontrollably with fear. Some were

31

vomiting; others cried as they advanced, and the tears, mixed with sweat and filth, streamed down their faces and blinded their eyes. Some have involuntarily urinated or defecated from the shock. Wild swearing and cursing filled the air.

Soviet troops grimly nicknamed these ceaseless, costly assaults 'the Rzhev meat-grinder'. Yet Stalin's High Command remained desperately concerned to tie down Wehrmacht soldiers who might otherwise reinforce the offensive in southern Russia. 'We all understood the terrible logic behind these actions,' said Red Army lieutenant Alexander Bodnar. 'At all costs we had to prevent the Germans from redeploying more troops to Stalingrad.'

For in the south, the Germans were poised to make a major breakthrough. On the afternoon of Sunday, 23 August, Red Army lieutenant Anatoly Mereshko was in command of a regiment of cadets at Malaya Rossoshka. The troops had been warned that German Panzers had broken through Soviet lines and were heading towards the Volga. They were ordered to dig in, and hold the road at all costs. But the odds were desperately unequal. These were young infantrymen, mostly eighteen-year-olds, with just a few months' training under their belts. They had no artillery or air support. When the German tanks appeared, they simply 'ironed the trenches', reversing over them and burying the defenders alive. It was all over in minutes. 'We watched our friends die,' said Mereshko, stationed on higher ground above the carnage, 'and were unable to help them. We felt absolutely powerless.'

And then the sky darkened. 'We saw masses of German planes, heading towards Stalingrad,' Mereshko continued. 'We felt a deep sense of dread. We knew how vulnerable the city was – that its civilian population was heavily swollen by evacuees, many of them children who had escaped the siege of Leningrad. And now this new horror was approaching. Within minutes we could see smoke and flames rising above the horizon.'

Stalingrad had been caught completely unawares. 'It was a warm and sunny day,' said Evgenia Siliverstova. 'We were having our tea when we heard the noise of planes, and went out on to the porch to look.' Others did the same. 'At precisely 4.08 p.m. – a time I shall remember for the rest of my life – we heard a terrible rumbling sound coming from behind the woods on the far bank of the river,' said Nikolai Orlov. 'And then an armada of planes appeared. We thought they were ours – and that they were on an exercise. And then we heard the howling of sirens and the first bombs went off.'

'The whole sky was filled with aircraft,' said Evgenia Siliverstova.

> I had never seen so many before. They were flying in small groups, and the whole sky was dotted with them, like a pattern on a cloth – polka dots or small flowers. And then, at about 4.20 p.m., there was a terrible roaring sound. I saw a huge burst of black earth lifting into the sky. The windows shattered, and the door blew off its hinges. From nowhere, a strong wind was blowing. Flecks of sand and grit crunched in our teeth. And there was an acrid smell of smoke and burning.

'It was so hard to comprehend,' Siliverstova continued. 'Hardly thinking, I grabbed my schoolbag with its books for the fifth grade, pens and pencils, and for some reason the small clock on the mantelpiece as well. Then all of us children ran out to the slit-trench in the garden to take shelter.'

> My grandmother and aunt stayed in the house to gather a few more belongings. But as I ran outside the sky suddenly went completely dark. All the wooden fences had blown over, and a huge black cloud was lifting in the sky. Lumps of burning wood

were flying around, carried in the air – some landing on nearby houses and setting them alight immediately. Entire house chimneys were collapsing from the shock waves of the explosions. A searing heat hit my face. And in bewilderment and terror I saw that everything in our kitchen garden – the pumpkins, tomatoes, corn – had been baked black.

When Anatoly Kuryshov got back to his house he found that it had received a direct hit. All his family had been killed. He thought with horror: 'What can I do now?' Albert Burkovski also found his house had been reduced to rubble. He could hear a terrible moaning coming from under the ruins. 'Everyone had been sheltering in the basement,' Burkovski recalled. 'They had been crushed by the falling masonry. At that moment I actually wanted to die – I could not stand the grief and misery of being all alone.'

'I had just returned from market,' recalled Anna Streltasova.

I had bought a watermelon – and we had put it on the table to eat. We heard air-raid sirens, but we didn't pay much attention to them – they had gone off many times before, and nothing had ever happened. The melon was red and ripe, and looked delicious. And then a bomb crashed into our building. Broken glass flew everywhere. My little sister was cut by some shards of glass and began bleeding badly. My mother grabbed a cloth and desperately attempted to staunch the bleeding. It was covered with red blood and red chunks of watermelon. She ran outside – saying she had to take her to hospital. I never saw them again. More and more bombs were falling. I struggled to help the wounded, to get them down to the ferry to escape the city. There was a crowd of people milling about in the street – many badly hurt.

'By the Volga shoreline were masses of people,' remembered Katia Bogdanova, including many children. And these children were terrified – using small spades and their bare hands they tried to dig holes in the sand, by the river's edge, to hide from the bullets and shells. And then German planes appeared, low over the Volga. They flew in relays, hovering over the ferries, which they first bombed and then machine-gunned. It was clear that these were civilians waiting to be evacuated, but the German pilots opened fire on unarmed women and children. They dropped bombs on a crowd of passengers just about to board a boat, then fired at those crowded on the decks. They bombed the Volga islands, on which hundreds of wounded had gathered, for people were fleeing the city on everything they could find – logs, barrels and makeshift rafts. The Germans pursued everything on the river that moved.

'The Volga embankment was strewn with bodies,' recalled Boris Kryzhanovsky, 'and people were running in all directions – panic-stricken, trying to save themselves.' Vladimir Beregovoy had joined a crowd of people trying desperately to get on board a river steamer. His mother – terrified of losing him – tied him to her chest with a towel. They managed to get on board – but the ship broke down in mid-river, and they had to transfer to another, already full of wounded soldiers, with bombs exploding all around them. Miraculously, Beregovoy reached the far bank unscathed.

Colonel Nikolai Skripko of the Fifth Soviet Air Fleet was in Stalingrad that afternoon. 'It was a massive Nazi raid,' he said.

German bombers were flying in groups of six or nine, at different levels, attacking in relays. Over 2,000 sorties were counted. It was a terrible scene – the howling of falling bombs, the chaos in the city. The main German attack was on central Stalingrad, where there were no industrial or military facilities. The Nazis wanted to spread panic among the inhabitants of the city, so that law and order would break down in the streets and on the river crossings. They struck with high-explosive bombs and incendiaries – the whole residential area was ablaze.

Colonel General Andrei Yeremenko, head of the Stalingrad front, wrote:

No one will ever forget that day – it was a living nightmare. We had been through a lot in the war up to that time, but what we saw in Stalingrad on 23 August was something completely different. The sky was filled with columns of fiery smoke. Asphalt on the streets emitted choking fumes and telegraph poles flared up like matches. The earth of Stalingrad was crumpled and blackened. The city seemed to have been struck by a terrible hurricane, which whirled it in the air, showering the streets and squares with rubble.

Yeremenko noted that the summer had been particularly hot, with no rain over the city for more than two months. In Stalingrad's centre, many wooden buildings were crammed together – and these burnt up in seconds. 'In this chaos', he added, 'we could clearly hear the screams and curses of the dying, the cries for help from little children, the weeping of women. Our hearts ached with compassion for these innocent victims.'

Gamlet Dallakian, one of the staff at Yeremenko's HQ, added: 'At least 40,000 civilians were killed in this attack, all of them peaceful civilians. War is war of course, but this was the worst act we had experienced from the Germans: they deliberately singled out our civilians as a target. They were not fighting soldiers but killing defenceless women and children.' Hate propaganda against the Germans was now thrown into stark relief.

It was the heaviest bombing raid that had ever taken place on the eastern front. Over one thousand German aircraft were involved – of which more than six hundred were above the city at any one time. Luftwaffe pilot Theo Rottiger of the 51st Bomber Squadron was one of the first to reach Stalingrad. 'I saw a city below me – a flourishing city. We were the first to drop our bombs there. Other planes quickly followed. The ground below us turned into a blazing inferno.' A huge weight of explosives and incendiaries had been unleashed – targeting the residential districts where most of the civilians lived. 'We had orders to wipe Stalingrad off the face of the earth,' Rottiger concluded.

German private Gerhard Dengler recalled the aftermath of the bombing: 'A huge black cloud of smoke hung over the city – it was held by thermal currents, so that it formed the shape of a giant black cross. We saw it as a gravestone for Stalingrad.'

Sixteen-year-old Nikolai Orlov had loved the city. Now everything fell apart before his eyes. 'I was living near the bank of the Volga, less than a mile from the city centre,' Orlov recalled. 'They bombed the residential area. And when I saw the first explosions I realized that that was it – a new terrible time had begun, it was irrevocable.'

In his bunker in the Tsaritsa Gorge, Alexei Chuyanov, chairman of the Stalingrad defence committee, was struggling to cope with a truly desperate situation. He had heard news that a Panzer division had reached the Volga at Rynok, in the northern suburbs of the city, and that German tanks were already pushing towards Stalingrad's tractor factory. There were hardly any regular Red Army troops to oppose them. The Germans would have to be held off by police and workers' detachments. And the Luftwaffe's bombing was paralysing the city centre. German planes were smashing buildings to rubble with high explosives and setting alight residential areas with incendiaries, leaving houses, schools and hospitals in flames. In a moment's lull, Chuyanov noticed his pet dog was no longer in the bunker. He asked an adjutant to see where it might have got to. Amid the horror of the day, he never forgot the reply: 'Comrade Chuyanov, your dog is fine. It is outside, playing with an elephant.' The bombing had breached the compound of Stalingrad's zoo, and the terrified animals were now roaming through the city.

The bombing continued relentlessly. That night Soviet lieutenant Anatoly Kozlov was ordered to bring supplies by boat to the tractor factory in the north of Stalingrad. 'I will never forget that journey,' said Kozlov. 'The city was in flames. German planes were still hovering above it – our boat was attacked four times. In the river were burning logs and countless corpses. From the shore we could hear a terrible wailing – people were wandering around as if in a trance, groaning and crying.'

Soviet cameraman Valentin Orlyankin was also in the city, and was able to film the horror engulfing it. On 24 August he wrote:

> What I have shot here will be a damning indictment of the German Fascists. My footage reveals them acting like wild jackals. I show their victims – helpless women, children and old people, left without homes, cursing Hitler. Their eyes are full of tears and hatred. I have taken pictures of the city ablaze, its inhabitants caught in vicious air and artillery attacks. And I am right in the middle of this conflagration. I shoot a film sequence, and then stop to help put out a fire, or assist at a first-aid station.

On 25 August Wolfram von Richthofen, commander of the German Eighth Air Fleet, flew over the stricken city. In 1937 Richthofen had masterminded an infamous terror raid on the city of Guernica in the Spanish Civil War. Now he wished to survey his latest achievement. He noted that 'the sky was full of thick, black fire-clouds', some of which were more than 3,200 metres high. The sheer level of destruction was impressive to him. Flames leapt from huge oil storage containers and fuel tankers on the Volga, and spilt oil was burning all across the surface of the river. 'The city,' he noted dismissively in his diary, 'is destroyed and without any further worthwhile targets.'

Soviet war journalist Vasily Grossman reached Stalingrad later the same day. 'The city is in ashes,' he wrote. 'It is like Pompeii, seized by sudden disaster on a day when everything was flourishing . . . There are children wandering about – some seem half-insane.'

As Richthofen surveyed the burning city, the broader course of the war was running strongly in Germany's favour. In North Africa, Rommel had finally captured Tobruk from the British and had pushed on into Egypt. Richthofen also knew that Stalin and Churchill had met for the first time in Moscow, and noted it in his diary. This summit – held between 12 and 15 August – had been a difficult one. Churchill had to personally explain to the Soviet leader that the Arctic convoys, which carried British and American aid to Russia, had been suspended after heavy shipping losses, and there would be no Second Front this year. Four days after the conference closed, on 19 August 1942, an Allied raid on Dieppe ended in failure. The Soviet Union was left to face the German onslaught largely on its own. There were doubts in British circles whether Russia would be able to hold on. Richthofen wrote: 'With a mixture of bluff and bravado, Stalin will have declared to Churchill his absolute resolve to hold on at Stalingrad. Now he will have to prove it.'

Stalin knew that the stakes were high. Soviet air force captain Stepan Mikoyan – the son of Stalin's trade minister, Anastas Mikoyan – was employed on aerial surveillance missions, reporting directly to the Soviet leader himself. 'We all knew the importance of holding on at Stalingrad,' Mikoyan said.

> A military failure there would have terrible consequences. Stalingrad was a powerful symbol of our will to resist, both within our country and on the broader international stage. We knew that the Turkish army had mobilized in August 1942 and some of their regiments had already undertaken reconnaissance missions across our border. I was responsible for tracking their movements and my reports went directly to Stalin. We had no doubt that if Stalingrad fell Turkey would enter the war as an ally of Germany. Stalin desperately wanted to hold the city.

On 26 August, a letter from Alexander Voronin, the head of Stalingrad's NKVD (secret police), made clear that a complete breakdown in law and order was now a real danger: 'Over the past two days of bombing all the main housing blocks in the city are destroyed or in flames, most factories are now no longer able to function . . . Widespread looting is taking place within the city. Five ringleaders have been shot dead on the spot. The leadership and staff of the NKVD are trying to maintain order.'

A defiant proclamation from the city's defence committee exclaimed: 'We will not give up our native city, our native home, our native land. We will block every road with impenetrable barricades . . .' In reality, the city's few barricades could have been pushed over by a truck. Alexei Chuyanov, who headed the committee, had been trying for weeks to put an evacuation plan in place for Stalingrad's inhabitants. Stalin had vetoed the idea. He feared that Red Army soldiers would fight less strongly for an empty city.

The suffering of the remaining civilians was near indescribable. Anatoly Kuryshov had teamed up with another young boy, and – starving – they tried to strip dead bodies of bags of food. But a shell exploded near by in the street, and Kuryshov saw his friend blown up before his eyes. He was too terrified to continue. 'We foraged amid the ruins,' said Boris Kryzhanovsky. 'We would see a dead horse, and cut pieces of meat off it. Shells and bombs were exploding all around us.'

Thirteen-year-old Tania Korneeva lived near the Volga river, on Matrosskaya Street, between the Red October and Barrikady factories in northern Stalingrad. After the German bombing, most of the street's inhabitants fled, but Korneeva's family could not: one of her brothers had ventured out during an artillery bombardment and had been hit by shrapnel below his knees, and his legs were now swollen with infection. An incendiary bomb had burnt down their house, so they moved into the narrow trench they had dug in the yard.

'A little shed still stood there,' Korneeva related.

Our mother set up a stove in it, so she could prepare food for us. But when she went to cook a bomb exploded right next to it. We saw her crawling back towards us and rushed to help – but she lost consciousness. She died shortly afterwards. I felt so utterly alone. My younger brother Tolya – who was only five – cried, and with his little finger tried to wipe the blood from Mother's leg. He did not understand why she was silent. Victor was in a fever – his legs were festering – and I could only bind them with rags.

'There was nothing left to eat,' Korneeva continued. 'Tolya sat silently, only crying at night while dreaming. Around us there was no one – our street had become an empty, bare place. Everything was burnt. I tried to bury Mama. I cleared away the ashes and began to dig a hole. I dug that hole for three days. I had just succeeded in burying her when a shell landed directly on top of the grave and blew her to pieces.'

On 29 August Nikolai Sokolov, a political officer in the Soviet Fifty-Seventh Army, wrote: 'I no longer believe that we have wider goals and aspirations in this war. What are we trying to achieve? – probably nothing. Everything will perish here at Stalingrad.' Two days later, Lieutenant Arsenii Marikov – whose unit was about to depart for Stalingrad – confided to his parents in Siberia: 'I am tormented by fears for the future of our Motherland. Will she survive or not? It is almost physically painful to realize that question lies in the balance. Some people still do not seem to realize the terrible danger that hangs over our beloved Russia. The Motherland and my life have an identical meaning for me – they are one and the same.'

After the heavy bombing of Stalingrad, Hitler was jubilant. On 2 September he ordered that once the city was taken its entire male population was to be wiped out. All females would be deported back to Germany. A day later Stalin warned his newly appointed deputy supreme commander, General Georgi Zhukov: 'The situation is getting worse. The enemy is only a few miles from Stalingrad. They could take the city today or tomorrow . . .' In Stalingrad itself, a girl wrote in her diary on 4 September: 'For two weeks we have been bombed. Now there is nothing left. Will we survive? I am terrified. Barricades are being put up everywhere. But they say the real nightmare hasn't started yet.'

Red Army soldiers were now pulling back from Stalingrad's outer defences and entering the city. They were horrified by what they saw there. 'We reached the Volga river,' said Private Alexander Tsygankov of the Soviet 181st Rifle Division, 'and saw a patch of land where several thousand civilians had gathered for evacuation. They were all dead –

old people, women and children. The Nazi planes had bombed and machine-gunned them all. I cannot tell you the hatred we felt for these sadists. We swore that we would be avenged for everything – for the bloodshed they had caused, for the wanton destruction.'

The crisis point had arrived. On 12 September General Friedrich Paulus, the commander of the German Sixth Army, moved his troops into position on the high ground above Stalingrad and ordered a rapid assault on the city. On the same day, the new commander of the defending Soviet Sixty-Second Army was appointed – Lieutenant General Vasily Chuikov. His orders were to hold Stalingrad and stand to the death.

3

The Tide Turns

O N 12 SEPTEMBER 1942 General Friedrich Paulus, the commander of the German Sixth Army, and Colonel General Maximilian von Weichs, the head of Army Group B, arrived at Hitler's HQ at Vinnitsa in the Ukraine. The Führer demanded to know when Stalingrad would be captured. He exclaimed impatiently:

> Russia has exhausted nearly all its military reserves. I expect resistance at Stalingrad to be of a purely local character – the Red Army is no longer capable of mounting a strategic counter to our attack. Our northern flank, along the Don River, will be reinforced by the armies of our allies very soon now, and in these circumstances, I see no danger to our overall position. I expect us to capture Stalingrad quickly . . .

Plans for the German offensive in the summer of 1942 – Operation Blue – had not deemed it necessary to fully occupy Stalingrad. The objective of Operation Blue was economic – to deprive the Soviet Union of its oil reserves in the Caucasus. Once German troops reached the Volga north of Stalingrad and put the river under artillery bombardment, and once the Luftwaffe's attacks had crippled the city's industrial infrastructure, the aim of Operation Blue was achieved. But the Führer was becoming mesmerized by Stalingrad. This was the city that bore the Soviet leader's

44

name and Hitler was increasingly drawn to wresting it from his grasp.

The Soviet position in the city did indeed look desperate. When a new commander, Lieutenant General Vasily Chuikov, was appointed his orders were to hold on at Stalingrad or die in the attempt. At the start of the battle for the city, on 13 September, he moved into a command post on the Mamaev Kurgan. He was there for only a day – German bombing and artillery fire forced him to seek greater protection in a bunker in the Tsaritsa Gorge. Twenty-four hours later, approaching enemy troops forced Chuikov into another hurried departure. He pulled back to the other side of the Volga, but army morale was so fragile that Chuikov could not risk spending even one night on the far bank of the river. Jumping on to a ferry boat, he found that a number of his staff had slipped away in the confusion. The NKVD found and arrested the chief fugitive, the Sixty-Second Army's deputy chief of artillery, Colonel Belyakov, and charged him with 'anti-Soviet agitation'. Belyakov clearly believed it was impossible to defend the city. Standing and fighting in Stalingrad was regarded as a death sentence.

But the Red Army clung on. Between 13 and 15 September NKVD patrols stopped 1,218 Soviet troops attempting to flee the city. A report on conditions within Stalingrad was bleak. The Germans had reached the Volga 150 metres from the ferry crossing. They had captured the Mamaev Kurgan, the hill that dominated Stalingrad, and were fighting in the city centre. The defenders were desperately short of ammunition, food and medical supplies, and it was very difficult to transport wounded soldiers to the far bank. Some soldiers had crossed into Stalingrad without any equipment. German bombing and artillery bombardment of Soviet positions was relentless. The NKVD concluded that the defence was paper thin, with ammunition likely to run out within twenty-four hours, and was being conducted with little more than desperate improvisation. It asked for instructions from Moscow, 'in case the Red Army abandons Stalingrad'.

There were also remarkable acts of heroism. Soldiers from a reinforced reconnaissance battalion from the 13th Guards Division recaptured Stalingrad's central railway station from the Germans in a daring night attack. Within twenty-four hours these troops were driven out again, but they carried on fighting, falling back through the burning city and occupying the Univermag department store and the nail factory. Another desperate stand was made, but the Germans ejected them once more, and the last few survivors eventually reached a small house on the Volga's edge. A force of over five hundred men had been reduced to six, but the action showed that some of the defenders at least were not yet ready to surrender.

On 16 September the Mamaev Kurgan was regained from the Germans, at the cost of terrible casualties – the Soviet frontal assault was launched without any artillery preparation against well-defended German dugouts. Two days later a hand-picked Red Army force from the 35th Guards Division made a brave stand in the grain elevator in the southern part of the city. All Soviet attempts to break through to the defenders from the north or south failed – the only way to get men and supplies into Stalingrad was across the Volga river. During the day German planes hovered over the river, bombing any vessel that moved; at night, they illuminated it with flares and subjected it to constant artillery bombardment.

General Georgi Zhukov, struggling to organize a relief attempt to the north of Stalingrad, exclaimed in frustration:

'It is the second year of the war – it is time we learnt to fight more intelligently . . . We cannot simply rely on the patriotism, courage, and bravery of our soldiers – throwing them into battle without any detailed knowledge of the enemy's strength. Of course, our troops are compelled to obey orders, but we do not have the right to needlessly throw away their lives.' The Red Army was being let down by the poor quality of its reconnaissance and an alarming lack of coordination between its infantry, tanks, artillery and air support. The German system, in contrast, seemed to run like clockwork.

In the late summer of 1942, this experience was common to all sections of the front. At Rzhev, Soviet troops were battering themselves against the well-defended positions of German Army Group Centre, losing many lives for small territorial gains. And on 16 September, the day of Zhukov's *cri de coeur*, Lieutenant Vasily Churkin of the Soviet 80th Rifle Division wrote in his diary from the Leningrad front: 'Our troops were ordered to attack an enemy strongpoint, but the Germans brought down heavy artillery fire on our advancing infantry and the assault failed. We have suffered very high losses.' The 80th Rifle Division's attack was on the Siniavino Heights, a strongly defended German position 32 kilometres east of Leningrad and a linchpin of their blockade of the city. Churkin contrasted Red Army incompetence with German organization. 'It is openly said that our attack failed because of the inadequate artillery support,' he said, and then added:

> The Germans fortify their strongholds well. They occupy the high ground and construct well-built defences, concrete pillboxes and deep trench systems to protect their soldiers. And they easily anticipate our tactics. As our infantry runs up the slope, German heavy machine guns are trained on the entry points to their positions. A deadly hail of fire is unleashed . . .

47

Our press talks of 'local engagements' against the enemy. But the ground is littered with the corpses of our soldiers.

These issues now began to be addressed. In September 1942 Soviet lieutenant Leonid Bobrov of the 102nd Rifle Division was pulled out of combat on the Leningrad front and sent on an intensive training course. He wrote about his daily regimen:

> A month of intensive schooling is already behind me. I have learnt a lot. I can now issue a range of orders for offensive or defensive operations. The front commanders take good care of us. They've given us brand new uniforms and boots, greatcoats and forage caps. But they demand that we study well, especially in tactics and fire support. I am fascinated by new weaponry and now I have a new machine gun, a Shpagin, which I clean for half an hour after each training session.

The Shpagin – the PPSh-41 sub-machine gun – would become the staple automatic weapon of the Red Army in the Second World War. It was cheap to produce and easy to maintain. Then Bobrov said candidly, 'We have a lot to do before we can rout the Fascists . . . Only when we properly master the art of military command will we be able to smash Nazism once and for all. We are all responsible for our soldiers' lives – and we need to lead them into battle and do it well. Once we can do this, we will all be ready for the fiercest and most decisive fighting.'

In the south, German pressure on Stalingrad was building. Attempts to break through to the beleaguered Soviet Sixty-Second Army had failed. On 22 September it looked as if the Red Army's defence of the city would collapse completely. Early that morning the 92nd Infantry Brigade, holding the southern part of Stalingrad, abandoned its positions. The brigade's commander, Colonel Tarasov, fled to an island in the middle of the Volga and the infantry then rushed to the river's edge and attempted to follow suit in a flotilla of makeshift rafts. Tarasov was quickly arrested by the NKVD and put before a military tribunal. The commander admitted that 'he was overwhelmed by combat stress' and could no longer cope with conditions in the city. The judgement passed against him was stark: 'Brigade Commander Tarasov failed to organize an adequate defence line, and motivated by cowardice and without orders from his High Command, evacuated his HQ.' He was immediately shot in front of his soldiers – who were then sent back into the hell that was Stalingrad.

Soviet general Alexander Rodimtsev's 13th Guards Division held a shrinking promontory of land in central Stalingrad, and as the Germans pushed along the Volga its position began to splinter. Wehrmacht troops flooded Rodimtsev's HQ, located in a conduit pipe in the Volga embankment, and brought up their machine gunners to finish him off. But Rodimtsev rallied his troops and repulsed the enemy in hand-to-hand fighting. At the end of the day, the 13th Guards were still holding on to the river embankment. The Germans turned their attention to Stalingrad's northern factory district. Another assault on 26 September nearly flung all the defenders into the river. But the Red Army continued to fight, and that night fresh Soviet reinforcements were ferried across the Volga. At the beginning of October the Germans bombed the oil storage tanks around Lieutenant General Chuikov's command post. Chuikov continued to direct the battle in dugouts underneath the blazing inferno. Against all expectations, the Red Army was holding on.

The rest of the Soviet Union was captivated by Stalingrad's heroic stand. Vera Inber wrote from besieged Leningrad that her fellow citizens felt a special kinship for the courage and the suffering of the city on the Volga. War journalists flocked to Stalingrad to report on the battle, with Konstantin Simonov and Vasily Grossman at the forefront of the pack. Pavel Antokolsky, one of the many who wrote about Stalingrad, was also inspired to create a tribute to his son Vladimir, who had died in combat in the summer of 1942 – a tribute that would reach out to all those carrying unbearable loss. 'I shall live, work and create,' Antokolsky vowed.

Others, while feeling the battle's extraordinary power, struck a less heroic tone. On 3 October Sergeant Yuri Koriakin, a signaller with the Soviet Nineteenth Army, confessed that he was 'in a disgusting mood'. Koriakin did not like being stationed at the Army HQ, at a time 'when such great events are happening all around us'. But he was also thinking about women, admitting in a letter to a friend:

Before the war began, I started paying attention to one attractive girl in my school. I liked her a lot: she was a bright student, a mature person and rather good looking. She treated me nicely and I in turn helped her to compose essays and solve mathematics problems. Our relationship was great and I wondered where it might lead.

At first when I joined the army she wrote to me regularly, but then her letters stopped, and now not a word or phrase for months. I have sent her several letters: it can't be that she hasn't received them – she's just not responding. So now I am in a lousy mood. It may seem spineless that when our country is going through such epoch-making days I am distracted by such personal concerns, but she has treated me like shit, the slut – oh well, fuck her, I'll survive without her.

All this has made me think I need to do something, not just sit around at Army HQ. So I have decided I want to serve in a reconnaissance unit, and have put a request in to my superiors, asking to be sent to the front line. Who knows, I may even be dispatched to join a partisan band – that's where the life is! I will certainly let you know how things develop.

The Germans could not understand how Stalingrad was still holding out. Wehrmacht liaison officer Captain Wilhelm Hosenfeld – stationed in Warsaw – took a more dispassionate view of events than those actually fighting in the city. On 5 October he wrote:

> The fight for Stalingrad now surpasses all our previous struggles – it has rightly been compared to Verdun. We must hope that the outcome is different. For I believe that the city holds a similar power for the Bolsheviks as Verdun did for the French in the First World War. It has become a symbol. This is a decisive moment. The French would say: 'Whoever holds Verdun will win the war.' The Führer has spoken in similar fashion of Stalingrad – and the city still has not fallen to us.

The Red Army commander at Stalingrad, Lieutenant General Vasily Chuikov, used an array of novel approaches to frustrate his opponent. Chuikov well understood German strengths, and the clarity of their strategy – to pin the defenders against the bank of the Volga, cut them off from the support of their fellows, deny them reinforcement in men and ammunition by putting the river under air and artillery bombardment, then finish them off through sheer firepower. He sought to counter this. Recognizing German air superiority, he ordered his troops to get as close to the enemy as possible. In the novel conditions of fighting in a ruined city, Chuikov sought to use those ruins to confuse and disorient the enemy. He broke up his military formations into small units – 'storm groups' – and deployed them to capture and defend strongpoints in the city, which were then consolidated into larger defensive systems. He kept his artillery on the far bank of the Volga, and used it to deliver concentrated and accurate shelling against German troops' assembly points. And he encouraged a snipers' movement in the army, recognizing its capacity to wear down the enemy in close-quarters fighting.

Chuikov was an instinctive fighter, who could sense the mood of a battle. He had the gift of being able to reach out and motivate his men, even in the hellish conditions of Stalingrad. 'Without Chuikov's leadership, I do not believe we could have held out in the city,' said Lieutenant Anatoly Mereshko, a staff officer in the Soviet Sixty-Second Army. In contrast, his opponent, the German Sixth Army commander General Friedrich Paulus, was a sound planner but was also pedantic and hesitant, never truly adapting his approach to the particular demands of city fighting. Luftwaffe commander Wolfram von Richthofen bluntly appraised Paulus as 'worthy but uninspiring', adding that 'his attempts to motivate the troops were only theoretical'. German strengths were beginning to turn into weaknesses.

Hitler once more ordered Paulus to finish off the Red Army defenders in the city. On 14 October a ferocious German assault was launched against the Tractor factory in northern Stalingrad. It broke through to the Volga, splitting the defending Soviet Sixty-Second Army in two. Under devastating air and artillery attack Chuikov lost contact with many of his units and could no longer direct the battle. On 15 October German machine gunners closed to within a few hundred metres of his HQ. It no longer seemed possible to hold on.

But hold on the Red Army did. Showing astonishing ingenuity, desperate courage and a profound love for the embattled city and the Motherland it had come to represent, groups of Soviet soldiers defied the Germans on the Volga's very edge. Paulus hesitated, delaying throwing further rein-

forcements into the battle, and he paid for it. By 17 October
a fresh Russian force, Colonel Ivan Lyudnikov's 138th Rifle
Division, had entered the fray, bolstering Chuikov's tottering
defence line by taking up its positions behind the Barrikady
factory. Another opportunity to capture the remnants of
Stalin's city had been lost.

As Stalingrad fought off the German Sixth Army, in the
north Leningrad was bracing itself for the onset of another
winter under siege. It was vital that the city – which had
already lost more than a million of its inhabitants to starvation
– improve its food reserves. The Germans, realizing this, and
wishing to destroy Leningrad through hunger, attempted to
disrupt the one route open to the defenders, across the water
of Lake Ladoga to the east of the city.

On 22 October Semyon Goldberg, a supply officer on the
Leningrad front, saw one of the ships of the Baltic Fleet
attacked and sunk by German planes. 'The worst thing is
how you grow acclimatized to war,' he wrote, 'and accept its
sights and horrors. This is halfway to defeat. We must learn
from last year's mistakes.' The following day Goldberg was
momentarily distracted from the growing crisis, remarking:
'A grey sky – but then on the horizon a luminous tinge of
silver. I gaze at it transfixed. For a few moments it is a beguil-
ing distraction.' Then he returned to more pressing concerns,
in particular ensuring that Leningrad's factories continued to
work, and the city's inhabitants had light and heating. In the
previous winter all power supplies had run out. Goldberg
stressed in his journal: 'We are painfully aware that Leningrad
is still desperately short of fuel.'

Yet Leningrad's position was growing stronger. On 29
October Goldberg was delighted by the month's supply figures: 914 tonnes of foodstuffs had been brought into the
besieged city. He added:

Preparation for this year's 'Ice Road' across Lake Ladoga has started. Zhdanov [Andrei Zhdanov, the Communist Party leader of the city] has already approved the plans, which to me seem nothing short of miraculous. But will they work? Three railway tracks will be set up – one wide gauge, two narrow – supported by wooden plinths resting on the ice. The road will run in parallel. But I am wondering how the movement of the ice will affect the plinths – and a host of other uncertainties. And there is the constant threat of German air and artillery attacks. Oh God – can we pull this off?

The whole of Leningrad's workforce was mobilized, ready to begin construction work. On 31 October Goldberg wrote: 'The last few days have been very tough. German planes are very active – bombing our supply ships – and our losses are considerable. And today a thin covering of snow has appeared, bathing everything in a pinkish-blue hue, as if in a dream or fairy tale.'

'A sudden cold spell has brought the temperature down to −8 degrees Celsius,' Goldberg wrote on 5 November,

and it is already possible to walk on the frozen surface of Lake Ladoga. The air is charged – like the nucleus of an atom – and is powerfully refreshing. But we are losing more and more boats to the enemy. Fourteen supply barges have run aground. We see constant air fights above us and the air is rent by explosions. We are in a particularly vulnerable position, on the main landing berth, and everyone is looking up anxiously. As bombs go off around us we are all covered in ashes and soot. At 1.25 p.m. supply boat 4529 received a direct hit, and it sank carrying a full cargo.

'Another massive air raid,' Goldberg wrote on 8 November. 'At 3.25 p.m. a host of Junkers appeared, bombing us heavily and wreathing the landing jetty in smoke. One of our loaders was blown to pieces.' Yet Goldberg and his fellow citizens continued to bring supplies into the city, undaunted by the German attacks. Leningrad would not succumb to the enemy.

In Stalingrad, the outlook remained bleak. The ice that offered hope to the inhabitants of Leningrad – allowing a supply road to be constructed over frozen Lake Ladoga – was a mortal danger to the Red Army fighters along the Volga. Once the ice floes on the river grew in size, it would no longer be possible to ferry supplies or reinforcements into the city.

On 11 November 1942 Colonel Ivan Lyudnikov's 138th Rifle Division was cut off from the rest of the Sixty-Second Army. German troops reached the Volga on either side of their position – behind the Barrikady factory. The division's combat journal was painfully honest about their worsening predicament. On 13 November it noted that seventy German machine gunners had penetrated the combat lines and had to be repulsed by staff from the command HQ. A number of fortified houses were lost in hand-to-hand fighting. Throughout the day the enemy kept up a terrible artillery bombardment, and that evening it was noted: 'Ammunition and food are running out. One day's rations remain.'

The next day the Germans pushed forward again. The defenders held on grimly. Divisional staff, security detachments and even the wounded were fighting. That night they ran out of food and ammunition. They carried on – robbing the Germans of both. Such desperate heroism became the hallmark of the Red Army at Stalingrad.

On 18 November 1942 the Soviet Sixty-Second Army was clinging on at Stalingrad with a battle line less than 100 metres from the Volga. The army was split into three. The 'northern group' under Colonel Sergei Gorokhov held a small strip of territory in the city's northern suburbs – the settlements of Spartanovka and Rynok. Soviet colonel Ivan Lyudnikov's battered 138th Rifle Division held a shrinking piece of land behind the Barrikady factory. The Germans were on either side of him. The Sixty-Second Army's main defences lay further south, running from the Red October factory, past the slopes of the Mamaev Kurgan, to a small stretch of river embankment in downtown Stalingrad. Ice floes were appearing on the Volga, threatening to disrupt the Soviet fighters' fragile supply lines. The Red Army's position was so precarious it seemed that one last push from the Germans would send the whole tottering structure into the river.

And yet, the Wehrmacht's Sixth Army was utterly spent. A force priding itself on its fast movement that had advanced between 65 and 80 kilometres a day at the start of its summer offensive was now struggling for a few metres of purchase amid steel smelting furnaces and ruined workers' houses. The Soviet troops had fashioned a formidable defence system. They put their heavy guns on the far bank of the river, and when the Germans moved their forces called down a hail of fire on them from lookout positions amid the ruins. They created strongpoints: fortified houses held by storm groups and protected by minefields. And Red Army snipers constantly harassed the enemy.

The morale of the defenders had grown. They had gained confidence in city fighting and self-belief and resilience. In 'Pavlov's House', a Soviet stronghold 140 metres from the river in central Stalingrad, the garrison played gramophone music at the Germans after each attack. 'We found a record amid the ruins,' said Red Army private Georgi Potanski with a smile. 'It was an aria about unrequited love and sleepless nights. Well, the enemy was giving us a few sleepless nights too, so it seemed an appropriate rejoinder!' Then he added: 'We fought as a team – everyone was equal. We were determined not to let the Germans through.'

Private Mark Slavin of the Soviet 45th Rifle Division was fascinated by the mood of quiet heroism sweeping through the army. His comrades were fighting in the remnants of the Red October factory. Slavin saw raw, frightened recruits change into hardened fighters in a matter of days. He began writing up soldiers' exploits in the divisional newspaper. 'Something remarkable was happening at Stalingrad,' Slavin said, 'and I wanted to record it.' The Germans were baffled. Time and time again they had expected to take the city. Instead, they were caught in a battle that bled away their strength. They could not understand how the defenders were still holding out.

The Red Army had sustained massive casualties. Its losses on the entire Stalingrad front from July to November 1942 – those classified as killed, taken prisoner or missing in action – amounted to 324,000 out of a total of 547,000 soldiers. The rate of attrition within the city was even worse. General Alexander Rodimtsev's 10,000-strong 13th Guards Division suffered 30 per cent casualties in its first day of combat and 80 per cent by the end of its first week in Stalingrad. At the conclusion of the battle only 320 men were left. Yet the survivors found the will to carry on resisting – and fought with stupendous power.

'All of us were on the same level,' said Mark Slavin. 'The commanders mingled with their men, ate with them, swapped jokes and even chopped wood with them. Everyone counted. We had no space to manoeuvre and the German bombardment was relentless, but we were determined to hold on to that narrow strip of land.'

The Soviet Union's armament industries – evacuated beyond the Urals as the enemy advanced – were now increasing their output. By November 1942 they were producing 24,000 tanks a year; the Germans some 6,000. They were manufacturing 128,000 heavy and medium guns to the Germans' 41,000; 336,000 machine guns to the enemy's 117,000. Red Army divisions were now better equipped and better trained.

As the clash at Stalingrad reached its climax, the Red Army feared that a dynamic German commander like Field Marshal Erwin Rommel would be brought in to replace the hesitant General Friedrich Paulus. 'We thought that Rommel would quickly grasp the essentials of street fighting and impose his will on the battle,' said Soviet lieutenant Anatoly Mereshko. But Hitler, the head of the German army, chose to retain Paulus as the Sixth Army's commander. As the Wehrmacht made its last attempts to capture Stalingrad, in North Africa Rommel's Afrika Korps had been defeated at El Alamein by the British Eighth Army and was now in full retreat. British and US commanders had then launched Operation Torch, a series of landings in French-held Morocco and Algeria. The tide of war was turning.

The German military position was becoming dangerously overextended. As they engaged in the slugging match on the Volga, their flanks on the Don and Kalmyk steppe were held by the weaker armies of their allies, the Italians, Hungarians and Romanians. On 19 November the Red Army struck back, bringing up reinforcements and launching a counter-offensive codenamed Operation Uranus. Two separate forces – the Fifth Tank Army and Twenty-First Army – broke out from bridgeheads on the western side of the Don river, smashed through the Romanian forces opposing them, and swung behind the Germans at Stalingrad, aiming for the road and rail junction at Kalach. Soviet major Alexei Selenkov of the 204th Rifle Division wrote in his diary on 19 November: 'This date will never be forgotten in the story of Stalingrad – either by our friends or enemies. It has started!'

If Kalach fell, the supply lines of the German Sixth Army would be cut. But the Red Army was seeking a far greater prize. The following day Selenkov noted: 'We have been fighting all day long. By the evening we reached the designated positions. We repulsed a small enemy counter-attack. We can hear the roar of our artillery all around us.' On 20 November a southern attack was also launched by the Soviet Fifty-First Army, stationed on the Kalmyk steppe. The Wehrmacht was completely taken by surprise by this new assault. Their military intelligence was woefully inadequate, for the Soviet forces had deployed with secrecy and skill. The armies of the Romanians, which bore the brunt of the offensive, began to disintegrate. Two Russian pincers were closing on Kalach, with the aim of capturing the town and encircling the Germans in Stalingrad.

'Our attack continues,' Major Selenkov wrote on 21 November. 'We feel such pride in our new offensive. All the secrecy, all the careful preparation, has come to fruition. The Germans simply had no idea how many forces we had gathered.' By 23 November the two pincers had joined near Kalach and completely surrounded them.

The visceral hatred felt by Red Army soldiers towards their foe was caught in a diary entry of Lieutenant Mikhail Alekseyev, now a deputy commander of an artillery battery in the Soviet Sixty-Fourth Army. After the date – 25 November – he inscribed proudly: 'The sixth day of our counter-offensive', before adding: 'I stepped on the dead body of a German soldier. His face was coulourless and his eyes glassy. What is he? A "Fritz" yes – a "human being" no. My disgust was so great that I got stomach cramps. This animal deluded himself that he was a superhuman being who would enslave Russia. This ape came here to create the New Order.' Coruscating hatred lay at the heart of many Red

Army soldiers' resistance, and this had now been fashioned into a formidable will to resist.

'The ring has closed!' Major Selenkov exclaimed on 26 November. 'We have caught the enemy in an iron vice between the Volga and the Don. Now our task is to throttle the Hitlerites. We are killing more and more of these monsters – and we will not stop until we have wiped them out completely.'

Some of the German generals trapped in Stalingrad wanted to attempt an immediate breakout. But Paulus hesitated, and then Hitler forbade any retreat from the city, promising a relief effort would be made by troops gathered under Field Marshal Erich von Manstein. Meanwhile the German Sixth Army would be supplied by air. But the Luftwaffe was not able to get enough food, ammunition or fuel into the city. The German position steadily worsened. On 6 December 1942 Wehrmacht liaison officer Captain Wilhelm Hosenfeld wrote: 'The fighting at Stalingrad continues with unremitting ferocity – fifteen of our divisions have been surrounded by the Bolsheviks. It seems that we have overestimated the capacity of our forces, and underestimated those of our opponent – in fact, our knowledge of the real extent of Russian strength was misconceived or simply wrong.'

On 12 December Manstein launched his relief effort – Operation Winter Storm. Initially it made good progress, but by 24 December it had been fought to a standstill some fifty kilometres west of Stalingrad. It briefly stood on the line of the River Aksai, waiting to see whether Paulus might attempt to break out of the city and join it. Such an operation would have been fraught with risk, and would almost certainly have been vetoed by Hitler. But the collapse of the Italian Eighth Army – another weak German ally – forced Manstein to pull back and cover his flank. As Christmas came and went, it was clear the plight of Paulus's Sixth Army was hopeless.

The Red Army now began to prepare Operation Saturn (sometimes known as Ring), the annihilation of all German forces at Stalingrad. On 31 December Captain Wilhelm Hosenfeld wrote:

> Our soldiers at Stalingrad remain completely cut off. German troops are buttressing Romanian forces, through fear they will collapse if left on their own. On the central front, the Russians are besieging Velikye-Luki, an important railway junction. It seems that the year 1943 will begin badly for us. I hope we can recover. But the great promise made by the Führer in the spring of 1942 – that Russia would be struck a mortal blow – has not come to pass. On the contrary, the Red Army is attacking us in considerable strength.
>
> We were never able to completely capture Stalingrad, and we did not reach Moscow either. The attempt to take Baku and the Caucasus oilfields has of course failed. And what we achieved at the beginning of our fight with Russia seems impossible now. We have not mastered the Bolsheviks.

On 10 January 1943 Lieutenant Mikhail Alekseyev of the Soviet Sixty-Fourth Army at Stalingrad wrote starkly in his diary: 'We are close to complete victory now. The enemy will soon be annihilated. We will take vengeance for all the humiliation he inflicted on us in the summer of 1942.'

On the same day Soviet forces surrounding Stalingrad launched Operation Ring. German units – weakened by cold and hunger and short of ammunition – fought bravely, but were soon falling back from the steppe and into the city. A day later – inspired by the success of comrades in the south – Soviet general Leonid Govorov launched Operation Spark to break the blockade of Leningrad. Again, the Red Army employed a pincer movement, the troops of the Leningrad and Volkhov fronts advancing across the narrow German bottleneck east of Schlisselburg, which ran up to the shores of

Lake Ladoga. The Germans held the only road, from Ladoga to Mga, and had strongly defended it. But the corridor they were holding was dangerously narrow.

As the Russians pushed forward, a remarkable role in the fighting was played by a female sniper, Nina Petrova. Petrova was fifty years old and the only woman on the Leningrad front to have won the full Order of Glory, the most highly respected soldier's decoration. She personally trained more than 150 snipers, and had killed 107 Germans. Petrova had a special sniper's rifle with her name engraved on it – a present from Soviet general Ivan Fedyuninsky. She led a women's unit of snipers, attached to the 284th Rifle Regiment (part of the Soviet 86th Rifle Division). When the regimental commander was seriously wounded in the January offensive, she led a counter-attack – personally capturing three Germans. Irina Altshuller of the 284th Regiment also took part in Petrova's counter-attack, joining in hand-to-hand fighting in the trenches and shooting a German officer.

Petrova and Altshuller were strongly driven to fight by the horror inflicted on Leningrad by the besieging Germans, who were deliberately starving the city's civilian population. This desire to hit back at a cruel enemy was harnessed by the Red Army, which improved its own planning and organization with far stronger use of artillery to support the offensive. On 12 January Red Army lieutenant Vasily Churkin's 80th Rifle Division joined Govorov's assault on the German siege positions around Leningrad. 'Our artillery opened up with a deafening roar,' Churkin wrote, 'and a two-and-a-half-hour bombardment was unleashed. Then we heard the sound of our tanks moving forward . . .' Two days later Churkin added: 'The fighting is going on day and night – our artillery is repeatedly striking the German defences.'

On 15 January 1943 Soviet lieutenant Leonid Bobrov (who had finished his retraining programme and was once more fighting with his unit) was also in action on the Leningrad front. Fierce combat had begun – and morale among the men was good. 'They are great guys,' he said. 'I would give up my life for any of them. We have managed to hit the enemy hard,' Bobrov continued,

> but he is looking to strike back . . . We are preparing to move forward again. The weather is clear and sunny. German planes attempted to bomb us, but we sent off such a barrage of artillery fire that they quickly disappeared. Yesterday I was busy with my machine gun – you know how I love using it, I am a bit of an adolescent with his new toy! I kept on firing until the barrel glowed red and I burned my hand. It's bothering me a little today.

This burn made Bobrov think about life and luck in the war. 'I'm still alive!' he declared, 'despite all the laws of probability, all the accidents that might happen. I can't quite believe it myself. I've not even had the slightest scratch after a year and a half of front-line fighting. Not a single wound!' And then Bobrov's tone changed. 'If I continue to survive unscathed I will probably get killed in the last few weeks of the war. That is my premonition – and I'm rarely wrong!' As if taken aback by what he had pronounced, he then veered away from it. 'OK, let's leave the subject – I still hope to meet with you, to see my friends and family.' But the prediction had been made.

The gap between the two Soviet fronts was now little more than 1.5 kilometres, and the Red Army concentrated its efforts on two German redoubts, Workers' Settlements 1 and 5. Special night-time combat units were formed to give the Wehrmacht garrisons no rest and to hinder their deployment of reinforcements. On 18 January the blockade of Leningrad was breached. Nikolai Gorshkov wrote in his diary:

> From anywhere in the city you can hear the thundering of artillery salvoes. The time is 11.00 p.m., and the radio has broadcast: 'In the last hour the enemy ring around Leningrad has been broken. Our army is victorious and the circlet of German divisions enclosing our city has been pierced. Over 15,000 enemy soldiers lie dead on the battlefield; many more have been captured ...' After this broadcast, happiness was everywhere. Everyone went out on the streets. Tears, strangers kissing each other, happiness, happiness ... We have longed for this day so much – no one can sleep.

'We have liberated Schlisselburg and broken the blockade of Leningrad,' Red Army lieutenant Vasily Churkin wrote the same day. 'We now hold a narrow strip of land – in some places only six miles wide – which connects us to the rest of the country again. And this small piece of land, reclaimed with so much blood and suffering, is the source of an incredible upsurge of patriotism.'

That upsurge in patriotism was strongly present at Stalingrad, where the soldiers' watchword had become: 'There is no land for us beyond the Volga'. As Soviet lieutenant Anatoly Mereshko said: 'Every building, every river, every scrap of earth in the city became precious to us – as if it represented the Motherland herself.' Rage against the Germans combined with a deep love of imperilled Russia to create an incredible resilience and will to resist – something the enemy, for all his professionalism, was unable to match. By 26 January advancing Red Army soldiers had joined with their fellows in Stalingrad. Paulus's position was now hopeless and he surrendered to the Russians on 31 January. The last resistance of German forces in the north of the city ended two days later, on 2 February 1943.

The absence of shooting, after months of hellish combat, was eerie. On 3 February Red Army nurse Katya Gorodetskay wrote: 'The enemy's resistance has ended. Lots of German generals have been captured. The prisoners were led along our trenches and our soldiers watched, fists clenched, struggling not to hit them. Silence, silence . . . it is very strange. We have been waiting for it for so long.'

For the Germans, the loss of the Sixth Army was a devastating blow. On 11 February German captain Wilhelm Hosenfeld wrote:

> The terrible drama of Stalingrad has now drawn to a close. It is said that some 300,000 men have been lost there . . . The troops had run out of food – one officer, who was flown out shortly before the final surrender, said that the daily ration for soldiers had been reduced to a small slice of bread. About 30,000 vehicles have also been lost, including innumerable tanks. The effect this catastrophe will have on us is not really possible to calculate.

Hosenfeld looked at the bigger picture: 'All along the eastern front, we are hearing bad news. The Russians attack at Voronezh and Kursk. The Caucasus army is in full retreat, and Rostov is now in danger. Fighting is taking place around the Don delta. We have suffered a serious reverse at Leningrad, where Soviet forces have restored a land link to the city. The military situation is difficult for us everywhere. We are struggling to hold our positions all along the front.'

The battle of Stalingrad was the turning point of the Second World War. For many years the Western image has been that of a hell on earth, where Soviet defenders were coerced into fighting by a brutal regime and a bullying army commander, prevailing only because of the strategic mistakes of Hitler and the German High Command. But the Red Army soldiers were powerfully motivated to fight, and their generals found the right blend of tactics and organization to fashion an extraordinary victory.

Soviet lieutenant Ivan Kaberov of the 284th Rifle Division wrote on 12 February:

> We are happy that all our losses are not in vain – Stalingrad is free! We first arrived at the city at a time of terrible fighting. As we approached, we saw smoke and fire and everything burning. The Germans wanted Stalingrad at any price. Today there is silence. The front line has already moved hundreds of miles to the west. Only the ruins remind us of the severity of the fighting. Now, with a feeling of real pride, we can say that we – the defenders of Stalingrad – changed the fate of our Motherland and saved our people from Fascist slavery.

This idealism was genuine and deeply felt. The balance of power on the eastern front was shifting. It was the Red Army which now held the combat initiative, and had gained stronger morale and determination. Soviet forces had come of age. In a very real sense, Stalingrad was a psychological turning point.

Ida Segal had volunteered for the Red Army at the beginning of the war, and initially served in a communications unit. But she fought as a paratrooper at Stalingrad, where she became an officer and was decorated with the Order of the Red Banner. The battle, everything it stood for and the comradeship she experienced in the fight for the city on the Volga profoundly changed her, and on 23 February 1943 she wrote her family a letter describing that transformation:

> It is my duty to the Motherland to be where there are thundering cannonades, where the world's fate is being determined . . .

I voluntarily joined the Red Army. I am proud of that, and I hope you are proud of it too, my dears, that you have a volunteer in the Patriotic War. I have learnt a great amount from the moment when I left home, on 22 June 1941, and I continue to see what real life is like. This war, this army, has for me been the best school ever. I am now a mature person holding well-formed opinions. I am no longer a young brunette student from the University of Kiev. Rather, I am a commander in the Red Army . . .

Your daughter Ida deeply respects the honour of a Soviet soldier, the honour of a Soviet citizen, and has not brought shame to the Segal family name. You wouldn't recognize me now. I wear trousers, a military tunic, leather boots, a trench coat − and I look great. I have grown taller, I have grown stronger and I have grown older. I look older than my age − I look like a real adult now.

Segal concluded with a simple statement − yet its heartfelt pride spoke for thousands of her comrades-in-arms: 'There was a difficult situation on the Volga and our guards division was transferred there. It is sufficient to say: I was in the Sixty-Second Army at Stalingrad.'

4

Psychological Attack

ON 27 JANUARY 1943 fifteen-year-old Yitskhok Rudashevski wrote from the Jewish ghetto in Vilnius, Lithuania: 'German military reports concede there is a major Red Army offensive on all fronts ... and the all-conquering German Sixth Army, that proudly fought its way into Stalingrad, is now enclosed in a ring of Soviet steel.' On 7 February he added: 'We have good news, and everyone in the ghetto is celebrating. The Germans admit that Stalingrad has fallen.' Such celebration, of course, had to remain hidden from the Nazi occupiers. But it was jubilant nonetheless. 'I walk across the street and see people winking at each other happily,' Rudashevski continued. 'The entire Sixth Army has capitulated – and at last Hitler has suffered a major defeat. Stalin's city has become the enemy's grave.'

Rudashevski took a walk in the ghetto. It seemed to him that winter was finally leaving. The weather was warm and sunny, and the ice on the streets was beginning to melt. He allowed himself a moment of hope – the thought that liberation might come. But in the town of Bedzin in German-occupied Poland fourteen-year-old Rutka Laskier was less optimistic. She wrote: 'The Nazis have been defeated at Stalingrad, Krasnodar and now Kharkov. Maybe the fact that the Germans are in retreat on the eastern front signals a nearing of the end of the war. I'm only afraid that we – the Jews – will be finished before that ever happens.'

On 10 February Roman Kravchenko wrote from Kremenets in German-occupied Ukraine: 'The Germans have reported the fall of Stalingrad and the loss of the Sixth Army, trumpeted this army's "heroism, loyalty and sense of commitment" and announced three days of mourning . . . They compared Stalingrad to Thermopylae. But there was a major difference – the people who were defending Thermopylae were protecting their homeland. The Germans at Stalingrad were aggressors, in a place they should never have been.' Nevertheless, Kravchenko felt the epic quality of both clashes. 'Just as modern-day researchers dig the remains of ancient battlefields,' he continued, 'and find helmets, swords and bones – 3,000 years from now they will find amid the ruins of the Stalingrad tractor factory the remnants of tanks, machine guns and rifles. And they will try to understand the significance of these objects . . .'

Soviet war correspondent Pavel Antokolsky had composed a piece on the significance of Stalingrad entitled 'The Germans on the Volga', and felt, like many others, that a turning point in the war had been reached. By 10 February 1943 he had also finished a poem about his son Vladimir, who had died in his first engagement with the enemy. It would simply be called 'Son', and Antokolsky hoped it would speak for millions of bereaved Soviet parents who had lost sons and daughters in the war. The poem was to be printed in the magazine *Smena*, and also as a separate booklet. In it, Antokolsky took a conventional propagandist line, comparing the communist idealism and honest patriotism of his own son to the ruthless Nazi dogmatism of a German son, who had invaded the Soviet Union. But his poem began powerfully and unusually with the deceased son addressing his

father, in the aftermath of Stalingrad, as the dead and the
living march westwards against the Germans:

> Do not call me, Father. Do not seek me,
> Do not call me, do not wish me back.
> We are on a route uncharted, fire and blood erase our track.
> On we fly on wings of thunder, never more to sheathe our
>   swords –
> All of us in battle fallen, not to be brought back by words.

The poem concludes with the father in mourning:

> I will dream of you still as a baby,
> Treading the earth with little strong toes
> The earth where already so many lie buried –
> This song to my son, then, is come to its close.

It was, in part, a commemoration of his son's life, and
Antokolsky had hoped to publish a photo of Vladimir next to
it, but the Komsomol Central Committee vetoed the idea.
They saw its potential to reach out to the nation. 'I under-
stand their reasoning,' Antokolsky wrote on 10 February.
'They want the poem to have the widest possible appeal.'

Exploiting its victory at Stalingrad, the Red Army moved
on to the attack. Sergeant Mikhail Borisov, an artillery officer
in the Soviet II Tank Corps, was participating in a bold
attempt to liberate the Donbas industrial region in the eastern
Ukraine. On 11 February 1943, at the village of Petrovka,
south-west of Lugansk, his gun unit was separated from the
rest of its detachment. A Germany infantry force suddenly
appeared. 'They saw that we were weak and isolated, and
decided to terrify us,' Borisov recalled. 'It was a fresh
Wehrmacht division, just arrived in the Soviet Union from
garrison duty in France. They all knew about Stalingrad, and
wanted to take their revenge, to humiliate us. So they began
to move towards us, not crawling on the ground, but at full

height – in three lines, spaced apart, half a metre between each man – as if they were goading us to fire.'

Eighteen-year-old Borisov had experienced German psychological warfare before, in the Crimea, and on the Don steppe. Almost a year earlier, in March 1942, he had been foraging for food in a ruined Crimean village. A German plane had appeared in the sky, and the pilot spotted him. The plane began to circle above the village, spiralling lower and lower, and raking its buildings with machine-gun fire. Borisov had cowered, terrified, and then tried to run towards more substantial shelter. The Messerschmitt followed, shooting ahead of him. It was a game of cat and mouse. The German flew low over the village and Borisov clearly saw the pilot's grinning face. He realized that his assailant was toying with him – and enjoying his sport. Borisov expected to die. But after half an hour of torment, the pilot wearied of the game and abruptly flew off.

Borisov was from a small Siberian village. He had enlisted in the Red Army – under age – in a flush of patriotic enthusiasm as the Moscow counter-offensive got under way. His image of war had been romantic and naive, gleaned from films and books. As the Wehrmacht pulled back from Moscow in disarray, Borisov had been worried the Germans would be quickly defeated – he did not want to miss out on the action. But the reality proved very different. In 1942 Hitler's forces had the strength and confidence to turn the tables on their foe. The Crimea – Borisov's first theatre of war – was a debacle for the Red Army. And beneath his partial understanding of such factors as army composition, troop manoeuvres and modern technology, the young man began to grasp a deeper, more primal truth about the war – that it was a clash between the hunter and the hunted. He felt he had undergone a terrible initiation in that burnt-out Crimean village, and wrote a poem about it, which he called 'Target Number One'.

> A leaden hail of bullets –
> Beyond them lies the scent of wormwood
> And the rowan trees' red foam.
> And the Messer tightens its circles,
> Hunting me down – alone.

Red Army soldiers were strongly discouraged from keeping diaries. But for Borisov – and many others – poetry became a meaningful substitute.

'It started with a few lines, written on scraps of paper,' Borisov recalled. 'I had no great literary pretensions. But with constant fighting all around me – and death always a close companion – I found those scraps of poetry brought some meaning to my experiences.' And so the writing grew:

> A sigh like a distant groan
> A line of a poem, severed by a bullet
> Only a half-finished line . . .
> But streaming with blood
> So painfully dear to me,
> Holding charred ruins . . .
> And white snow, baptized by fire.

Instinctively, Borisov wanted to channel the powerful emotions thrown up by the war. On the Don steppe in 1942 the theme of 'Target Number One' was reprised, with even greater frustration and shame. Borisov's whole battalion was strung out across the open countryside. They had air cover, but the five Russian planes (I-16s – Polikarpov single-engine fighters) were ponderous and slow. A single German Messerschmitt appeared. The German deftly manoeuvred round the I-16s, and shot them down, one by one. Then he turned towards the infantry. There was no cover for them. 'A burst of machine-gun fire would have finished us off,' Borisov said. 'Instead, he merely flew over our column, again and again. Then he tipped his wings at us, in a derisory mock salute, and flew off.' The Red Army soldiers had been reprieved. But Borisov added: 'The shame and humiliation we felt was overwhelming. It would have been better to have been killed. We shook our fists at the German plane in helpless, agonizing rage.'

By 1943 the feeling had changed. Now, at Petrovka on 11 February, the Germans once again wanted to humiliate and mock. But on this cold clear February morning Stalingrad was in everybody's minds. The Germans had been deeply shocked by the loss of the entire Sixth Army and sought revenge for their comrades. But Borisov's gun unit had gained the self-belief to withstand a numerically superior foe.

The Wehrmacht could scarcely comprehend that the Red Army had outfought its own soldiers at Stalingrad. It sought other explanations for the defeat – the weather, the unreliability of Germany's allies, the Hungarians, Italians and Romanians, the problems of logistics and supply. In this small engagement at Petrovka, it sought once more to assert its dominance by using a psychological ploy. By standing up, and walking towards the enemy, the Germans deliberately made themselves a target. They were not yet in machine-gun range. But they drew themselves up in three lines, evenly spaced, across an open, snow-covered field, and began advancing towards the lone Russian unit. They would provoke their opponent into panic-firing. Some of their men would die, but the rest would overwhelm the Soviet soldiers. And as they did so, they would witness a last despairing resistance from their foe and demonstrate the triumph of their discipline and resolve.

Borisov watched the Germans draw closer. Time and

space contracted. He could no longer see the sky. All his attention was focused on his gunsight. He felt something against his cheek – his commanding officer was pushing a pistol against his face. 'Misha,' the officer yelled hoarsely. 'You're a Siberian, right – a hunter? Let them come close, as close as fucking possible! Then open up right in the middle of them.' Borisov felt strangely calm. The enemy was moving forward silently – then a clinking sound was magnified in the cold winter air. Borisov knew that the Germans had come from garrison duty in France. 'They are carrying cognac flasks,' he thought. 'So that's the basis of their courage!'

Borisov readied himself. The Germans were now about 300 metres away. He recalled what followed in a poem, 'Psychological Attack':

> I cannot see the sky,
> Only the black ring-end of our gun barrel.
> We let them come closer,
> And then a tornado unfurls:

The Red Army soldiers opened fire. Shells exploded among the advancing Germans, but they held their formation – and pushed on, now within machine-gun range.

> The enemy is almost at my trench
> And cold sweat is dripping down my neck.
> A hail of bullets rattles the gun shield
> And my mind is going mad with fear.

Borisov kept on firing, and more Germans fell to the ground. And then, suddenly, they broke, men running in different directions, colliding with each other – shooting wildly. Triumphant, Borisov let off a final salvo at the fleeing foe. The dead lay on the ground in heaps – he counted over a hundred of them. The phrase 'Psychological Attack' had a dual meaning – an attempt to intimidate an opponent, but also – in Red Army slang – an assault conducted under the influence of alcohol, lacking real confidence and belief. Amid the bodies, shattered cognac flasks lay on the snow.

Stalin's High Command now decided to push back the Germans on all fronts. But such objectives were unrealistic at this stage of the war. The Wehrmacht still had plenty of fight left in it, and attempts to dislodge German troops from the Siniavino Heights south-east of Leningrad proved fruitless.

Soviet lieutenant Nikolai Vasipov recalled:

> We were stationed in swampy ground that was difficult for our tanks to move across and the transport of supplies became more and more erratic. The peat was burning from the constant shell fire, letting off a heavy grey smoke until it was impossible to tell night from day. The trenches began to fill with the dead bodies of our troops. We pushed forward slowly – the cries of the wounded echoing all around us – with a mood of grim determination, but made little headway against the Germans. They dominated the high ground above us – and their system of fortification was well-constructed.

Lieutenant Vasily Churkin of the Red Army's 80th Rifle Division remembered one of these attacks, on 22 February 1943. 'We were supposed to take the heights in time for Red Army Day [on the 23rd],' he wrote in his diary.

> As we went up to the assembly point, we passed a young woman at the crossroads directing the military traffic. Our infantry moved on – but was unable to make progress against a pulverizing enemy artillery barrage. On our way back we passed the crossroads again. The young Red Army soldier lay by the side of the road. Only a few minutes earlier she had been standing there, alive, beautiful, smiling at us. Her body was torn to pieces by a shell blast.

Nikolai Vasipov recalled a visit by Leningrad Front commander Lieutenant General Leonid Govorov. Govorov was an expert artilleryman and a humane leader. He handed out extra rations to the soldiers and asked about the front-line conditions. 'We are losing too many men here, Comrade Commander,' an officer told him bluntly. Govorov had masterminded the breaking of the Leningrad blockade, but it was clear this latest offensive was asking too much of his troops. 'We cannot do it any other way,' he replied, but his voice was choking with emotion. Vasipov and his fellow fighters sensed Govorov did not want to continue these attacks, but had to obey orders from the High Command.

Yet the attitude of Stalin's High Command – ruthless and unrelenting as it was – began to change. In February 1943 Major General Konstantin Rokossovsky was appointed commander of the Soviet Central Front, with orders to push on to Bryansk and Orel, but once again German positions were too strong, and Red Army troops were exhausted. The length of campaigns, the high level of casualties and the seemingly endless combat were too much for many of these soldiers:

A report from the 121st Rifle Division of the Soviet Sixtieth Army on 31 March 1943 stated bluntly: 'Recently, many instances of drinking binges have been observed in the division's units – and these now have spread to the command personnel who – instead of enforcing discipline – are in some cases encouraging and actively participating in them.' The Sixty-Fifth Army was concerned about 'unstable elements' within its ranks that had carried out 'crimes motivated by cowardice', including self-inflicted wounds, in an attempt to avoid front-line service. Combat stress was taking its toll.

Rokossovsky wrote: 'It became abundantly clear to me that a successful offensive would only be achieved through proper and realistic preparation, allowing time to fully supply and organize our armies – particularly if the enemy had been able to prepare a strong defensive position.' He was critical of the high losses Red Army soldiers were suffering, and the fatalistic way some commanders pushed their men into near-suicidal attacks. He demanded that one army leader – Major General German Tarasov of the Soviet Seventieth Army – be sacked for launching an offensive without proper reconnaissance, and needlessly losing men's lives. The culture of Soviet military command had previously placed little concern on the well-being of the individual soldier – yet Stalin's High Command acceded to Rokossovsky's request, and Tarasov was removed.

The war had moved on from Stalingrad – and the image of the burning city on the Volga, which once had mesmerized the world, began to fade. In March 1943 Soviet lieutenant Vladimir Gelfand's 301st Rifle Division passed through Stalingrad on its way to a different section of the front. Gelfand and his comrades – who had been fighting in the Caucasus – were given two days' leave, and decided to look round the ruined city. 'We arrived at the site of this famous battle by military train,' Gelfand began.

> It was a struggle that brought glory to the Red Army and humiliation to the enemy. But a terrible picture of destruction unfolded before us. The river embankments on the Volga's edge were littered with German weaponry and equipment. A smashed plane emblazoned with the swastika lay between two gullies. We saw burnt and twisted tanks, jettisoned lorries, cars and guns – the relics of a once powerful army, now a mass of scrap iron. Dead bodies were everywhere. Some had been placed in heaps for burial; others lay on the ground, partially stripped of clothing . . .

As Gelfand surveyed the scene, he was struck by the raw heroism of Stalingrad's defenders. 'The city centre was utterly disfigured. I was moved by the scene of desolation at the entrance to one of its buildings. The doorway had once been adorned by two beautiful, carved lions. One had vanished; the other had been split by a shell blast. Red brick protruded from its white plasterwork. It gave the impression of blood running out of the body of a noble, wounded beast.'

In the far south, the Germans began to pull back from their last outposts in the Caucasus. Red Army soldiers were too exhausted to pursue them far. Russian sniper Maria Galyshkina of the 57th Marine Brigade remembered that by March 1943 supplies and ammunition were running out: 'The Brigade was starving. Soldiers were tossing grenades into the river to try and stun and catch a few fish. That was a luxury. I remember how happy I was to get a handful of rotten corn. And we had almost run out of bullets!' Galyshkina shared a tent with another female sniper, Anna, and the two became close friends.

On 3 March the brigade was ordered to attack a German-held village. Reconnaissance was poor. It was reported that the enemy had only one heavy machine gun – in fact they had nineteen of them. Galyshkina saw the leading soldiers running back, saying it was a massacre – everyone was being killed or wounded. Anna had gone missing. The Germans often targeted Red Army women soldiers for particularly cruel treatment, and Galyshkina feared the worst. Two days later she went on a sniping 'hunt' and managed to kill four Germans. She wanted revenge for her friend, but the killing didn't really satisfy her.

On 8 March – International Women's Day – Galyshkina and other women snipers in the unit got together. The occasion was not a happy one. Anna was no longer with them, and two of the newest snipers had been killed by an enemy marksman that very morning. Two days later, the Germans pulled back from the village. The Red Army soldiers found Anna strung up in a barn, in her military-issue blue underwear, raped, with a broken bottle between her legs. She was covered in blood and one side of her face had been hacked away. Galyshkina could not stop crying. But then she gathered herself. In front of her fellow soldiers she swore an oath of revenge on the mutilated body, for Anna, and for all Soviet civilians murdered by the enemy.

The Red Army needed to regroup. In the south, the Germans' ablest commander, Field Marshal Erich von Manstein, had counter-attacked in the Ukraine and recovered Belgorod and Kharkov. Hitler and his generals were hoping to bring in reinforcements from the west and resume a general offensive in the summer. They sought vengeance for Stalingrad and wanted to reassure Germany's wavering allies that recent events were merely setbacks in a campaign whose success was still assured. Their attention focused on the exposed Soviet salient around Kursk. On 15 April preliminary plans were drawn up to launch a pincer attack on the Russian position from the north and south and to entrap the Red Army forces stationed there.

The offensive would be supported by a range of new weapons that were frightening in their destructive power, the heavy Tiger tank, the medium Panther tank and the heavily armoured self-propelled gun, the Ferdinand. To counter this onslaught, the Red Army had to decide whether to launch an attack of its own, to forestall Hitler's plan, or to go on the defensive, allowing the Germans to wear out their strength before counter-attacking. Stalin was now prepared to listen to his generals, and when a trio of his ablest commanders – Zhukov, Vasilevsky and Rokossovsky – argued strongly for the latter course, their views carried the day.

On 4 May 1943 Soviet private Alexei Zhiburt read a piece

in the army newspaper *Red Star* by the war correspondent Ilya Ehrenburg. It was called 'The Return of Proserpina', and this legend from ancient Greece – and Ehrenburg's interpretation of it – deeply touched Zhiburt and his fellow soldiers. 'I read it out aloud in the trench,' Zhiburt began, 'and I tried to put as much expression into my reading as I could.'

First Zhiburt gave a short résumé of Ehrenburg's argument: 'It has been a long time since Proserpina, the lovely goddess of spring, has paid a visit to our ruined, burnt and desolate land. But she will return to us, Ehrenburg says, when the hateful Hitlerites are finally beaten. And Ehrenburg is right. We must now muster all our strength, so that the poor, weeping Prosperina can be restored to her youth and beauty, so that she can complete her work as quickly as possible.'

And then Zhiburt let his own imagination run free: 'And when she returns to us, escaping from the Hitlerite underworld, how much she will achieve, how generously she will bestow her gifts. Bright green leaves will unfurl from trees split open by shells, flowers will appear among the churned-up debris of war . . .'

Both sides were now feverishly preparing for a great summer battle at Kursk. The Germans were bringing up more and more troops, supplies and weaponry; the Red Army was constructing a series of elaborate defence lines, heavily mined and protected to blunt the force of the German attack. On the northern flank of the Kursk bulge, General Rokossovsky's Central Front was built up to a strength of 712,000 men and 1,800 tanks and self-propelled guns. Over 5,000 kilometres of trenches were dug, and anti-tank strongpoints (ATSPs) set up at regular intervals. Each ATSP had twenty anti-tank guns and several dozen anti-tank rifles. The distance between each ATSP was no more than 600–800 metres, and around them were at least a thousand mines.

Major General Nikolai Antipenko – the head of supplies on the Soviet Central Front – remembered Rokossovsky's thoroughness – his front-line visits, to check that troops were properly equipped and ammunition stocks replenished. 'We must be patient,' he told Antipenko. 'Let the Germans exhaust themselves attacking our defences. Once that happens, we will show them what we are made of.'

Rokossovsky would be faced by Field Marshal Walther Model, commander of the German Ninth Army. Although Model would be attacking, he had a substantially smaller force, some 332,000 men and 1,000 tanks and self-propelled guns. The commander of Army Group Centre, Field Marshal von Kluge, was opposed to the offensive and took no part in it – and Model was concerned about the depth of the Soviet fortifications. To offset these disadvantages he was promised the new giant self-propelled gun, the Ferdinand, but a lot of reliance was being placed on this super-weapon, which was as yet untested in battle. And the terrain of the northern flank of the Kursk bulge also favoured the defenders – only 90 kilometres of front line was good tank country.

On the southern flank the Germans were stronger. The Voronezh Front of Soviet general Nikolai Vatutin, with 626,000 men and 1,700 tanks, was facing some 445,000 men and 1,500 tanks from Army Group South, commanded by the Wehrmacht's ablest general, Field Marshal Erich von Manstein. Vatutin's troops had dug a massive 4,200 kilometres of trenches, studded with ATSPs and minefields, in three lines of defence. Although the German attacking force was again smaller than that of the Soviet defenders, it contained some superb fighting divisions – including the elite SS Totenkopf and Leibstandarte – and was buttressed with the powerful new Tiger tank. And in the south, the terrain favoured the attacker. Vatutin's forces were deployed on the steppe in open ground – the Germans had greater freedom to vary the point of impact of their assault.

The skill and temperament of the rival commanders would play their part. To the north of Kursk, Field Marshal Walther Model had won his reputation as a master of defence. He had no real experience of attack at army level of command, and was daunted by the strength of Russian positions. His opponent, newly promoted General Konstantin Rokossovsky, believed in the correctness of the Soviet strategy, and had the confidence to make a transition from defence to attack when the occasion was right.

The southern flank offered a sharp contrast. Field Marshal Erich von Manstein revelled in open, fast-moving warfare and the skilful coordination of tanks, assault artillery and air power. His opponent, General Nikolai Vatutin, a clear and intelligent military thinker, preferred the role of attack to defence. Vatutin was in his element directing an offensive – his finest was Operation Uranus, encircling the Germans at Stalingrad. As time passed, and the German offensive still had not started, Vatutin became uneasy. 'We are oversleeping and will miss our chance,' he complained to Marshal Alexander Vasilevsky, chief of the Soviet general staff. 'The enemy is not attacking. Soon it will be autumn, and all our plans will have failed. Let us stop digging in – and start our offensive first.' Vasilevsky refused Vatutin's request.

Hitler's postponement of his great Kursk offensive – Operation Citadel – gave his Russian opponents more time to strengthen their defences. But it had a different psycho-logical effect, building up a near-intolerable level of strain. Everyone was in training to meet the new German super-weapons, carrying out 'ironing' exercises where T-34s drove over trenches of infantry to combat 'tank fright', using Molotov cocktails and tank grenades, studying pamphlets on how to combat the new German tanks and guns. And so the weight of expectation grew. On three different occasions Stalin's High Command warned the fronts of an 'imminent German attack'. Lev Malikin, a Soviet reconnaissance scout with the 222nd Guards Infantry Regiment, said: 'Everyone was expecting the German offensive – and people were really feeling the stress. All units were on a state of high alert. Officers were manning observation posts all day long. The artillery was "tucked up" close to the front line and ready. The suspense was unbearable.'

On 5 July 1943 Hitler ordered his troops forward.

'Soldiers,' the Führer enjoined,

today you will be beginning an offensive, the outcome of which will be crucial to the war. Your victory will show the world – more strongly than ever before – that all resistance to the might of the German Army is ultimately useless. Until now, those partial successes the Russians have achieved have been because of their tanks. My soldiers! Finally you have a tank superior to anything they possess. Our new weapons will shake the Soviet Army to its very foundations. Remember – everything depends on success in this battle.

Hitler was fixated by these new super-weapons – the Tigers, Panthers and Ferdinands – armoured juggernauts that he believed would carry all before them. Some of his troops shared this confidence. German radio operator Wilhelm Roes of II SS Panzer Corps exclaimed: 'We thought nobody could resist such might – we were confident of winning.' Yet the Panthers and Ferdinands were being pushed into battle too quickly, without full testing and preparation. By July 1943 the Red Army had a colossal strength of its own – some 9,580 tanks and self-propelled guns – to match these monsters. There was a strong psychological aspect to Hitler's new offensive – relying on these terrifying weapons and German military skill and professionalism to overawe the Red Army, and undermine its will to resist. But the Russians had learnt from their mistakes in the spring of 1943, and had prepared thoroughly. They had good intelligence on the design of the new German weaponry, and had devised battlefield tactics to counter it.

The German offensive began with a colossal artillery bombardment. Soviet reconnaissance scout Lev Malikin recalled:

> The thunder of explosions literally threw us from our bunks in our dugouts. We grabbed our guns and manned the slit-trenches. Between the trenches and the command posts was a whirlwind of flame, smoke and earth – thrown up by the force of the bombardment. The enemy's artillery preparation lasted about an hour – then the guns began to subside. Under the cover of a huge smokescreen, the Germans began to advance . . .

On Kursk's northern salient, the German attack under Colonel General Walther Model pushed forward 11 kilometres on 5 July, but ran into well-fortified defences and determined resistance. On the following day it repulsed Soviet counter-attacks, but advanced only another 3 kilometres. 'I don't know how we managed to withstand this armada of German tanks, self-propelled guns and infantry,' said Private Mikhail Bulatov, an engineer in the Soviet 235th Rifle Division. 'It was a quite terrifying sight – but we fought them to a standstill.'

Bulatov's unit was stationed at the small town of Ponyri – 48 kilometres north-east of Kursk – which turned into a miniature Stalingrad. Every building was fought over. 'The fortified railway station was the key to our position,' Bulatov continued. 'The Germans threw tanks and self-propelled guns into the battle for it, but we resisted strongly. At the end of two days' fighting our division had lost more than 2,500 men – but the railway station remained in our hands.' Fearing his offensive was losing momentum, Model swung fresh forces south-west of Ponyri to the Olkhovatka Heights. If he captured this vital piece of high ground, Ponyri could safely be bypassed and the road to Kursk – now only 40 kilometres away – would be open. Barring his way was the Soviet 75th Guards Division.

There were fears that Model might still break through, for his 70-tonne Ferdinands – equipped with formidable 88mm guns – had the armoured strength to open up the Red Army defences. Model had ninety of them. Major General Antipenko asked Rokossovsky if they should evacuate supply and ammunition dumps ahead of the German attack. 'No,' Rokossovksy replied. 'We will stand fast. Even if the enemy encircles my troops, we will carry on fighting. I will take command of them personally.'

The Soviet 75th Guards Division – manning the Olkhovatka Heights – had been formed around a nucleus of Stalingrad veterans under the command of Major General Vasily Gorishny. They were tough seasoned fighters, with the will to withstand the German onslaught. 'The early morning of 8 July was completely quiet,' recalled Sergeant Andrei Puzikov, commander of an artillery unit in the 75th Guards. 'We were struck by the beauty of the sunrise. For a few brief moments it felt as if the war no longer existed . . .' Then a German reconnaissance plane appeared overhead, dropping a mass of leaflets. They read: 'Stalingrad bandits – we know you are here! We have come to finish the job. We will wipe you out.'

Rokossovsky had reinforced the Olkhovatka Heights with dug-in tanks, in camouflaged positions, from Lieutenant General Georgi Rodin's Second Tank Army. He had also created 'fire bags', where Soviet artillery would be used as bait to lure German tanks into an ambush. The 'fire bag' put in place 'flirtatious guns', the nickname for artillery deliberately firing from open, unprotected positions, to draw German tank formations forward. As the tanks came closer, they would be bombarded on the flanks by concealed anti-tank batteries. It was a tactic that required enormous courage and presence of mind from Soviet artillerymen. They had to let the enemy come within 200 metres of their position to allow the anti-tank ambush to be fully effective.

The Soviet troops were subdued yet determined. Puzikov and his comrades knew a major German attack was in the offing, but there was a bizarre prelude to it. As the enemy approached they began to broadcast music from speakers rigged up on the back of their lorries. Red Army soldiers looked at each other in astonishment. It was another psychological trick, and as if sensing the mood of the defenders, the Germans chose to play Russian folk tunes. 'It had a strong impact,' Puzikov said. 'First there was sadness, then rage. Some shot their machine guns in the air in frustration. But the anger galvanized our men. We would not let the enemy through.' The music stopped. Line after line of German tanks appeared, rumbling menacingly towards the Soviet positions. A day of ferocious fighting followed. At the end of it, Puzikov was the sole survivor of his gun battery. But the Red Army line had held.

That night, Sergeant Konstantin Glukhovsky was counting the cost of this desperate stand. Out of 105 men in his company, only eighteen were now left. He wondered whether they could carry on. But then Rokossovsky arrived in person. 'We told him how tough things were,' Glukhovsky said. 'Our commander replied that he knew – he had been watching how well we were fighting. And these simple words of encouragement had an enormous effect on us.' Major General Rokossovsky – the commander of the Soviet Central Front – then stayed and shared supper with Glukhovsky's decimated company. He radiated self-belief, telling the men that they would hold the Germans here – and then go on to the offensive themselves. This gesture invigorated the defenders, and the following day they once more held their position. The power of Model's assault began to diminish.

Combat on Kursk's southern salient was even more furious, for here the Germans deployed their Tiger tanks. The Wehrmacht commander, Field Marshal Erich von Manstein, formed his armour into a powerful battering ram, and began to make substantial inroads into the Soviet defences. 'Early each morning the Germans would hit our positions hard,' recalled Soviet war correspondent Yuri Zhukov, attached to General Katukov's First Tank Army. 'They would close in on any weak point. With a thunderous reverberation more than a hundred vehicles would move forward. Leading the way were the Tigers and Panthers, followed by self-propelled guns and other tanks. In the sky we would hear the howling of their bombers; all around us their artillery would open up.'

'It seemed impossible to withstand such an onslaught,' Zhukov continued.

> The Tigers moved forward ponderously, but were an absolutely terrifying sight. They would manoeuvre in ravines and gullies and then re-emerge close to our positions. The long-barrelled guns gave their shells a formidable velocity – and they were able to smash through most of our armoured protection. When faced by an anti-tank ditch these monsters simply moved down the incline, turned, and started grinding down the packed soil. They were like a herd of angry elephants. The earthen ramparts would crumble – and then, out they crawled, moving forward inexorably.

The 76-tonne Tiger tank had 10 centimetres of frontal armour and 7.5 centimetres of side armour. Its 88mm gun had an accurate range of 1,370 metres, which was more than three times that of the Soviet T-34 tank. Yuri Zhukov added: 'Tactics to counter the Tigers had been worked out by our High Command and circulated among our troops. But only those who have heard the roar of this colossal tank, and seen the damage inflicted by its diabolical gun, can understand the reserves of courage needed to combat it.'

Red Army lieutenant Vasily Chernyshev, commanding an artillery battalion in the 183rd Rifle Division – part of the Sixty-Ninth Army – had to face this onslaught. 'We were fighting for every trench, every dugout,' Chernyshev remembered. 'After the fierce daytime combat, during the short summer nights we had to try and repair our damaged defences, get in ammunition and supplies, evacuate the wounded and bury our dead. We had hardly finished these tasks when – in the early morning light – German planes would appear in the sky, bombing our positions. This kind of fighting was going on day by day.' By 11 July Chernyshev had been pushed back to the small settlement of Prokhorovka, 65 kilometres south-east of Kursk. Manstein was now close to a decisive breakthrough. He had breached many of the Russian defences and knew that Stalin's High Command was desperately rushing up reinforcements. He hoped his armoured strength could now win him victory before these arrived.

But it was at Prokhorovka that the Red Army turned and confronted some of the best German divisions and their new and fearsome weaponry. Major General Popov – the commander of the Red Army defending force, II Tank Corps – was determined to block the German advance here and buy time for fresh Soviet troops – the remainder of the Fifth

Guards Tank Army – to join him. He would hold his ground or die in the attempt.

This was a moment of truth for the Red Army, and there was to be no holding back. On the night of 10 July Lieutenant Polunskii of the 284th Rifle Division was ordered to occupy a defence line close to the German positions. Polunskii claimed to have done this – but, frightened of the enemy, was found directing proceedings from a dugout 3 kilometres in the rear. He was immediately dismissed from his post and placed before a military tribunal. Soviet discipline was ruthless, but men were also rewarded for their courage. That night, Lieutenant Mozorov – a platoon commander in the same division – was honoured for being the first to jump into a German trench, where he destroyed two mortars and other military equipment. Sergeant Kopylev – a reconnaissance scout – was rewarded for killing a Wehrmacht officer and capturing valuable German documents and a map.

The following morning, battle commenced south of Prokhorovka. 'At about 7.00 a.m. the fog lifted, and the slight, drizzling rain stopped,' recalled Soviet major Vasily Sazhinov.

> German artillery and mortars began to bombard our position and then their tanks emerged. The atmosphere among our troops was tense. We were all combat-experienced, but none of us had seen so many tanks before – and then there were the Tigers, placed along the enemy line, which stood out because of their size and long gun barrels. We were hit by a wave of explosions, engulfing us in a cloud of black dust, a dense fog of dirt, through which we glimpsed the purple-black flames of burning vehicles.

Mikhail Borisov's artillery unit collided with an SS reconnaissance force. The Soviet troops had just moved out of some woodland, and saw that the state farm ahead of them was ablaze. Then everyone heard a terrible rumbling sound. The earth began to shake. A column of enemy heavy tanks was approaching from the opposite direction. For a few brief moments Borisov's position was shielded by the billowing smoke. Four Soviet guns were matched against nineteen German tanks.

Borisov felt sick with fear. He had never seen tanks as large as this before. He had heard stories about the new German monster tank – the Tiger – and how its relentless, shuddering progress drove Soviet soldiers mad with terror. He wondered whether he was going to die. In a year and a half of fighting, Borisov had led a charmed life. He had been the only sur-vivor of five different artillery batteries. He had been wounded twice – and by an odd quirk of fate, on both occa-sions it was on his birthday, 22 March – but each time he had recovered quickly. But these present odds were just too great. It seemed as if fortune had finally deserted him.

Borisov was jolted back to the present. His commanding officer gave an order, they opened up on the middle of the column, and two tanks immediately caught fire. The others turned towards them. German artillery also ranged in on their position, and Stuka dive-bombers appeared in the sky above.

'The ground was rocking from side to side from the force of the explosions,' Borisov said. 'We were grabbing the wounded, trying to bandage them, and then returning to the guns.' But one by one those guns fell silent. Borisov and two of his comrades manned the last, and kept on firing. They fell into a desperate rhythm – loading, shooting, load-ing and shooting. More tanks were hit. Then, as Borisov called out for ammunition, there was no longer any response – his two comrades lay dead on the ground. Borisov was left on his own. He rammed shell after shell into the gun. There was no time to aim properly. But the enemy was so close he hit another three of them. A German tank was now only 45 metres away and had him in its sights. Both fired at the same moment. Borisov's last memory was of a patch of blue sky, and a wheel of the gun flying through the air, then darkness.

Borisov's heroic stand had been noticed by Major General Popov – the commander of the Soviet forces – and, moved by the artilleryman's defiant bravery, he ordered his chief of staff to retrieve his body from the field of combat. Borisov was found covered in debris from the last, exploded tank. Miraculously, he was still alive.

Borisov spent the next few weeks recovering in hospital. Once more his life had been spared. He was awarded the title of Hero of the Soviet Union – the highest award for bravery in the Red Army. His comrades quickly learnt of his exploit, which was publicized in front-line army newspapers.

The courage of Red Army fighters like Borisov held the Germans at bay, and allowed time for the Soviet Fifth Tank Army to reach Prokhorovka. On 12 July 1943 both sides clashed in a great and terrible tank battle in the open countryside. Here Soviet general Nikolai Vatutin – impatient to counter-attack – made a bad blunder. He should have assumed a strong defensive position, as Rokossovsky had done on the Olkhovatka Heights. General Pavel Rotmistrov's full tank force had not yet arrived, and the men were exhausted after travelling day and night at speed to reach the battlefield. They should have been ordered to dig in. Instead, they were flung into a frontal assault against the German position. They would face the elite SS divisions Totenkopf and Leibstandarte.

Major General Helmut Becker of the SS Totenkopf recalled in astonishment: 'I noticed a cloud of dust on the horizon, and soon, from these clouds, emerged a mass of

Russian tanks.' Rotmistrov – the Fifth Tank Army's commander – had appealed to Vatutin to cancel this ill-judged assault. Although he had the advantage of numbers – more than 400 of his tanks were in position on the morning of 12 July – his T-34 tanks needed to get within 500 metres of the German Tigers and Panthers for their fire to be effective, whereas the Germans could destroy a T-34 at a range of 2 kilometres. To have any chance of success, Rotmistrov needed to attack at speed on a wide front. But at Prokhorovka, the vital factor of terrain was working against him.

Rotmistrov's tanks had to advance along a narrow corridor between the River Pysol and the railway line. And this corridor was partially blocked by an impassable ravine. The Germans – who knew the features of the battlefield – were training their guns on this point. Once round this obstacle, the attacking tank brigades would have to reform, lining up in rows, back to back, in full view of the enemy.

The Soviet Fifth Tank began to move forward. As the first wave reached the ravine the German guns opened up. Tank after tank was hit. Losses were so severe that the force had to wait for the second wave to join it. The result was carnage. Red Army lieutenant Vasily Bryukhov remembered: 'Tanks were bursting into flames all around me. Five-tonne turrets were blown off their hatches and flew 15–20 metres into the air though the force of the explosions. Sometimes the upper armoured plate of the turret broke off and soared high into the sky. Often, the artillery blasts were so strong that a whole tank would crumple into a heap of metal.' In a matter of minutes, two of Rotmistrov's tank brigades had suffered more than 50 per cent losses. And they still had not engaged the enemy.

Soviet general Vatutin's tactical ineptitude was rescued by raw Red Army courage. Rotmistrov's remaining tankers abandoned the planned frontal assault and decided to work their way around the Germans. Russian tanks broke through along the riverbank of the Pysol and got behind SS Totenkopf's position. Others veered off and attacked the massed artillery of SS Leibstandarte. To counter this threat, the Germans flung their Tigers into the fray.

'As the German and Russian forces engaged, the battlefield was wreathed in fire and smoke,' said Red Army lieutenant Vasily Chernyshev. 'Tanks were on fire, houses were on fire, the wheat was on fire – everything was burning. We fought amid a fume-cloud that the sun could hardly penetrate. Above us, we heard the sounds of a bitter aerial dogfight. Destroyed planes – trailing clouds of thick smoke – would fall on to the battlefield. Hundreds of guns were shooting all around us – and somehow we had to survive in that hell. The fight lasted well into the evening.'

'It wasn't a battle – it was a slaughterhouse of tanks,' said Red Army lieutenant Vasily Bryukhov. 'Everything was burning. An indescribable stench hung in the air. Everything was enveloped in smoke, dust and fire.' T-34 driver Anatoly Volkov remembered: 'The atmosphere was choking. I was gasping for breath, with perspiration running down my face. I expected to be killed at any moment.'

Soviet lieutenant Boris Ivanov was with the 31st Armoured Brigade by Prokhorovka's state farm: 'The constant din, the roar of tanks, the rattle of machine guns, artillery and dive-bombers – the noise was terrible,' Ivanov recalled. 'Neither side was able to make much progress. That night there was a lull in the fighting, and I saw a destroyed Tiger tank close to our position – it was on its side, its barrel pointing up at the sky. It had been rammed by several of our T-34s. All of our tanks had been incinerated.' This terrible image stayed in Ivanov's mind. Battle resumed the following day – by the end of it, his unit had advanced a mere 275 metres.

On 14 July an eerie silence fell over Prokhorovka. Both sides were utterly exhausted. The trenches were full of corpses. Soviet war correspondents – fascinated by the mighty clash of armour – counted 432 wrecked Soviet and German tanks littering the battlefield. The majority of these were Russian – Rotmistrov's tank brigades had lost more than two-thirds of their strength. But they had fought the Germans to a standstill. Red Army soldiers fell asleep where they stood.

Although the outcome at Prokhorovka was inconclusive, German confidence in their offensive was now waning. Their losses in men and tanks had also been substantial. Model's attack on the northern Kursk salient had been called off – and the Soviet Central, Western and Bryansk Fronts were now counter-attacking in force. The German Ninth Army was forced to retreat. Manstein still hoped to make something of his advance from the south but Hitler, alarmed by the news of Allied landings in Sicily, began recalling divisions from the eastern front to combat this new threat. The Red Army had bravely withstood the German onslaught.

The Germans had always fought best in the summer, and the summers of 1941 and 1942 had brought them great victories in Russia. But by 1943 the Red Army had the strength and self-belief to withstand them. It now began to drive the Germans back. Its actions were a formidable success, but bought at a terrible price from Soviet soldiers – a price that called for considerable self-sacrifice.

As the Red Army pushed forward at Kursk, Sergeant Boris Komsky decided to chronicle the savage losses suffered by his regiment. Although keeping diaries was strongly discouraged, Komsky chose to defy the order. On 22 July he recorded: 'Trapped by enemy fire in a deep ravine. We extricated ourselves after ten minutes. The Germans pound us with their artillery. Sasha Ogloblin suffered a head wound and was stretchered out. Yesterday the chief of staff of our regiment was killed. They recovered his body – he had been burnt alive . . .' On the 23rd he added: 'Another hard day. The Germans have apparently pulled back some 15 kilometres, but keep bombarding us with artillery and mortars.'

On 26 July Komsky wrote: 'Ahead of us lies an important railway station. We have to capture it. But the battalion has been badly thinned out. Its remaining strength amounts to little more than two platoons. Today the battalion commander had both his legs torn off by an exploding shell. The chief of staff was also badly wounded. That evening two sergeants carried food out to our front-line positions. One of them played the harmonica for us. Both were killed on the return journey.'

The Germans were on the retreat, but still resisting strongly. There was no general collapse, instead a dogged determination to inflict casualties on the Red Army. On 28 July Komsky noted:

In the morning we found out that the railway station we were supposed to take, on the Orel–Kursk line, had been abandoned by the enemy. We started moving towards it. It was a trap. It turned out that the Germans had not pulled back, but had dug themselves in about a kilometre behind the station, and had called in reinforcements. We immediately came under heavy artillery fire. We stopped about three kilometres from the station, and took up positions along a country road. Suddenly we heard the roar of an artillery strike right over our heads. We dived for cover in a roadside ditch. When the firing stopped, and we returned to our previous positions, my heart started pounding. The exact spot where I had been was now a gaping shell-hole. The barrel of my mortar was squashed like a tin can; my gas mask had completely disintegrated. My trench coat, which I had discarded, had been punctured by shell fragments in 15 different places – if I was still wearing it, just one of these would have ensured I no longer needed the coat or anything else. Misha Indechenko is seriously wounded; Semenov is hurt in the leg. My mortar is out of commission. Will they give me a new one? If not, then it's off to Mother Infantry. Immediately after the attack 10 katyushas took revenge on 'Fritz', for my mortar, and for Misha.

There was a mood of pride among Soviet commanders at their progress, but this was tempered by mindfulness of how dangerous the war still was. On 29 July General Konstantin Rokossovsky wrote to his family about the Kursk battle: 'Having at last a little free time, I would like to tell you what has been happening,' he began.

> Early on the morning of 5 July the Germans began their offensive – throwing into battle a massive amount of tanks, artillery and planes. They deployed their newest armoured monsters: the Tigers, Panthers and Ferdinands. The assault went on for eight days – never stopping, either day or night. You have probably read about the results of the fighting in the newspapers. We have beaten the Fritz. We have captured a lot of prisoners and enemy equipment. To put it simply, we have given the Germans a sound thrashing. We have started our counter-offensive, and are now pushing the enemy back, westwards. Every day we liberate hundreds of towns and villages.

Rokossovsky added revealingly that he wished to avoid the military censor: 'You are offended that I don't write often,' he continued. 'Believe me, there are days when I practically collapse with exhaustion. But that is not the main reason for the delay. I am waiting for an opportunity to send you my letters, not through the post, but by a trusted courier who can deliver them to you personally.'

Then he confided: 'My lucky star is still with me – for somehow I remain healthy and energetic, and still in one piece! On one occasion I only survived by a miracle – *and I have started believing in miracles* [my italics]. The house that I was using as my command post received a direct hit and was blown to bits. I survived without a single scratch. For the first time, I have started to believe in fate. I do not think I am supposed to die yet.'

Others well understood Rokossovsky's sentiments. On 1 August 1943 Lieutenant Nikolai Benesh wrote an astonishing letter to his family:

> I don't know whether news of my death has reached you yet, but a notice was sent out from my unit – everyone thinking that I had been killed. But I am alive – and writing this letter. No one imagined that I could have survived, but I was saved by a pure miracle. I fought for three days in an enemy-occupied village. The rest of our unit had retreated. I was surrounded by Germans. They disarmed me and another Red Army soldier and decided to shoot us. I stood against the wall of one of the village farmhouses with two German soldiers aiming submachine guns at me. In a frenzy, I threw myself at them. They opened fire, but not a single bullet touched me. I grabbed a gun and killed one of the soldiers, then shot the other at point-blank range. The other Red Army man was only wounded in the arm. Together, we ran for it. I still don't understand how I managed to pull this off. When I came to my senses, having gone some distance, I was simply stunned. But, well, that's how it happened . . .

'When I came to my senses . . .' was a telling phrase. Soviet sergeant Mikhail Borisov remembered fleeing from a low-flying German plane, holding an empty ammunition box over his head. This was not a rational decision – the wooden box would provide no protection whatsoever from the plane's machine-gun fire. 'It was a powerful reflex action,' Borisov said, 'but one that had nothing to do with reality. Several minutes later I found myself standing in the middle of a deserted road. The plane had disappeared. I had no idea how I got there – it was as if I had awoken from a dream.'

The Soviet advance continued. On 3 August Boris Komsky wrote: 'Our Political Officer, Tyrkalev, who had fought with our unit for two years, was killed by an exploding mine. He had recommended me as a member of the [Communist] Party, and only yesterday wrote a testimonial that I should be awarded a military medal for bravery.' The terrible attrition rate among officers was one reason why many deserving soldiers did not get medals; there was simply no one left to recommend them. As Soviet signalman Petyr Simonov put it: 'Today the section and platoon commanders get killed, tomorrow the company commander – several days later there's no battalion commander any more. Who's going to propose the award?' Komsky's entry for 3 August concluded: 'Three men were wounded when our battalion commander – who was completely drunk – ordered us into an attack without any artillery preparation.' Although the Red Army's fighting performance had improved dramatically, Komsky's diary extracts show that the failings in army leadership criticized by Rokossovsky in March 1943 had not been fully eliminated.

On 5 August Soviet troops recaptured Orel and Belgorod. This triumph – which removed any last, lingering threat to the Russian capital – was marked by a celebratory firework display in Moscow. But the everyday combat picture on the ground remained harsh and unremitting. A day later, Komsky's much-depleted company was thrown into an attack on a German-held village: 'One by one our people are being killed,' he began.

Again, we were forced to leave someone behind at the onset of the attack. Oshkov crawled over, and promised to get the medics to him as soon as we could. My machine gun opened up on the Germans. They saw us – and their own guns responded. My second-in-command was wounded in the leg. Oshkov was also hurt. To try and get them to our first aid station was so very difficult – 700 metres away, across an open rye field. Nevertheless we began to do it. Then my turn – I was hit in the arm by a shell fragment. As one of my comrades bandaged it I experienced a strange calm, almost relief, as if the end had come. The machine gun had to be abandoned – and the intensity of enemy fire forced us all on our hands and knees. Somehow, all of us managed to get back in one piece. That evening I was admitted to hospital.

In the course of the Red Army counter-offensive the Germans had been pushed back more than 210 kilometres, and Soviet troops now stood on the borders of Belorussia. Victory had been bought with the blood of countless Red Army soldiers. It was in hospital on 19 August that Boris Komsky learnt about the fate of the rest of his company: 'A hard day,' he began.

Kravetz, who has just been admitted to the same ward, told me what happened. On the 9th of August, three days after me, he was wounded in the leg. The idiotic battalion commander decided, on a whim, to adjust our front-line positions. This 'improvement' to our lines ran straight into a German artillery barrage. The last five from my platoon – Yasha Maliyev, Islam, Oshkov, Mikhailov and Lieutenant Kushnerev – were all killed. This news is devastating. I am particularly saddened by the loss of Yasha – we had become close friends. The division is now so weakened it has now been pulled out of combat altogether, and will be re-formed.

In the opening stages of the battle of Kursk, from 5 to 13 July 1943, 69,000 Red Army soldiers had been killed, captured or were missing in action. In the Soviet counter-offensive against Orel in July and early August, 113,000 Russian troops were lost. And the actions against Belgorod and Kharkov, which brought the campaign to a close, accounted for another 72,000. The total of 271,000 Red Army losses forms a stark contrast to the casualty rate during Operation Husky, the Allied invasion of Sicily, from 10 July to 17 August. Here US forces lost 2,572 killed and 1,012 missing and captured; the British 2,721 dead and the Canadians 562. The hell of the eastern front was incomparably worse than any other theatre of war.

But the Kursk counter-offensive was a great Soviet triumph nonetheless. 'The Soviet Armed Forces had dealt the enemy a buffeting from which Nazi Germany would never recover,' wrote Marshal Alexander Vasilevsky, chief of the Soviet general staff. 'The big defeat at the Kursk bulge was the beginning of a fatal crisis for the German Army.' One hundred and eighty Russian soldiers were awarded the title of Hero of the Soviet Union after the battle. Hitler's 'psychological attack' had failed to overawe the Red Army – and the tables were turned on the Wehrmacht. The Germans would never mount another major offensive in Russia.

5

The Dam

ON 24 AUGUST 1943, a day after the Red Army had recaptured Kharkov, Stalin's High Command intended a major new offensive, to cross the Dnieper river in force and regain the industrial regions of the Ukraine. Two weeks earlier, Hitler had belatedly agreed on the construction of a series of fortifications along the western bank of the Dnieper. The Führer imagined a great eastern wall, one that would keep the Slavic hordes at bay; in reality, there was only time to build strongpoints in those areas where a river crossing by the Russians was most likely.

As the Germans pulled back, Hitler ordered a ruthless scorched-earth policy to create supply shortages that would slow the Red Army's progress. Retreating German soldiers carried off all the foodstuffs and raw materials they could find. The Wehrmacht took more than 200,000 cattle, 270,000 sheep, 153,000 horses and 40,000 cartloads of food from the Donets region in the eastern Ukraine. And whatever could not be removed was destroyed – every house, bridge, road or barn. The advancing Russians would enter a wilderness. Field Marshal Erich von Manstein, commander of Army Group South, said simply: 'The food situation at home makes it essential that the troops should be fed off the land, and that the largest possible stock should be placed at the disposal of the homeland.'

'Mile after mile of devastation and misery,' said Private Gabriel Temkin of the Soviet 78th Rifle Division. 'The Germans were certainly very good at this job. In numerous villages, the barns and storage facilities were burnt down, the grain silos blown up and famers left without grain to tide them over to the next harvest. The Germans set fire to houses and shot any inhabitants who resisted.'

On 29 August a group of Soviet war journalists visited the recently liberated town of Orel. One of them was Pavel Antokolsky. They were hoping to write a collaborative book about the region's experience under German occupation, and the terrible destruction wrought by the invader, but the project never came to fruition. Antokolsky was also hoping to borrow a military vehicle and try to locate his son's grave. He was not able to – all available vehicles were requisitioned for the new Soviet offensive.

Red Army soldiers – witnessing this tide of destruction – wanted to free the Ukraine as quickly as possible. On 10 September 1943 Ariadna Dobrosmislova, a medical instructor in the Soviet 308th Rifle Division, wrote:

We are driving the vile Germans from our homeland, liberating villages, towns, thousands of people. Oh, if you could experience this! What you read in the papers, or hear about from stories, can never move you as much as when you see it with your own eyes. I choke with tears when I remember our encounters with the local population. People ran to meet us, hugged and kissed us, wept, fell to their knees. As soon as we entered a village people immediately surrounded us on all sides, pulling at us, talking endlessly, with tears and laughter, of grief for what they had suffered, and joy that that suffering had come to an end. An old village teacher said to us: 'History has never seen such atrocities as those wrought by the German barbarians.'

Pavel Antokolsky, the Soviet war correspondent whose moving tribute to his lost son caught a nation's pain

The son – Vladimir Antokolsky – killed in action on 6 July 1942, in his first clash with the Germans

Stalingrad in flames, 23 August 1942

Red Army soldiers
defending 'Pavlov's
House' in Stalingrad

'A village on the Volga': the Soviet 62nd Army clings to the Stalingrad river embankment

Russian artilleryman and war poet Mikhail Borisov

A cartoon from a front-line Red Army newspaper shows Borisov garlanded with the remnants of an exploded German tank at Prokhorovka

Комсорг батареи Михаил Борисов сжег 7 „тигров".

Любуйтесь!
Радуйтесь!
Дивитесь!

Картина сделана
с натуры!

Пред вами комсо-
мольский витязь!

В семи тигровых
шкурах.

(из фронтовой газеты)

A dead Red
Army soldier
during the battle
of Kursk

Soviet tanks and
infantry on the
move at Kursk

Destroyed
German tank,
Kursk

Red Army lieutenant Boris Komsky

Komsky's diary recorded the high cost of success as Soviet forces
counter-attacked at Kursk

The joy of liberation: Red Army troops free a village in the Ukraine, September 1943. Many were destroyed in a ruthless German scorched earth policy

Red Army forces crossing the River Dnieper near Kremenchug

The dam at Zaporozhye

The smashed control room at the hydroelectric power station,
Zaporozhye, 14 October 1943

Soviet machine gunner
Alexandra Bocharova.
Bocharova saw a Jewish
family, and those who had
helped them, strung up near
Kiev. The memory haunted
her for the rest of her life

Survivors and victims: the typhoid camp at Ozarichi shortly after its liberation
by the Red Army, March 1944

The Soviet assault was planned in three stages. The first was to push hard after the retreating Germans, not allowing them time to reinforce their position on the Dnieper. The second was to launch a massive attack, crossing the Dnieper river on a broad front and keeping up the pressure on the enemy. Finally, when their position on the western bank of the Dnieper was strong enough, Soviet troops would advance on their key targets. The prize was the liberation of the Ukrainian capital, Kiev – and Stalin wanted to achieve this in time for the anniversary of the Bolshevik revolution on 7 November.

On 22 September the first Soviet bridgehead was established on the western bank of the Dnieper, where it joined the River Pripyat. On 25 September another was created, near the Ukrainian town of Dnepropetrovsk. The assault was conducted along a 400-kilometre section of the front, and – with resources at full stretch – all means of transport were used to get troops across the river, including small fishing boats and rafts. The crossings were often carried out under heavy German fire, and Soviet soldiers then had to dig in along the ravines of the Dnieper's western shore. Most of the bridgeheads were little more than 10 kilometres wide and 2 kilometres deep. It was vital that supplies, reinforcements and heavy equipment were brought up as quickly as possible – the Germans would soon launch major attacks on every Red Army position.

There was hard fighting to be done, however, before more Russian soldiers even reached the river. Major General Ivan Russiyanov's I Guards Mechanized Corps – part of the Soviet South-Western Front – specialized in deep operations, the creation and exploitation of rapid breakthroughs. But its route to the Dnieper was blocked by the German 9th Panzer Division, which was pulling back through the southern

Ukraine. And the Panzers had been reinforced by a heavy tank battalion that included the mighty Tigers.

Colonel Viktor Iskrov, a battalion commander in the 116th Guards Artillery Regiment, ran into a column of heavy German tanks at the village of Shevchenko on 26 September. 'I was at my command post when I spotted them,' Iskrov recalled. 'They had broken through our infantry positions and were coming straight towards us. I got through to the regimental commander on the phone and asked what to do. He answered: "Use your initiative!" So we ran as fast as we could towards our artillery battery. The guns were camouflaged among some hedgerows. Recognizing the danger of tank fright [the fear felt by raw recruits when confronted by tanks at close range], we pulled "green" gun-loaders out of the line, and replaced them with experienced officers.'

Iskrov found a vantage point on a small hillock behind the battery. He ordered his crews to fire at the tanks' lighter side armour on his command, which would be the lifting of a red flag. But when the tanks rumbled into view one of the gunners panicked. Sergeant Serdyuk was unnerved by the size of the monsters, let off a shot and missed. The Germans immediately spotted his position, and blasted his gun. After the battle, Serdyuk's head was found 20 metres from the rest of his body. He had been decapitated by the sheer force of the explosion.

The tanks began to turn, exposing their flank armour – and Iskrov raised his flag. His gunners let off a volley of shots. One of Iskrov's best artillerymen – Lieutenant Semyon Markin – had boasted to his comrades that he was going to destroy his first Tiger that day. He hit two of them. But the shells ricocheted off the armour, the tanks swung round and fired back. A shell tore his body in two.

'It was a terrible duel,' Iskrov said. Eventually the Germans pulled back. And then, before the Soviet colonel could gather himself, he heard that his commander, Major General Russiyanov, was about to visit his battery. 'As battalion commander I tried to maintain military formalities,' Iskrov recalled. 'I saluted the general and began to make my official report. But my nerves were so shaken that I could not carry on.'

'The general took in the nightmare of the battle's aftermath,' Iskrov remembered, 'the moans of the wounded, the dead lying right up against the guns, some of the bodies ripped apart by direct hits. He took off his cap, made a deep bow, and said – with tears in his eyes: "A report will not be necessary, Comrade Colonel. May eternal memory and glory be with the defenders of our Motherland." He reached into his pocket and awarded me a medal on the spot – the Order of the Red Banner. Then he told me that all the men in my unit would be recommended for decorations.'

The brave stand of Iskrov's artillery battery was a tribute to the growing skill and courage of the Red Army. But when forced to prepare an offensive hastily, under pressure from Stalin's High Command, it was still profligate with human lives. By the end of September no less than twenty-three Soviet bridgeheads had been created on the right shore of the Dnieper. Some of these were reinforced, ready for an eventual break-out. Others – with cold calculation – were deliberately left to their own devices.

Red Army nurse Natalia Peshkova, serving with a mechanized brigade of the Third Tank Army, had crossed the Dnieper near Bukrin on 27 September. The troops were forced to swim across the river, because there were no boats or pontoon bridges. They dug in on the steep western slope of the riverbank, but had no heavy weapons and suffered increasing casualties – the Germans were attacking incessantly.

'We were shelled day after day,' Peshkova recalled, 'and the sky overhead was black with enemy planes. It was really frightening. We were just left on our own, without food or reinforcement. We realized that we were being used as decoys, to tie down German forces.'

By the end of September 1943 the Bukrin bridgehead was some 20 kilometres wide and 3 kilometres deep, and contained an assortment of Soviet units from the Third, Twenty-Seventh and Fortieth Tank Armies. They were opposed by up to ten German divisions. 'So many people were killed,' Peshkova continued. 'There were 280 new recruits in a neighbouring battalion. At the end of the battle only sixteen of them were left. We were crawling around on our hands and knees, sheltering from the incessant bombing and scavenging for food. We were being sacrificed – so that other Red Army units could liberate Kiev by 7 November.'

Soviet private Mikhail Kuznetsov of the 367th Artillery Battalion remembered the unit next to him being sent on a suicidal assault on a well-defended German position.

> At 8.00 a.m. the soldiers were ordered to attack. Their political officers yelled out: 'For the Motherland! For Stalin! Hurrah!' Within seconds, most of them were mown down by German heavy machine guns. The survivors crawled back, and all became quiet. But some three hours later we again heard: 'For the Motherland! For Stalin!' The rest of the unit was then wiped out – and what for? It was clear that the Germans had several machine guns, so an artillery or air strike should have been ordered before the attack. Instead, the entire field was covered with corpses.

Soviet lieutenant Georgi Osadchinsky added: 'At the Dnieper in September 1943 we suffered needless casualties. This had happened before, during the Moscow counter-offensive and at Rzhev in 1942. Our army had improved, and our commanders were now more skilful – but more should have been done to save our soldiers' lives.'

Red Army private Mansur Abdulin's 66th Guards Rifle Division had reached Kremenchug, on the eastern bank of the Dnieper, on 29 September. It marched through ruins of burnt-down towns, villages and farms. 'Ashes, smoke – everywhere,' Abdulin remembered, 'only brick chimney stacks were left of what were once homes.' At Kremenchug the soldiers found the remains of a German POW camp. About a hundred Soviet soldiers were still hanging on wooden gallows. On the main street, Abdulin witnessed an extraordinary commotion: 'Peasant women, armed with axes, pitchforks, sticks, even pokers, were driving several captured Germans along the road. The women were terribly agitated, screaming loudly in Ukrainian. Then they stopped near a pit and started pushing their prisoners into it. One Nazi, trying to resist, shrieked that he had three children. "What about our children?" a woman bellowed. He was thrown in – and buried alive with his fellows.'

Everywhere the Red Army soldiers saw slogans: 'Give us the Dnieper!' 'The Ukraine is expecting us – forward!' But now they had reached the river, they found no boats had been provided for their crossing. Instead, each rifleman was instructed to make a special device to keep him afloat: sheaves of straw tied up in a waterproof wrapping. It looked like a large pillow – but it seemed to work. On the night of 5 October the men began to cross the river. Their first objective was the island of Peschanny, partway across the Dnieper. But the Germans were waiting for them there. As they clambered ashore, the Soviet soldiers were met by a withering hail of fire.

'The Nazis were battering the hell out of the island,' Abdulin recalled. 'And we could do nothing in reply. Our sub-machine guns wouldn't work – they were clogged with sand. The grenades were also useless. In fact, the only weapons we now had were entrenching shovels.'

The Germans had heavy machine-gun posts on the island, and were also directing artillery strikes against the hapless Soviet soldiers – who were left cowering in the sand. They had no artillery or air support, and were trapped without working weapons. 'I thought I had seen all the horrors of war,' Abdulin said, 'at Stalingrad, at Kalach, in the battle for the Kursk bulge. But nothing compared to this. We had been left to the mercy of fate.'

In desperation, the men waited until dawn, and then – with the sun behind them, shining into the eyes of the German gunners – charged en masse towards the enemy. Many were killed. But the Germans were utterly taken aback. 'A black tidal wave of 500 desperadoes rushed towards the Nazi positions,' Abdulin remembered. 'I saw a German staring at us – paralysed with horror. I ran faster and faster, with one thought in my mind: "Kill him!"'

Surviving Russians hurled themselves into the trenches, leaping on to their opponents and wrenching weapons from their grasp. Abdulin saw a frenzied Red Army soldier riding a German piggyback, beating his opponent's head with a jammed gun. The remainder of the enemy fled. Abdulin and his comrades were still under artillery bombardment – but now they had food and weapons. Five days later, the shelling stopped – and the men reached the western bank of the river. They had been cynically ordered to undertake what was known as a 'false crossing'. While enemy guns were firing on these hapless soldiers, other troops were able to cross the Dnieper safely upstream and downstream. Only one thought lodged in Abdulin's mind: 'Accursed war!'

The Soviet advance was gathering momentum. It was now

crucial to eliminate the few surviving German bridgeheads on the eastern bank of the Dnieper. The existence of these strongpoints made it easier for the Wehrmacht to conduct an orderly retreat, and they could serve as possible bases for counter-attack. One was at the city of Zaporozhye, where a giant dam spanned the Dnieper. Here on 13 October the assembled Russian forces devised a bold night-time assault, to surprise the enemy and capture the dam intact. Its execution was a remarkable triumph that showed the very best of which the Red Army was capable.

Russian reconnaissance scout Gabriel Temkin, with the 78th Rifle Division, said: 'Zaporozhye was a city of great importance to us. Under the Soviet state its huge dam – the biggest in Europe – and its gigantic power station had become a technological showpiece, supplying power to the whole Ukrainian industrial region. For the same reason, it was important to the Germans, because its generating capacity was more than half a million kilowatts, supplying the running power for the Krivoy Rog iron mines and the Kirovograd metallurgical plants.'

Zaporozhye was on the eastern bank of the Dnieper, and the dam at its northern end an imposing structure, over 800 metres long and some 60 metres high. The Germans had heavily fortified the area around it with trenches and dugouts interspersed with barbed wire, minefields and anti-tank ditches. The city's garrison – drawn from three infantry divisions – totalled nearly 25,000 men, and was supported by an armoured reserve that included the formidable Tiger tanks and Ferdinands.

Faced with such enemy strength, General Rodion Malinovsky, commander of the Soviet South-Western Front, decided to attack Zaporozhye from three different directions. Lieutenant General Vasily Chuikov's Eighth Guards Army would strike from the east, Lieutenant General Dmitry Lelyushenko's Third Guards Army from the south-east and a combat group of four infantry divisions from the Soviet Twelfth Army from the north. But first, the Red Army needed to gain accurate intelligence on the Germans' plan to blow up the dam.

On the night of 10 October Soviet reconnaissance scout Gabriel Temkin captured a German infantry grenadier. The interrogation went smoothly. The German told Temkin about preparations to destroy the dam, and was immediately sent to the divisional HQ. Two hundred tonnes of dynamite had been stacked in the turbine hall of the power station on the far side of the river, and an additional 40 tonnes placed in the mine chambers of the dam itself, along with about a hundred aerial bombs. The Red Army response was swift. A special combat group of thirty-four tanks was set up, drawn from Major General Russiyanov's I Mechanized Corps. Joining it would be a squad of infantry and engineers from the Eighth Guards Army – men who had considerable expertise in neutralizing explosives.

Lieutenant General Vasily Chuikov's Eighth Guards Army – formerly the Sixty-Second Army, the defenders of Stalingrad – had particular skill in night-time fighting. 'The important thing,' Chuikov remarked, 'was to keep overall control of the emerging shape of battle.' The experience of Stalingrad now paid a handsome dividend. Stakes with white tips were used to mark the approach routes for Soviet tanks and infantry. White symbols were painted on the turrets and sides of the tanks; Red Army troops signalled to each other with flashlights. 'Tank destroyer' assault teams were organized, small groups that would infiltrate the German lines and seek out their Tiger and Panther tanks and Ferdinand guns, and signal their whereabouts with flare rockets. Air strikes would then be called in to destroy or immobilize the enemy's heavy weaponry. By 13 October everything was ready.

The plan was daring and entirely novel – a major night-time assault on an occupied city had never been undertaken before. An intense artillery bombardment would open up on the German positions. Then a mass of searchlights would be turned on, to dazzle the defenders, and Red Army soldiers would attack. While the enemy was attempting to regroup, Russiyanov's combat group would push into the city centre, then drive straight for the dam.

At 11 p.m. the Russians struck. 'The horizon was crimson from the flare of hundreds of our guns,' Private Temkin said. 'It was the first time I had witnessed such concentrated artillery fire – it was as if the God of War had spoken. The bombardment was devastating.' More than 200 Soviet tanks and self-propelled guns moved into the attack, infantry following swiftly behind, and a mass of searchlights lit up the German positions. Major General Russiyanov described its effect:

> Our aim was psychological disorientation of the enemy. Immediately after the powerful artillery barrage – directed along the entire German line – their troops were blinded by the dazzle of searchlights. Then our tanks rolled forward en masse, with our infantry behind them, spraying the trenches with machine-gun fire. The enemy was completely surprised by our attack, and – badly shaken – some soldiers simply threw down their weapons and fled in panic. Others, blinded by the headlights, ran into the path of our oncoming tanks.

Advancing at full speed, Soviet assault groups smashed through the German lines of defence, spraying their occupants with flame-throwers and machine-gun fire. Just after midnight Russiyanov's combat group broke into the city centre. The German artillery battery protecting the approaches to the dam was overrun, and the leading tanks accelerated towards the entry road that ran along the top of its massive structure. But they had been spotted. Suddenly the power station was ablaze with light, and an explosion ripped the fabric of the dam. Three Soviet tanks rammed the station wall, and the infantry and engineers hurled themselves into the building, spraying its defenders with machine-gun fire. They were able to stop the charges going off. The Zaporozhye dam had been saved – and in a special broadcast the following day, Stalin paid tribute to the Red Army for its daring success.

Soviet troops were ready to push further forward. As they swung towards Kiev, fighting was particularly fierce, the Germans putting up a desperate resistance. On 29 October 1943 Red Army medical instructor Ariadna Dobrosmislova wrote of the death of her closest friend Katyusha:

> We gave her a military burial – simple and solemn. In place of a coffin we laid her on a stretcher. It felt strange to see our brisk, lively Katyusha lying motionless there. Her face was pale but peaceful. Only the breeze lifted a lock of her hair. We raised the stretcher on to our shoulders and carried her to her grave. Our guns opened fire at that moment on the Germans, and this served as her salute. We decorated her grave with pine cones and bilberries. I wrote on the board: 'Here lies Sergeant Katyusha Smirnova, born 1922, died heroically for our Soviet Motherland 26/10/1943. Sleep peacefully, dear friend – we shall avenge your death.'

At the beginning of November 1943, on the western bank of the Dnieper not far from Kiev, Sergeant Nina Lutsenko of the Soviet Sixtieth Army's 121st Rifle Division took charge of her first artillery battery. Lutsenko had been motivated to fight by the cruelty of the German occupation in the Ukraine, and its indiscriminate killing of innocent civilians. Her village had witnessed a mass execution: the men were rounded up, forced to undress and shot dead in the meadow next to the village school. The victims included Lutsenko's uncle and two of her school friends. She had watched her two young cousins – girls aged eight and six – crying as they picked up their father's clothing and took it home. In that moment Lutsenko felt the tangible presence of evil. She made a promise: 'I will do whatever it takes to avenge you!'

In the summer of 1943 Lutsenko was sent to the front line as a nurse. The regimental commander asked her to become his lover, and offered her a safe job – as a typist at army HQ – if she accepted. But Lutsenko wanted to fight. During the battle of Kursk – as casualties mounted – she had stayed on with the crew, carrying shells and working as a loader. In the hellish conditions of fighting near Prokhorovka, when the gun's barrel glowed red from constant firing, she won her fellow soldiers' respect: 'They treated me as a brother-in-arms,' Lutsenko said proudly. In September 1943 she became an artillery spotter, and the following month led an attack on a German heavy machine-gun post. 'I suppressed all fear,' Lutsenko said, 'and allowed myself to be consumed by anger – anger for all the suffering the enemy had inflicted.' In such a heightened emotional state, cowardice could not be tolerated – and when one Red Army soldier was reluctant to join the attack, Lutsenko held a pistol to his head and threatened to shoot him.

Now she would lead her unit in an assault on the Ukrainian capital. 'Conditions during our attack on Kiev were horrific,' Lutsenko remembered.

We broke out of our bridgehead on 3 November. The Germans clung desperately on to the city's approaches, bombing and shelling our positions. We were constantly on the move – and for three days no field kitchen was able to reach us. In the midst of these fierce clashes with the enemy, I felt particularly responsible for the lives of my crew. I was giving the orders to destroy German tanks, and I knew that a bad decision would cost lives. When I saw a friend or comrade hurt, I gathered myself and kept strong. Every fight was hard.

Red Army soldiers broke into Kiev three days later, on 6 November. They had kept to Stalin's timetable.

A clutch of Soviet war correspondents had followed the progress of the Soviet armies. Boris Polevoy – moving forward with the First Ukrainian Front, wrote about the symbolic power of Red Army soldiers crossing the mighty Dnieper river. Pavel Antokolsky also wrote a piece entitled 'The Right Bank of the Dnieper' – but whereas Polevoy contributed regularly to *Pravda*, and was one of the Soviet Union's most popular writers, Antokolsky was struggling to get his own work chosen by the much smaller *Komsomolskaya Pravda*. But Antokolsky was already receiving hundreds of letters from bereaved parents who had read his poem, 'Son'. As the Red Army fought its way westwards, sometimes with considerable loss of life, Antokolsky had touched a chord.

At the Tehran Conference from 28 November to 1 December 1943 the 'Big Three' – the Allied leaders Roosevelt, Churchill and Stalin – met for the first time, and Stalin received an assurance from Roosevelt that British and US forces would open a Second Front in France – Operation Overlord – in the late spring of 1944. The Western Allies now held most of southern Italy, a campaign that had cost their forces 2,009 killed and 3,501 missing or captured. The Red Army had lost 103,000 soldiers in its advance through the eastern Ukraine and another 173,000 crossing the Dnieper river and capturing Kiev.

In a special ceremony on 29 November, the British prime minister, Winston Churchill, handed the Soviet leader Joseph Stalin the sword of Stalingrad, a gift from King George VI to the people of Stalingrad in recognition of their extraordinary courage during the battle. Soviet intelligence officer Zoya Zarubina remembered that Stalin was moved by the gift: 'He had a speech of thanks prepared,' she said, 'but when Churchill presented the sword Stalin's voice wavered, and he could not give it. Instead, he just said thank you, several times.'

Zarubina added:

A group of our military attachés had been diverted to Stalingrad on their way to Tehran. They spent a night in the city, and were struck by the efforts of the citizens to rebuild, amid so much destruction. They were deeply affected by this, and had shared their impressions with Stalin, who listened attentively. At that time, the view of our government was that Stalingrad would have to be abandoned – the scale of devastation was simply too great. A new city would be built along the Volga, further south, and a site had already been earmarked. But the image of the devastated city stayed in Stalin's mind, and when Churchill commented, in private conversation with the Soviet leader, that of course Stalingrad would have to be reconstructed in a different place, Stalin had a change of heart. Shortly after the conference ended, he announced that the city would be rebuilt in exactly the same place, however expensive and time-consuming that process would be.

Zarubina recalled that a group of Western diplomats from Moscow had been on the same diverted plane. She believed that they were embarrassed by the scale of destruction at Stalingrad and felt guilty – by delaying the opening of the Second Front they had let the Russian people shoulder the main burden of the war. This was a partisan, Soviet viewpoint. But the massive casualties suffered by the Red Army in turning the tide of war in the east gave Stalin a powerful moral authority at the conference.

German Army Group South was now in full retreat, but Manstein's skilful generalship could still cause the Red Army problems. Nina Lutsenko remembered a German counter-attack at Zhitomir in December 1943. 'We saw 12 enemy tanks approaching,' Lutsenko said.

> We positioned our gun behind the ruins of a bombed-out house, and waited for them. One tank got up so close that as I watched it through the gunsight I felt its presence with my whole body. I experienced an intense awareness of what was going on around me, as if time was standing still. Then I gave the command: 'Shrapnel shell – aim under the turret.' And we hit it! The next tank turned, showing its side, and we shot at its fuel tank – everything was going up in flames. Altogether we managed to hit four tanks.

It was a remarkable tally, but now the other eight German tanks surrounded the lone Russian gun. 'It seemed that this was the end,' Lutsenko acknowledged, 'but we had called in a "katyusha" strike – and just at that moment, with a deafening roar, a volley of our rockets landed amid the enemy. More tanks caught alight and the remainder retreated.'

'I never wanted to be seen as weaker than men – or as a less effective soldier,' Lutsenko continued. 'I was determined to prove myself, again and again. When we liberated villages in the Ukraine, and the young women greeted us in traditional costume, presenting us with flowers, I no longer felt I was one of them. Something had changed in me. When we were off duty, and I ironed another soldier's tunic or sewed the buttons back on, it was as if I was reminding myself of a previous life.'

As the Red Army pushed on, through the Ukraine,

soldiers were unsure what they would find there. 'We were liberating village after village,' said Soviet private Alexander Fein. 'One day in December 1943 we entered a village that had been burnt down completely – only the chimneys were left. It was completely deserted. Suddenly a young boy emerged from the ruins – about 13 years old – unwashed, covered in dirt and completely alone. We took him with us, and looked after him. He was fed and taken care of. But he could not speak at all.'

After a fresh round of combat, the Red Army unit halted for a few days. An elderly serviceman befriended the boy, and made an overcoat and boots for him. Then, one morning, Fein heard him singing – it was as if he was coming back to life. A few days later he told the Red Army soldiers his story. The boy had been evacuated from Leningrad with his mother and sister, and they had decided to go to his grandfather's village in the Ukraine. The train they were on was bombed by the Germans, and his mother was killed. He and his sister reached the village, but the enemy occupied it soon afterwards, and his sister was sent away to Germany as a slave labourer. As the Germans pulled back they set light to all the homes, and the terrified boy hid with his grandfather in the cellar. Later the grandfather went out to search for food, but he was shot by a retreating enemy soldier. The boy waited in the darkness, covered in soot and dirt, until the Red Army arrived. 'That was the kind of childhood many had in this war,' Fein said sadly.

For all the ruthlessness of the German scorched-earth policy, some communities were left intact, since the speed of the Red Army's advance could force the enemy back before he had completed his grim task. But there were other explanations. Soviet artilleryman Alexander Zhuravlev always remembered the liberation of the Ukrainian village of

Divochki. There was no sign of damage whatsoever. Not a single home was ruined. 'In previous towns and villages we had been greeted warmly – people had embraced and kissed us. But here there was a strange silence. People would not look us in the eye.' It was likely that the village had collaborated with the Germans. 'I felt like laying down an artillery barrage in its midst,' one of Zhuravlev's comrades said. 'Their indifference appalled me.'

For the most part, it was the atrocities which shocked Red Army soldiers. 'We would approach a ruined village,' said Lieutenant Anatoly Mereshko of the Eighth Guards Army, 'and see inhabitants strung up on trees ahead of us with crude placards tied around their necks, and find others massacred in barns or outbuildings. We advanced through the countryside with a growing sense of dread.'

'At dawn we arrived at a village,' noted Red Army lieutenant Vladimir Gelfand, marching through the Ukraine with the Soviet 301st Rifle Division. 'There was not a single person around. The Germans had taken everything, even the livestock and poultry. But they had shown some consideration – they had left the dogs alive.'

Soviet lieutenant Vasily Bryukhov recalled the horror experienced by a fellow tank commander, Lieutenant Ivanov. The brigade had passed near Ivanov's home village, and he requested permission to visit it. But his family was not there. 'Ivanov was told that they were herded into a barn with other young villagers,' Bryukhov said, 'and the building was then drenched with petrol and set alight. That was how his wife and two children died. When Ivanov rejoined us he was a different man. He no longer took prisoners – if someone tried to surrender he killed them immediately. And he fought with desperate bravery – as if he could no longer bear living and was seeking out death.'

Mark Slavin, the editor of the Eighth Guards Army news-paper, remembered: 'We were passing through areas that once had been home to thriving Jewish communities. Now there was nothing. For three months, we advanced through the Ukraine without seeing a single living Jew. Our soldiers grew so disturbed by this that we had Jewish reconnaissance scouts posted in the vanguard of our army, trying to find out what had happened to them.'

An answer to Slavin's question was beginning to emerge. At Boyarka in the Ukraine, 20 kilometres south-west of Kiev, Alexandra Bocharova – a Jewish machine gunner with the Soviet Sixteenth Army – made a terrible discovery: 'In a hut, by the corner of a garden, we found an old man who had been hanged. Strung up next to him were two young women, and three small children – the youngest of whom was only three years old. A young man lay dead on the ground next to them, a broken rope still around his neck. It was a horrible, horrible sight. For a long time we stood there in silence, we couldn't really take it in.'

Surviving inhabitants joined the Red Army soldiers and explained what had happened. They were the remains of two families. The first – the old man, his daughter-in-law and his two grandchildren, aged six and three – had lived in the house. The second – a young Jewish couple and their child – had been in hiding in the cellar; the local family had been trying to protect them. For two years they had cared for them, digging a tunnel and passing food down at night, knowing all the while that if they were found out they would be shot. And then the German soldiers left the village. The Red Army was approaching – and a reconnaissance detach-ment of Russian soldiers had already passed through. The old man saw this, and told the Jewish family it was safe to come out.

The old man wanted to celebrate their survival. He invited the Jewish couple and their child to join his own family for a meal. They sat down together at the table. But their joy was short lived. A detachment of SS troops pulled back through the village. They burst into the house, realized what was going on – and hanged them all, there and then. 'We couldn't put this episode out of our minds,' Bocharova said. 'It haunted us.'

Soviet war journalist Vasily Grossman decided to visit the Ukrainian town of Berdichev, which had just been liberated by the Red Army. Grossman was a Jew, and he wrote to his wife: 'I am going to Berdichev today – my comrades have already been there. They say that the town had been devastated, and only a handful of people, out of the tens of thousands of Jews who lived there, have survived. I have no hope of finding Mama alive. The only thing I am hoping for is to find out about her last days, and her death.'

Grossman found out that his mother had almost certainly died in a mass execution in the town on 15 September 1941. Red Army private Roman Yagel visited Berdichev at the same time as Grossman. While German atrocities against Soviet citizens were reported by Stalin's regime, there was no specific emphasis on the extermination of the Jews. Front-line soldiers encountered anecdotal evidence but nothing more. Yagel chatted to a few of the Jewish survivors, and as he did so, the vague rumours about the fate of Jews in German-occupied territories became real. They told Yagel about the mass killings, and about Babi Yar, the ravine on the outskirts of Kiev, where more than thirty thousand Jews were killed on a single day. Yagel was part of a large Jewish family, and had always imagined returning to them at the end of the war. Now all that changed.

'I felt that something was terribly wrong,' Yagel said. 'I

had always imagined that if I made it through the war, if I stayed alive, I could come home and tell my father that I was a hero. But now I had a strong sense that there was no one left alive to tell.' Yagel was pierced by an aching loneliness, as if a darkness once held at bay was rushing down upon him.

'There are no Jews in the Ukraine,' Vasily Grossman wrote. 'In none of the cities, towns or villages will you see the black, tear-filled eyes of little girls; you will not hear the pained voice of an old woman; you will not see the dark face of a hungry baby. All is silence. Everything is still.'

More than 500,000 Jews fought with the Red Army during the war, and about 180,000 of them perished at the front. Sometimes they encountered anti-Semitism among their comrades; more often, they were accepted by their fellow fighters, and respected as brave and patriotic soldiers. But these Jewish soldiers felt a particular need to demonstrate their courage. It was in part a response to the old prejudice against their race, but as they learnt of Hitler's murderous war against their people, their fight also became an increasingly personal one.

That fight was moving westwards. For Red Army soldiers, days of continuous marching became part of infantry life. Soviet private Efim Golbraikh recalled:

A foot soldier is loaded like a donkey: trench coat, backpack, gas mask – stuffed with hand grenades – steel helmet, entrenching tools, a mess tin, map-case and ammunition pouches, and a rifle or sub-machine gun. We would sweat all over – white salt stains appeared on our tunics, and when we took them off, they would stand upright on their own! And as we marched, we would be given sunflower seeds by liberated villagers. The seeds would pass time on the road. By the time you had chewed your way through a pocketful, 10 kilometres had gone – that was the soldier's speedometer!

On longer marches soldiers would sometimes fall asleep on their feet, stumble out of formation and even fall into roadside ditches from sheer exhaustion. As a precaution, they marched three abreast – the man in the middle asleep, supported by his comrades on either side, then they would swap over. 'On top of everything else they would sometimes hang four 82mm mortar shells on each of us,' Golbraikh added. 'It was not advisable to fall down asleep with a shell garlanded around your neck. And so we walked, our bodies itching from sweat and lice, our stomachs sticking to our backbones through hunger.'

As the Red Army liberated swathes of Ukrainian territory abandoned during the first months of the war, they encountered men of call-up age previously untouched by mobilization – teenagers who had reached the age of eighteen, ex-soldiers who had managed to settle in the occupied territories and partisans. This mass of new recruits was immediately called up, and sometimes thrown into combat even before receiving a uniform. Soviet private Dmitry Boulgakov recalled: 'An HQ was set up in an unburnt shack in a village that we had just liberated, and the drafting of all men born between 1890 and 1924 was announced. There was no medical examination and no uniform. They were given rifles – but most of them had never served in the army and could not handle firearms.'

Not surprisingly, regular Red Army soldiers treated these new arrivals with disdain. At this stage of the war most were from the Ukraine – and they were scornfully nicknamed 'Warriors of the Fifth Ukrainian Front'. There were in fact only four Ukrainian Fronts – the 'Fifth' implied, however unfairly, the enjoyment of a peaceful and comfortable life for two and a half years while millions of Red Army soldiers had been dying in battle.

And these deaths would continue. 'A man sometimes foresees his time of passing,' said Soviet artilleryman Alexander Zhuravlev.

Once we undertook a night march and passed through a village. We were supposed to take a turn in the road by a chapel – and as we had been warned that the Germans frequently shelled that spot we moved across quickly, only to find the turning was becoming narrower and narrower, until it led to a sheer precipice. A nearby soldier yelled at us 'Where are you going? – the Fascists are on the other side.' And then we realized that our reconnaissance group, who should have checked the route, had simply vanished, leaving us to the mercy of fate. When we caught up with them I asked the leader 'Why didn't you tell us we were going the wrong way?' He replied: 'It's completely my fault. I don't know what has happened to me – I just froze.' I looked hard at him – he seemed not to be with me. And then, at that very moment, there was the sound of a shell. I threw myself to the ground – but he remained standing, and was instantly killed.

The reconnaissance leader's paralysis was so untypical that afterwards, Zhuravlev was left wondering whether the man had somehow sensed his own demise.

This was now a war for women as well as men. By the end of 1943, 102,333 female snipers were serving with the Red Army, alongside 49,509 signallers, 15,290 sub-machine gun operators and the 6,097 women who were fighting with artillery units. More than 800,000 women served with the Soviet armed forces during the Second World War, constituting about 8 per cent of its military personnel, and about 200,000 of these were decorated. They were not forced to fight – they wanted to. Sergeant Nina Lutsenko said: 'It was a natural reaction to the crisis that we faced – our Motherland had to be defended.' Prejudice against women fighters, however, remained common in the Red Army. 'What is the difference between an artillery shell and a front-line girl?' the soldiers' joke ran. 'The shell is "stuffed" in the rear and taken to the front. With the girl, it's the other way around.'

On 6 February 1944 Soviet medical instructor Ariadna Dobrosmislova of the 308th Rifle Division spent a few days with a different unit. She had been awarded the Order of the Red Star for the defence of Stalingrad, where she had been badly wounded, and she had always been treated with courtesy by her fellow soldiers. She knew how to fight as well as tend the wounded, and took pride in polishing her Mosin-Nagant rifle – which she nicknamed 'Boris' – until it shone like a mirror, boasting that it was the cleanest gun in the company. But Dobrosmislova was shaken by her encounter: 'In our own unit girls are regarded as girls,' she wrote to her mother,

> we are shown respect and attentiveness and most certainly never insulted in any way. When we briefly dispersed to another company I came up against attitudes to 'soldier girls' which were wounding to the point of tears. Some didn't even regard us as females, calling us 'ersatz women' and other undeserved names. Others tell us that 'after the war, no one will want to marry you' and 'you will never be a wife or mother'. One lieutenant declared that in the army every girl becomes a whore. You can imagine how hurtful it is to hear such things! No one in our own unit had ever made such comments. I loathe these men – and the five days we spent in their company seemed like five years of penal servitude.

It was inevitable that the Soviet forces contained a kaleidoscope of attitudes. But they were learning how to master their enemy. On 16 February 1944 the Red Army destroyed six encircled German divisions at Korsun in the southern Ukraine. Some of the enemy soldiers managed to break out.

Thousands more were annihilated where they stood. Soviet private Gabriel Temkin would never forget the scenes of carnage: 'The large valley that opened up before me was covered with greyish-white snow, and dotted up to the horizon with heaps of dead bodies.' The German corpses had been systematically stripped of their clothing.

On 15 March 1944 Soviet lieutenant Vladimir Gelfand began noting evidence of German massacres of Jews in the Ukraine. He recorded in his diary: 'Passed a village farm. Local people told us that the enemy shot all the Jews here, including little children, and buried them in an anti-tank ditch.' Two days later Gelfand wrote: 'Stayed at the home of a good, kind woman. She had managed to save the lives of two Jews, who were in a miserable state. She spoke of a terrible tragedy – the murder of Jewish people by the German bandit robbers.' Gelfand added, 'There are seven Jews in my platoon, including myself. We all actively seek out the toughest combat missions against the enemy.'

Korsun was a triumph for the First and Second Ukrainian Fronts of Marshal Ivan Konev and General Nikolai Vatutin. General Rodion Malinovsky's South-Western Front – which had been renamed the Third Ukrainian Front in the aftermath of its triumph at Zaporozhye – was now advancing on Odessa. He drew up his battle plans on 24 March 1944, and Red Army troops fought their way into the city on 10 April. Leading the way was Lieutenant General Vasily Chuikov's Eighth Guards Army. Its combat engineers managed to defuse German explosives, saving Odessa's beautiful Opera Theatre from destruction. A day later, Red Army nurse Miriam Kogan received a letter from her brother: 'Our dreams have come true at last – I was fortunate enough to visit the city the day after its liberation. The Opera Theatre is still intact – and this is very good news. But there are many tragic things that took place in Odessa, which I am obliged to share with you . . .'

The Kogans were Jewish. Miriam's brother continued:

> In the city's suburbs, the enemy shot around 1,000 women and children as he was about to pull out. I saw some of the bodies in a ditch close to the brick factory – it was a horrible sight . . . And Uncle Syoma and his family – it is hard to say this, but it seems they are no longer alive. I spoke to their old neighbours, who said that Uncle did not want to move out . . . he said that in their previous occupation of the area in 1918 the Germans had not done much harm, so they wouldn't do much now. And so they paid the price . . .

By early 1944 Russia was winning the war against Nazi Germany. Under the stress of intensive campaigning, and influenced by an ideology that emphasized the collective good above the welfare of the individual, it is clear that the Soviet Union needlessly threw away the lives of many of its soldiers. These men and women were not fighting as part of a robotic mass, however. Red Army soldiers' voices testify to the desperate pain felt over the loss of each individual life.

6

Killing Fields

O N 6 JANUARY 1944 Wehrmacht soldier Hans Jürgen Hartmann, fighting against Soviet partisans near Minsk in Belorussia, recorded in his diary: 'The nights are filling with a new tension. They send out reconnaissance groups – watching, observing and reporting back. They keep out of the way of our own patrols. And if we move on them in strength, it fails – because they know exactly when we are coming . . . We need so many more troops . . .'

By the beginning of 1944 many German troops were feeling increasingly lost in the vast and alien landscape of Russia. The combat strength of the Wehrmacht was so depleted that many infantry divisions now consisted of little more than the complement of one or two battalions – and such weakened units could muster only eight or nine men along a 90-metre stretch of front. The strength of Soviet forces opposing them in the same area was usually substantially higher, sometimes reaching between seventy and eighty soldiers. Colonel General Kurt Zeitzler, chief of staff of the Wehrmacht, wrote: 'Such an unfavourable ratio of men to space had a profound psychological effect. A feeling of isolation and depression grew among our soldiers – particularly if the region they were stationed in was desolate, dreary or deserted. The effect was intensified by the numerical superiority of the enemy.'

The German Army Group Centre, holding the vital road link from Smolensk to Minsk, the capital of Belorussia, clung on nonetheless. General Gotthard Heinrici, commander of the Wehrmacht's Fourth Army, fought a series of skilful winter battles to defend the town of Orsha – although considerably outnumbered by his Russian foes. In Vitebsk, Colonel General Hans-Georg Reinhardt's Third Panzer Army was defiantly holding out against superior Red Army forces. But in the south, the German Ninth Army was under pressure from Soviet general Konstantin Rokossovsky's First Belorussian Front, which had launched a fresh winter offensive.

Hans Jürgen Hartmann continued:

> We move along the trenches in silence during these foggy nights, hearing only the muffled calls from sentries in the distance, and suddenly one starts before a shadow, a sound, a nearby movement. It must be the wearing effect on our nerves, the cumulative tension, one see forms, ghosts, when in reality there is nothing. All around us everything is so frighteningly quiet – the snow absorbs every sound. And then one is jolted by a comrade crunching his boots on the ice, startled by a sudden burst of moonlight illuminating the white field before us as if it is alive, or standing – rigid with shock – in the sudden light of a tracer flare.

The tide of war was flowing ever more strongly against the Wehrmacht. 'The Germans are pulling back from Leningrad,' Lieutenant Vasily Churkin of the Soviet 80th Rifle Division wrote in his diary on 22 January 1944. 'At night the horizon is ablaze – the Germans are burning houses and mining roads as they retreat . . . It has been terrible to see our beautiful city suffer so much. We want to push the Fascist scum away, once and for all.' On 27 January 1944 the 900-day German siege of

Leningrad was finally broken, and Army Group North forced to leave the city's suburbs. Over a million civilians had died in this brutal siege.

Red Amy soldiers pursued the Germans vigorously. 'We saw enemy soldiers from one of their rear garrisons running about in panic,' recalled Soviet lieutenant Leonid Bobrov of the 102nd Rifle Division.

> They had been surprised by the speed of our advance, and had only just awoken. They were running from one dugout to another – only partially dressed and still barefoot. An order came through from our commander: 'I am concerned about the state of health of our opponents. Make a surgical intervention.' And so we did, crawling towards their trenches in our camouflage suits, then rushing the position and finishing the Germans off with grenades.

Soviet troops entered Estonia on 1 February and pushed the Germans back to the Narva river. 'The enemy is in a hurry,' Lieutenant Vasily Churkin recorded on 8 February. 'Abandoned vehicles lie by the side of the road, marking his retreat. Our planes are pursuing him, swooping low over the forest.' The Wehrmacht resisted tenaciously, but was forced to concede more ground. On 18 February Red Army soldier Yuri Sarkisov wrote to his family from the Leningrad front. 'You've asked me to speak frankly about my army life, about conditions in winter – but during all the time we have been fighting I either chose to write brief, amusing letters or none at all. Now I want to be honest with you about my daily routine.'

Sarkisov chose to relay two episodes:

> On the 15th I went out on reconnaissance. Orientating myself with the map I led a group of men about 800 metres from our first line of defence . . . We came to a mass of barbed wire and

I noticed some trenches near by. They used to belong to the enemy but I assumed they were now ours . . . Suddenly I heard a shout of alarm . . . Four German machine guns were pointing straight at us. I leapt sideways, ran, fell, kept going. Miraculously, I was not even injured – although I later found four bullet holes had ripped through my coat. On the 17th I fought with a 'Ferdinand'. There were five of us manning our own gun. Three were killed, one seriously wounded and the gun was destroyed by a direct hit. I remained completely unscathed – without even a mark on my uniform. I feel I have returned from another world.

Then Sarkisov added a postscript: 'I still can't get over what happened yesterday. I can't forget our platoon commander, a lieutenant, who played the guitar beautifully; the sergeant, who told wonderful stories and jokes. The gun-layer and the other soldier were great singers. It was my favourite unit – I jokingly gave us the nickname of "jazz bandits". Now it has been wiped out.'

The Germans' position in the north was weakening – leaving their ally, Finland, increasingly isolated. In mid-February secret exploratory talks were held between Finland and the Soviet Union – but Russian terms for ending the war were deemed too harsh, and the negotiations were broken off. The Baltic States – incorporated by Stalin into the Soviet Union in 1940 and invaded by the Germans the following year, with many of the population broadly sympathetic to the Nazis – were also in jeopardy.

On 21 February 1944 a Soviet female partisan – Ina Konstantinova – in a detachment behind German lines south-west of Leningrad – wrote:

In the early morning, the commander wakes me up for a reconnaissance mission. I remember how, long ago, my nanny woke

130

me up to go to school. I didn't want to get up – I wanted to have a long lie in the warm bed, but now it's so different . . . I walk in the woods, thinking and remembering . . . We are experiencing cold weather here. Probably it's cold at home too. In my mind's eye, I see the frost-fashioned flowery patterns on the windows of my room . . . We no longer hear the sound of artillery from the war zone beyond us . . . The enemy is losing his strength. Lately, a series of punitive expeditions have been sent out against us, but our losses are small.

German Army Group Centre's southern flank was also feeling the strain, as attacks from Soviet general Rokossovsky's advancing forces grew in strength and confidence – and these were coordinated with an increasingly threatening partisan movement operating behind German lines. A Wehrmacht priest, Josef Perau, who was stationed with the German 129th Infantry Division south of Bobruisk in Belorussia, also wrote in his diary on 21 February:

It seems that the war here is particularly savage, and conducted in a most cruel way. A 'partisan republic' has been set up in this area, and its commander resided for a while in a nearby village. In graveyards, crosses marking the dead have been ripped out – out of sheer enjoyment it seems – to be replaced by a solitary placard displaying the Soviet star. It reminds me of the 'death runes' on the graves of SS men. It is frightening to see this conscious discarding of the Christian cross.

Hitler strongly disapproved of Christianity but reluctantly tolerated the existence of divisional chaplains within the German army – recognizing that some soldiers at least both wanted and needed their presence, and that army morale would suffer if they were removed. And with that army in full retreat, Perau remained witness to a violent and brutal conflict, for the most part entirely lacking in higher moral qualities. Hate was the driving force behind the war in the east.

The partisan movement in Belorussia had now become a serious threat to the Wehrmacht, for German military defeats and increasingly harsh treatment of civilians had alienated many of the local inhabitants. Yadviga Savitskaya had joined a partisan group near Minsk: 'We were warned how dangerous it was, and that there was little chance of staying alive,' Savitskaya said. 'But we didn't think about ourselves. We were opposed to this enemy not just with our hearts but with our whole being – everything . . . Hatred overwhelmed me. It was stronger than my fear for those close to me – or my own death. The Nazis must not remain in our land.'

In the first months of the war the partisan movement in Belorussia had been relatively small. Stalin had called for partisans to rise and fight the Germans as early as 3 July 1941, but the initial response was muted: they had numbered little more than 12,000 in mid-August 1941, a month after the region had been fully occupied by the Germans, and had grown to some 30,000 by the end of that year. Their military operations were not properly organized by the Soviet High Command – at this stage of the war, over 90 per cent of partisan bands were without radios – and consisted largely of random attacks on transport installations and the plundering of villages in German-occupied territory.

The partisans certainly did not enjoy universal support among the peasantry – and were often seen as a threat rather than a source of support. Ivan Treskovski – a teenager living with his family on a farm in the village of Usayazha, deep in the Belorussian countryside, remembered cowering with fear when partisans called on his father. They were drunk and threatening, yelling out: 'Give us some bacon fat – or we will kill you,' Treskovski said. 'Their visits were a regular source of terror.'

But after German defeats at Stalingrad and Kursk the number of partisans grew steadily, as even those who had been afraid earlier rallied to the cause, and their actions began to be properly coordinated by Moscow, which parachute-dropped agents, supplies and equipment into partisan-controlled regions. By the beginning of 1944 there were over 180,000 armed partisans in Belorussia alone. In the aftermath of the battle of Kursk, some 167 partisan units – totalling well over 100,000 men – ran a two-month campaign targeting Army Group Centre's transport links, which played havoc with German supply lines.

The German response was an increasingly brutal series of retaliations which made less and less distinction between partisan bands and innocent civilians. In the aftermath of one operation, conducted in the summer of 1943, it was noted that while a figure of 4,500 enemy dead was reported, only 492 rifles had been recovered. Since every partisan was obliged to own and carry a rifle, this discrepancy was alarming. Reich Commissar Heinrich Lose was sufficiently concerned to note: 'Such figures strongly suggest that the majority of "partisan suspects" are in fact nothing more than innocent peasants, the majority of them being women and children.' Lose added: 'To lock old men, women and children in barns and set fire to these buildings does not appear to be a suitable method of combating partisan bands.' Lose was a Nazi, was imbued with Hitler's race doctrines – and regarded Slavs as subhumans. He added to the last sentence a chilling, clinical postscript: 'Even if it is desired to exterminate the population . . .' – lack of efficacy would therefore appear to be his only objection to this method.

German Police Regiment 23, operating in the countryside

near Minsk in the spring and summer of 1943, now routinely prefaced its military instructions with the statement: 'Everything that may give shelter or protection to the partisans is to be destroyed. The area is to become a no man's land. All inhabitants are to be shot.'

By the beginning of 1944 over 140 punitive operations had taken place in Belorussia, and 5,295 villages had been burnt – all their cattle and grain seized, the able-bodied deported to Germany and the remaining inhabitants killed. More than 700,000 civilians had been killed by the German occupiers, including at least 250,000 Jews; a further 400,000 Soviet POWs had been starved to death or executed; 377,000 people had been transported to Germany as slave labourers. Whole regions had been turned into desert.

Belorussian settlements were an easy target for security forces, whether their inhabitants had been helping the partisans or not. Mere proximity to a partisan band was often a death sentence. Civilians would be rounded up and ordered into a large building or barn, which was then cordoned off and set alight. When Germans forced the villagers of Oktyabrysky into a communal building and then set fire to it, Teklya Kruglova survived the blaze by leaping out of an upper-storey window. She fell into a ditch and lay hidden under a pile of snow and brushwood. When the screaming subsided there was utter silence. The fire had died down and the Germans were nowhere to be seen. Kruglova was concussed, partially burnt and in a deep state of shock. She picked herself up gingerly. 'If only I could hear something,' she thought, 'even the sound of an animal, or a bird. But there is nothing, absolutely nothing. It is so silent.' And then a terrible idea came to her. 'What if I am the only person left in the world?'

The horror was hard to comprehend. But those Russians

who survived such measures were suffused with hatred. Valentina Ilkevich had joined the Minsk partisans. She remembered:

> We picked up a woman who was lying almost senseless. She could not walk and had been crawling along the road. She said that she had thought she was already dead. She had felt blood running over her, but had decided she was feeling this in the other world. When she came to a little, she told us that she had been taken out to be shot with her five children. They were led out to a barn and four of her children were shot in front of her. The last that was left was a baby boy. One of the Germans wanted to amuse himself. He motioned to her that she should throw her baby into the air, and that then he would shoot. In despair, she threw her child against the side of the wall, killing him first, before the German had a chance to fire. She said that she did not want to live, that after everything that had happened she could not live in this world, only in the next.

'I did not want to kill, I wasn't born to kill,' said Ilkevich. 'I wanted to become a teacher. But they came to our land to kill and burn. I saw them set fire to a village and could not cry out or weep loudly – we were on reconnaissance – I could only gnaw at my hands. I still have the scars. I remember the people crying out, and the cows and the hens with them. And everything seemed to cry out with a human voice – everything alive.'

Antonina Kondrashova fought in a partisan detachment in Belorussia.

> I still have in my ears the cry of a child as it was thrown into a well. It was impossible to bear that terrible sound. The child went down and down, and screamed and screamed, as if from under the ground, from the other world. It was not a child's cry, and not a human cry. It was a cry from beyond the grave. After that, whenever I went on a mission, my whole spirit urged me

to do only one thing, to kill them as quickly as possible, to kill as many as possible – to destroy them . . .

They did awful, abnormal things to people. Imagine how you would feel if a big bonfire had been lit in front of you – in the middle of the village – and an old schoolteacher who had once taught you had been thrown on it . . . A person that you knew had been shot, burnt or torn to pieces by dogs. I learnt that my mother had been shot, and dumped into a large anti-tank ditch and the ground flattened by trucks. I ran there and dug, turning over corpses. I recognized my mother by the ring on her hand. When I saw her I cried out and lost consciousness. Some women pulled her out of the ditch, washed her with water from a little can and buried her properly. I always kept that can with me.

In the past, such atrocities had not usually been committed by regular soldiers but the security detachments and police regiments that oversaw the occupied territories. But by the beginning of 1944, the German army itself had become increasingly involved in anti-partisan operations, and also the forcible evacuation of civilians. As German forces retreated, a savage scorched-earth policy was put into effect to deny the Red Army shelter, economic resources and potential man-power. In November 1943 Army Group North created a fall-back defensive position, the Panther Line, and forced the native population in the zone in front of it to abandon their homes and march several hundred kilometres to camps in the German rear. But in February 1944, Army Group Centre planned a very different evacuation strategy, one in which civilians were not removed from the fighting, but placed in camps directly in the military zone.

German soldier Hans Jürgen Hartmann had now moved up to front-line positions. The battalions of his division were now down to fifty to sixty men, and no reinforcements were arriving. 'No one is going to confess to defeatism among his comrades,' he wrote in his diary. But on 27 February Hartmann penned a longer entry:

> If the Russians shift the emphasis of their attack – today, tomorrow, here and there – they may win some territory, straighten out their line, push us back a little, but all this can still be borne, because the space and land we hold are enough at present. It may never happen that our opponent makes a crucial breakthrough. But that possibility remains my great secret worry – one that I cannot confide to anyone, a fear that continues to haunt me at every stage of my travels through this land. This vast, boundless country we hold is partisan-infested – and upon that everything, really everything, now depends. There is little economic strength left in its hinterland, and we have no proper reserve positions, or at least nothing deserving of that name. Nothing, nothing, nothing . . .
>
> At this terminus point, this end station, one wanders from village to village, each with only a few poor inhabitants left, and then – finally – the front: a lousy trench with a few comrades in it, our men standing in their camouflaged winter coats, our lookout posts, the dark, dirty bunkers . . . and behind the foremost trench lies Bolshevism, the Red Army and infinite Russia.

The Red Army was advancing rapidly into the western Ukraine, and General Rokossovsky's First Belorussian Front was also moving forward in support of this offensive. As it did so, Army Group Centre's southern flank was becoming increasingly vulnerable. The German Ninth Army began to prepare fresh defensive positions further west. It sought to buy time in order to pull its troops back safely.

On 9 March 1944 Colonel General Josef Harpe, the Ninth Army's commander, put in place arrangements for the construction of a new series of camps close to the front line, strung out along the marshland region of Polesie, directly in the path of Rokossovsky's forces. Three days later Army Group Centre's commander, Field Marshal Ernst Busch, authorized that 'evacuation measures' – the forcible deportation of civilians to these camps from all surrounding towns and villages – would begin immediately.

The operation was coordinated by General Friedrich Hossbach of LVI Panzer Corps. In support of this, the German 129th Infantry Division was ordered to move with engineers and equipment and quickly construct a camp close to the small town of Rudobelka, about 80 kilometres southwest of Bobruisk. On 13 March Wehrmacht priest Josef Perau – serving with the division – wrote in his diary: 'The planned Sunday service cannot now be held. The troops are suddenly required to assist with the evacuation of civilians.' The men departed later that morning.

Perau had struggled to connect with the men of the 129th Division since his assignment to the unit that winter. Fighting was bitter – the Russians were pressing hard on this section of the front – and there was now little interest in church services among the soldiers. Everyone knew how exposed their position was – and with Soviet forces pushing forward the mood was uneasy and fearful. The troops were anxious to pull back to the new defence line as quickly as possible. 'All the time, our men are haunted by the spectre of capture by the Russians,' Perau observed. 'This dread stalks us, terrifying and unknown.'

As the Red Army advanced it sought to coordinate its actions with Belorussian partisan units, working behind the German lines. The 129th Division had been bombarded with commands about this additional threat. An order of 19 February 1944 warned the men that partisans were infiltrating nearby villages: 'These people will often look like harmless, hungry suffering civilians,' the troops were told. 'In reality, they are fanatical partisans. The enemy is frequently using women on reconnaissance missions behind our lines. We have only managed to capture a few of them. It is now no longer possible to differentiate between the innocent and the guilty.'

Construction work on the new camp began immediately. It had no buildings. An open field was surrounded by barbed-wire fencing and sentry watchtowers. It had been readied by the division on the morning of 15 March, and the next stage of the German operation began. Later that day, Perau wrote in his diary:

I thought I had seen all the horrors of this war, but in the last few days a tragedy has unfolded in front of me that even Dostoevsky would have shied away from depicting. Our troops are herding together all the civilians from the surrounding areas into a big camp. In it, there is no form of shelter whatsoever ... The reason given is that villages are breeding grounds for typhus, and are partisan hideouts – at least, that's what they tell me.

I came across the camp completely unexpectedly, returning from the front line. There was a light drizzle and it was beginning to get dark. I began to hear an odd sound, distant yet strangely disconcerting. As I drew closer, I realized it was wailing from a mass of human voices. I found the ground was scattered with the belongings of those who were too weak to carry them any further. And then I saw solders hauling away the body of an old man as if he were an animal. A rope was tied around one of his legs. A woman was lying by the side of the road, a fresh bullet wound in her forehead. There were what seemed to be small bundles left in the dirt. A sentry from the Field Police explained that they were bodies of little children that he had covered with a few old blankets. The mothers had left them by the wayside – too weak to carry them any further. So they had been shot, just as they 'eliminate' anyone who can't continue – whether through illness, old age or general weakness.

I went up to a Medical Officer, but he said dismissively: 'Father, leave this to us. I have shot a few helpless children myself, out of pity. Germany will return to the ranks of the civilized nations after this war has been won.' Some ordinary soldiers speak like that too. Others find it repugnant.

Perau's testimony reveals that some soldiers – brutalized by the war or firm believers in Hitler's race doctrines – showed not a shred of compassion for these hapless civilians, and actively participated in this atrocity. Others were uneasy about what they were doing. There were still qualms of conscience within the Wehrmacht about the horror being inflicted on the Belorussian population. And there was also a real fear of Soviet retribution. 'They are worried what will happen to them if they are captured by the enemy, what will happen to Germany if this war is lost,' Perau added. 'They blame it on the security detachments – although regular troops are involved too.'

It was in fact a regular army operation – planned and co-ordinated by the staff of the German Ninth Army and executed by General Friedrich Hossbach of LVI Panzer Corps. Security detachments were involved only in a supporting capacity. Hossbach had ordered the creation of task forces to raid unsuspecting Belorussian villages in the early hours of the morning, a selection process, where those fit for work were separated from their families and forcibly transported to Germany, and 'collection points', where the remainder – the old, the weak, mothers and children – were assembled. They were then force-marched to the camps – all stragglers being immediately shot. The number of survivors was carefully inventoried. On 16 March Hossbach reported to the German Ninth Army: 'We have already assembled some 39,597 civilians – of whom many thousands are little children.'

The next stage of the plan began – one of particular interest to German army commanders. Perau continued: 'In the distance, I saw an army staff car moving along the road. A general was inside it. I wonder what high-ranking officers think when they see these things.'

General Friedrich Hossbach was in fact well satisfied by the 'energetic' execution of his orders. Rank-and-file soldiers either participated in the atrocity or disengaged from it all. Perau intervened to stop troops plundering the belongings of those unfortunates killed on their way to the camp. These were mostly women and children, weak with hunger, who had struggled in the thick mud on the approach roads. Mothers had halted, trying to wrap their little children against the cold. German sentries had immediately shot them. Soldiers in Perau's division had then attempted to seize their embroidered blankets, to send back to their wives in Germany.

By 17 March over 47,000 civilians were inside the camps. Convoys of vehicles began to draw up outside the fences, and seriously ill hospital patients were carried out and interspersed among the prisoners. Thousands of people began to fall ill. The camp surrounds were mined, and the Wehrmacht troops withdrew further west. They waited for their Red Army opponents to discover them.

Advancing Soviet soldiers did so on 19 March. Reconnaissance units from the Sixty-Fifth Army's 37th Guards Division reported seeing large concentration camps in the marshland area of Polesie. 'They are enclosed by barbed wire and in them thousands of civilians are huddled together, without any form of shelter whatsoever,' one Red Army soldier related. 'It is almost too terrible to look at.' The division's commander, General Ushakov, immediately sent several units to overpower the camp guards and release the prisoners.

Whatever the barbarity of these camps, which were merely pens in which civilians could be left to die of exposure, the reality was worse. The German plan was to infect the inmates with typhus and thus create an epidemic among advancing soldiers and civilians alike. And the plan was working – most of the prisoners were now ill. As Soviet soldiers rushed into the camp to help the weak and sick, they had no inkling that typhus, carried by lice and thriving in unsanitary conditions, was now rampant in the camp – and that the disease would now be transmitted to them.

'It was the most heinous crime of the German army we had yet experienced,' said General Pavel Batov, commander of the Soviet Sixty-Fifth Army. On 21 March the head of the army's intelligence section sent an urgent report to Moscow:

> The camps were in open fields – surrounded by barbed wire. Their approaches had been mined. There was no shelter at all, not even of the flimsiest kind. Those imprisoned inside it were forced to lie on the ground. Many of them – already weak – lost the ability to move, and lay unconscious in the mud. The prisoners were forbidden to collect brushwood to make fires – for the slightest breach of this rule the Germans would shoot people. These camps have been deliberately put on the edge of a military zone. Most of the occupants are women, children and the elderly.

The cruelty was unspeakable. One of the prisoners told her liberators:

> At night we were driven through knee-deep mud into a camp. On the forced march the Germans beat us – and anyone who lagged behind was immediately finished off. One of the women had three small children. The youngest slipped in the mud, and a German soldier immediately shot him. When the other two turned round, frozen in terror, the soldier shot them as well.

The mother let out a heart-rending cry – but this was cut short by the final bullet.

Filip Ivanovic related: 'The Germans brought us into a camp in an area of marshland. There was no shelter, food or water – and any food people were carrying was confiscated by the soldiers, along with coats, boots and warm clothing. It was forbidden to make a fire. On the first night more than five hundred people died, mostly small children . . .'

Particular attention was paid to the testimony of another prisoner, Zinaida Gavrilchuk: 'In the camps, disease was spreading rapidly,' she began.

> During the night of 15 March hundreds of people died of typhus. The sick and the dying were dragged into heaps. I spoke to one of the German sentries, who was an ethnic Pole, and asked him in Polish what was going to happen to us. He waited until no other German guards were near, and then told me that in 16 hours' time all German sentries had been ordered to depart from the camp, leaving it to the advancing Red Army. When I asked why the camp was being abandoned, he said the object was to infect the Red Army with typhus.

'A burial pit had already been dug,' remembered Matruna Budnik. 'Wherever we went, we had to step over corpses. We were unable to eat or drink, and had been forced to lie for days in the snow and mud. When we saw our own army approaching, our relief was indescribable.' Red Army soldiers, doctors and nurses had rushed into the camps to help rescue the prisoners. 'The horror was unimaginable,' one Soviet nurse said. 'The swampy ground, the barbed wire, the minefields – and thousands of people in a delirium, sweating, with high temperatures on icy, half-frozen muddy ground.' Over 32,000 people were liberated from the camps, including 15,213 children under the age of thirteen; 517 of these children were now orphans: their mothers had been shot, or had died in the camps from typhus, hunger and cold. The rescuers were themselves rapidly infected. 'We had an epidemic on our hands,' said General Pavel Batov, commander of the Sixty-Fifth Army. 'The whole of our XIX Army Corps had to be quarantined.'

Mikhail Gulyakin, a Soviet military surgeon with the 37th Guards Division, recalled:

> When we reached the region of Ozarichi, in the Polesie marshes, our soldiers began falling ill with typhus. When we investigated the cause, we found that the Fascists had erected several concentration camps, in open fields, where thousands of Soviet citizens were forced to lie in the mud. The Nazis specifically brought typhoid patients here, with the intention of creating an epidemic after the liberation of the camps by the Red Army. Their calculation was that Soviet soldiers would rush in to help the prisoners – and contact with them would lead to wholesale contamination.

The Germans had left informers in the camps – inoculated against typhus – to relay further information on the spread of the disease. On 20 March Field Marshal Ernst Busch, the commander of Army Group Centre, received a full report of the operation. It was deemed a success. More typhoid camps were now set up in other endangered sections of the front – one near Mogilev, on the eastern bank of the Dnieper river, and another south-east of Vitebsk.

But the Red Army responded quickly and efficiently to this threat. Surgeon Mikhail Gulyakin continued: 'Fortunately, we had recently created an effective vaccine against typhus – which had first been tested at the front in December 1943. Large stocks of this were readily available, and thousands of Russian soldiers were quickly inoculated. We dispersed the sick – both soldiers and civilians – among 27 different hospitals, where we treated them, and we were able to contain the disease.'

This grotesque German plan shocked even hardened veterans of eastern front fighting. Nothing like it had been seen before. Once the danger of contracting typhus had passed, a full-scale commission was dispatched to Ozarichi, presided over by the deputy head of the Supreme Soviet, and the chiefs of the Red Army medical services. It found that the Germans had brought over two thousand typhus patients into the camp in order to create an epidemic as rapidly as possible. A network of informers was then set up: 'to monitor the spread of epidemic typhus in the Red Army and report details back to the Germans.'

German disregard for human life was flagrant – and was now seemingly institutionalized within the command structure of the Wehrmacht. The commission concluded that this plan 'for the mass extermination of peaceful Soviet citizens and Red Army soldiers' had been orchestrated at the highest level of Army Group Centre and put into effect by corps and divisional commanders of the German Ninth Army. The condition of the camp inmates – particularly the children – was filmed and photographed, and publicized in Red Army newspapers and newsreels. Soviet Sixty-Fifth Army commander General Pavel Batov said simply: 'These atrocities we would neither forgive nor forget.'

7

A Lucky Star

IN APRIL 1944 Stalin and his deputy commander, Marshal Georgi Zhukov, discussed plans for a major summer offensive. They wanted to strike a decisive blow against Germany's last major troop concentration – Army Group Centre – and to liberate Belorussia. Zhukov was confident this plan would come as a complete surprise to the enemy, and that a Soviet pincer operation would first encircle and then overwhelm his forces. The Red Army began to build up the necessary superiority in manpower and equipment to deliver the Germans a devastating blow. Over the next two months 406,000 tonnes of ammunition were delivered to the Russian troops, along with 304,000 tonnes of fuel and 508,000 tonnes of food and supplies. It was the most thoroughly planned operation of the war.

Field Marshal Erich von Manstein – the Wehrmacht's most gifted commander – had been dismissed by Hitler on 31 March, and replaced by Field Marshal Walther Model. Manstein had skilfully extricated some of the German forces from the Korsun pocket in the southern Ukraine, defying the Führer's strict injunction to hold fast. Hitler recognized Manstein's military ability, but at this stage of the war wanted only generals who were totally obedient to his commands. Manstein's Army Group South had also evacuated the Crimea, and was now holding a line along the River Dniester, close to the Romanian frontier. Army Group North had been forced to pull back from Leningrad. Only the position of Army Group Centre in Belorussia seemed stable. Here the German defences jutted into the Soviet line – forming what was called the 'Belorussian balcony'. The group was commanded by Field Marshal Ernst Busch, a solid but uninspiring leader, appointed largely because of his slavish loyalty to the Führer.

The successful advance of the Red Army into the Ukraine in the spring of 1944 made the German High Command believe its summer offensive would also be launched there. The main strength of the Germans – in tanks and aircraft – was therefore committed to the south. This redeployment left Army Group Centre vulnerable. Of the 5,000 tanks available to the Wehrmacht on the eastern front, fewer than six hundred were now in Belorussia. Seven Luftwaffe fighter groups were stationed in the Ukraine; only two in Belorussia. This imbalance made the Soviet High Command all the more eager to attack. In Belorussia in the summer of 1941, the Red Army had been badly mauled by the Germans. Now it was time to settle the score.

Stalin named the attack Operation Bagration, after Prince Pyotr Bagration, a general from a noble Georgian family who died a heroic death fighting against Napoleon's army in 1812. The Soviet leader – a Georgian himself – hoped that by invoking this illustrious predecessor he would bring his own operation good luck. Operation Bagration was certainly ambitious in scope. First, there would be pincer operations on the German flanks, to destroy the concentrations of enemy forces at Vitebsk and Bobruisk. Then Soviet troops would move rapidly to Minsk, cutting off the escape route of the Army Group along the motor highway. Thus the Soviet High Command planned to destroy the whole of Army Group Centre.

147

Ordinary Red Army soldiers remained unaware of such grand designs. Spring was in the air, and many thought of home. On 26 April 1944 Soviet lieutenant Leonid Bobrov wrote to a friend, with greetings for the First of May holiday. There would be no proper holiday for most Soviet soldiers – the pressure of the war was unremitting. But Bobrov was upbeat: 'The First of May, a martial anniversary, and a fiesta of spring,' he declared. 'We are celebrating it for the third and hopefully last time in war conditions. We are not doing anything particularly special. We push through to the rear of German positions, attack their garrisons, take enemy soldiers prisoner.' Bobrov looked to the future, imagining when the war would be over, and concluded with youthful bravado: 'I've lost three springs of my life – and of course I mean lost for fun, and flirting with girls. But wait, I will make up for everything. All girls will be mine!'

On 20 May Stalin called his deputy supreme commander, Marshal Georgi Zhukov, and his chief of staff, Marshal Alexander Vasilevsky, to Moscow to finalize details of Bagration. Vasilevsky would oversee plans for the northern pincer movement, the attack of the First Baltic and Third Belorussian Fronts on Vitebsk. Zhukov would do the same for the southern movement, which would be launched by the First Belorussian Front against Bobruisk. The jumping-off point for this southern pincer was the German stronghold of Rogachev. Two days later General Konstantin Rokossovsky also arrived. Rokossovsky, the commander of the First Belorussian Front, would be commanding the southern pincer thrust against Rogachev and then on to Bobruisk. But he now proposed a surprising alteration to the original plan.

On 22 May, in front of Stalin's entire High Command, Rokossovsky argued strongly that the southern pincer movement against Bobruisk should consist of not one but two different strikes against the enemy. Rokossovsky's idea ran against accepted military theory, which prescribed for encircling operations one main strike on each flank. But Rokossovsky believed that the Red Army needed more flexibility in its approach. He knew that the German positions at Rogachev were strongly fortified, and they would bring up their tank reserves behind the threatened point. He believed that two separate thrusts of equal weight would catch the enemy off balance, making him unsure where best to deploy his armour.

The meeting was dramatic. Rokossovsky insisted on two Red Army attacks on the southern flank, one at Rogachev, the other further south, at Parichi. He was strongly criticized, and twice was invited to leave the room and reflect on his proposal. After each exit and return he defended his decision again. Rokossovsky's perseverance won over Stalin, who was now at last genuinely listening to his generals. The Soviet leader intervened, praised Rokossovsky and added: 'The Front commander's persistence in this argument shows he has carefully thought through the organization of this offensive – and that is a good guarantee of success.' Rokossovsky's proposal was accepted.

Major Makhmud Gareev, an operations officer in the Soviet XLV Infantry Corps, was struck by this. 'The new idea was well thought out. And the way Stalin listened to Rokossovsky, and was willing to adapt the plan for Bagration accordingly, showed how far he had come from the incompetent military leadership of the summer of 1941.'

While Stalin was becoming more flexible in his thinking, Hitler grew increasingly dogmatic. The Führer now designated a number of Belorussian towns and cities as 'fortresses', including Vitebsk, Orsha, Mogilev, Bobruisk and Minsk. A commander of one of these fortified areas had to hold out at all costs, even when completely surrounded. A fortress could be abandoned only with Hitler's personal permission, and in May 1944 all commanders of fortified areas in Belorussia were summoned to the HQ of Army Group Centre, where they were required to give written pledges that they would hold their fortresses to the last man and last round of ammunition.

Hitler declared that his fortress policy 'would fulfill the function of the great castles of earlier times. It would ensure that the enemy did not occupy areas of decisive importance. The fortresses would allow themselves to be surrounded, thereby holding down the largest possible numbers of enemy forces, and establishing conditions favourable for counter-attacks.' General Hans Jordan, commander of the German Ninth Army, was less enthusiastic, stating: 'We consider the orders establishing fortresses particularly dangerous. They bind us to tactical measures that we cannot in good conscience accept as correct.' This rigid insistence on fortress defence deprived the Wehrmacht of its combat flexibility, which in the past had been one of its greatest strengths.

On 6 June 1944 Stalin wrote to British prime minister Winston Churchill, congratulating him on D-Day and the opening of the Second Front. Such was the concern for secrecy, the Soviet leader merely said: 'The summer offensive of Soviet troops – as agreed by us at the Tehran Conference – will begin in mid-June at one of the most important sectors of the Front.' Where exactly was not specified – even to the Western Allies.

The Germans had fielded just over thirty divisions in the west, to meet the Allied landings in Normandy. In the east they had in place 165 divisions, more than five times as many. But by June 1944 the Red Army held powerful superiority over Army Group Centre: 1,700,000 Soviet troops from three different fronts were now opposing some 800,000 Wehrmacht soldiers; 24,000 Soviet artillery pieces faced around 9,500 German ones. But the most telling disparity was in tanks and planes, where 6,834 Russian aircraft were opposed by 839 belonging to the Luftwaffe; 4,080 Red Army tanks were assembled against 551 German ones. To keep such a powerful advantage, it was vital that the Germans remain unaware of the forthcoming offensive, and did not bring up reinforcements.

The Russians put in place a remarkable deception operation. The build-up for Operation Bagration continued in strict secrecy. All troop movements took place at night. Vehicles moved without lights, orienting themselves by white roadside signposts and white painted markings on the front and back of every transport. Speed was regulated and overtaking strictly forbidden. Movement was allowed only between the hours of 10 p.m. and 4 a.m.; at dawn all army formations went into camouflaged positions. Only cars with special passes were allowed to travel during the day, and each army was allowed only a hundred of these. Special air patrols were made over areas of troop concentration. If the pilot noticed the location of a Soviet unit he would drop a pennant. Receiving a pennant meant the position of the troops was visible from the air and the commander should take immediate steps to improve camouflage.

This secrecy was observed from top to bottom of each army. Strict radio silence was observed, and daytime measures put in place to confuse the enemy. Troops deliberately drove away from the combat area, as if redeploying elsewhere or engaged in routine maintenance work. At night feverish preparations continued – soldiers training to move through swampy ground, creating special marsh skis and making rafts and sledges for the guns, so they could easily be transported cross-country, and bringing in beams and bundles of wood to build temporary trackways for tanks. Again, all activity ceased at dawn. The Germans continued to believe that the Red Army's offensive would be launched further south, in the Ukraine. Three days before Operation Bagration began the commander of Army Group Centre, Field Marshal Busch, unaware of any danger, left his HQ and went on a short holiday.

The Red Army maintained close contact with Belorussian partisans, who would be responsible for sabotage operations against German supply lines once Operation Bagration got under way. It was through these partisan reports that Soviet generals became increasingly aware of the atrocities committed by the German army against the Belorussian civilian population. Soviet captain Makhmud Gareev said: 'These blood-chilling accounts gave our preparations a terrible urgency.' There were delays nonetheless, as the logistical operations to supply the armies of three separate Fronts were enormous. The date finally chosen for Bagration was powerfully symbolic – the third anniversary of the German invasion of the Soviet Union.

On 22 June 1944 Major Vasily Ingor of the Soviet 308th Rifle Division wrote:

> During three cruel years of war we have fought over distances of thousands of kilometres, in endless steppe lands, in forests and on the shattered streets of burnt-out cities. We shall never forget the dozens of rivers and lakes, the hundreds of villages – many of which do not even appear on maps. We shall always remember them – because we seized them in battle from the accursed Germans. We are proud to have liberated Orel and Bryansk. But most of all we are proud of Stalingrad. We defended our Mother Volga and stood to the death under our commander

Leonti Gurtiev – our father, hero and general. At Stalingrad we delivered the decisive blow to the German Fascist troops. After three years we have grown and become strengthened by the rich experience of battle. We have learnt to hate and love with ever greater intensity.

The Red Army struck its first blow against Vitebsk. On the night of 22 June troops from the First Baltic and Third Belorussian Fronts stormed the town's outlying defence positions. The German garrison was soon in deadly danger. On 23 June Colonel General Hans-Georg Reinhardt asked permission to pull Wehrmacht forces back. Field Marshal Busch – making a rapid return from his holiday – countermanded Reinhardt and insisted Vitebsk be held. On 25 June Soviet troops encircled the town. That evening Hitler grudgingly authorized a partial withdrawal – leaving a division to man Vitebsk's defences – but the decision came too late. The German break-out attempt was cornered in a forest southwest of the city, and the troops annihilated by artillery fire and air strikes. Vitebsk's depleted garrison was overrun the following day.

As Operation Bagration was unleashed, Hans Jürgen Hartmann, a German officer with XXXIX Panzer Corps, recorded in his diary on 23 June 1944: 'In the central section of our front, the Russians have begun another major offensive. They have often given themselves a bloody nose attacking Orsha and Vitebsk, so we remain quite confident. Nevertheless, our thoughts go out to our fighting comrades.'

By the following day, Hartmann was less optimistic:

I visited the HQ to find out more news of the Russian offensive against Army Group Centre. Things have been rapidly worsening since 22 June, the enemy's attack is widening – and every day the situation looks more serious ... Here everything is quiet for the moment, but all of us suspect that it will not last much longer – our army bulletins warn that strong enemy tank and infantry forces have penetrated east of Mogilev – pushing forward on both sides of the motor highway – aiming for Vitebsk.

To the south, Rokossovsky's offensive against Bobruisk began two days later, on 24 June. One force hit hard at Rogachev, blasting German defences with air and artillery strikes; the other struck through the marshland at Parichi. It was here, in the region of Polesie, that Rokossovsky's troops had discovered the typhus camps, in which the German army had deliberately infected thousands of Belorussian civilians. In these circumstances it was not difficult to motivate the advancing Red Army soldiers. Rokossovsky gave a leading role in this attack to the Soviet Sixty-Fifth Army – the army that the Germans had hoped would succumb to a typhus epidemic. The Wehrmacht briefly clung on at Rogachev, but Rokossovsky achieved a complete breakthrough at Parichi, where the Russians fought with a savage ferocity. 'I wanted to kill as many of the enemy as I could', said Nikolai Litvin of the Sixty-Fifth Army. The decision to launch two attacks against the enemy was completely vindicated. Army Group Centre's meagre tank reserve was committed first to one sector and then the other. As a result, it was unable to deploy effectively in either area. Rokossovsky kept advancing.

On 25 June Josef Perau, the Wehrmacht priest serving with the German 129th Division, wrote:

> Just before noon a warning reached us that we are in imminent danger of encirclement. The Russians are now ahead of us, and the route to Bobruisk is blocked. Ammunition is running low . . . As we begin to load up the wounded on to lorries the first enemy shells burst overhead. But the first village we pass through

remains strangely peaceful. It nestles high above a riverbank. Storks sit happily on their nests, tending their young, as if there is no war. But the rooftops where they have built their homes will surely go up in flames before their young can ever fly.

By 28 June the whole of the German Ninth Army had been surrounded in the Bobruisk pocket. That day Josef Perau continued:

> News has reached us of the fall of Vitebsk and Bobruisk. The collapse of the entire central front now seems imminent . . . A dull apathy settles over people. For a while I just sit, drained and exhausted. For two days we have had nothing to eat. The heat is utterly soporific. Then more bad news jolts us to our senses. The 427th Regiment is surrounded. Its commander – leading an attempted break-out at the head of his men – was killed. The wounded have had to be left behind. Many of them asked to be shot rather than fall into the hands of the enemy.

The Russians now flung their tank forces through the broken German lines. On 30 June Josef Perau noted in his diary: 'The Russians have recaptured Lyuban – 30 kilometres north-west of us – and Orsha is about to fall into their hands. The division – all of it that remains – is entirely focused on finding an escape route. Harassing fire from the enemy's planes and artillery has suddenly ceased, and an eerie silence hangs over the forest. Everyone is preoccupied by one unanswerable question: is there still a way out?'

The same day German officer Hans Jürgen Hartmann wrote grimly: 'Yesterday the enemy reached Orsha and Vitebsk – the combat zone is moving ever westwards, to the Berezina, to Mogilev. Then the Russians will advance on Minsk. My God – when will this stop? Why does our position, which for years has withstood every storm, every onslaught, now break asunder?'

Soviet private Veniamin Fyodorov of the 77th Guards Infantry Regiment remembered that: 'In 1944 we were advancing like the Germans used to advance in 1941. The German reliance on fortified areas was stupid – it condemned their troops to death or captivity. They were an easy target: our artillery shelling and air strikes simply smashed them to pieces.'

General Rotmistrov's Fifth Guards Tank Army was now bearing down on Minsk, the Belorussian capital, with more than five hundred tanks. Hitler sacked Field Marshal Busch and brought in Field Marshal Model to command Army Group Centre. Reinforcements were urgently summoned from the Ukraine. But Army Group Centre was disintegrating even as these fresh dispositions were being made. Wehrmacht forces now fled towards the Berezina river and the one bridge – on the Mogilev–Minsk highway – that remained in German hands. Thousands of vehicles, wagons and marching infantry converged on it, in scenes reminiscent of the final collapse of Napoleon's *Grande Armée* at the Berezina in 1812. One Wehrmacht officer recorded: 'Not far from the bridge our retreat is turning into a stampede. It is utterly shocking. Carts and cars ram each other, push each other off the roadway, in a desperate attempt to get on the bridge. There is swearing and cursing, then fights break out. The few remaining field police stand by, helpless.'

Soviet planes hovered over the fleeing troops, bombing and strafing. Army Group Centre's once-proud divisions were now falling apart, with no effective command or control. On the night of 1 July the remnants of Josef Perau's 129th Infantry Division tried to evade the Russians, moving cross-country along forest tracks. 'Vehicle breakdowns and lack of spare parts have slowed down our attempt,' Perau recorded.

Violent arguments broke out. The infantry insulted the motorized units, the motorized units the artillerymen – now without
their guns, which had hurriedly been blown up before our
retreat. It was a result of the sheer stress of our situation. But
underneath these disagreements we all need each other – and
everyone knows it. It is incredibly demanding work. Each lorry
or car has to be hauled across the swampland on wooden rails.
Sometimes they get stuck, and angry swearing breaks out.

The Germans' painful progress continued. At midnight on
2 July the exhausted soldiers gathered for a couple of hours'
halt in the forest. 'There was a strong sense that all depended
on the next stage of our journey,' Perau said. 'Our survival
hung on a knife edge. Partisans were in the area – and the
Russians were ahead of us. The final push towards our
retreating front line began in the grey light of dawn. The
order was passed along the line: "Ready weapons for firing!
Drive fast!"'

The soldiers passed terrible evidence of an enemy bombing
attack. Another division had pulled back along the same
route before them. It had been caught by Soviet planes, and
dead men and horses littered the track. But now all was quiet.
'The Russians have broken through to the north – and are
rushing towards Minsk,' Perau recorded. 'They are preoccupied with bigger gains.' The Germans drove on – evading
the trap. Minsk – the capital of Belorussia – fell to the Red
Army a day later, closing the ring of encirclement around the
battered remnants of three German armies.

On 3 July German officer Hans Jürgen Hartmann wrote:
'in the central section of our front, three of our commanding generals have been killed: General Martinek – who only
a few months ago visited us – Schunemann – his replace-
ment, and Zutavern . . . Our surroundings have been burning for days, the stench is in our noses, the sky is red from

the flashes of guns and the smouldering ruins and around us everything is hissing and cracking. We are all terrified for the future.'

Hartmann's unit – like so many others – was in full retreat:

At 8.00 p.m. our convoy began to roll out – the field kitchens are in the first group, the engineers are further back, to deal with any breakdowns. Extra machine guns and ammunition have been distributed among the infantry. Signal rockets herald our progress – the Russians will not easily see them because so much is burning. The last explosions are heard in the city, as the remaining equipment is blown up . . . Our vehicles pause on the outskirts of town, loaded with everything we can carry. We are fleeing westwards, and behind us, the houses on both sides of the road are burning. Overhead, the pale sky is wreathed in smoke. Destroyed bridges, piles of jettisoned equipment and flames engulfing everything behind us – is it all some terrible dream?

War journalist Pavel Antokolsky was moved by the triumph of Bagration, and on 6 July, to mark the second anniversary of his son Vladimir's death, he wrote a letter to him. 'Son' was gaining an increasingly large readership. Antokolsky now added – as if he were speaking to Vladimir in person: 'Through this poem tens of thousands of people have come to know you and love you: fathers, mothers, sons and daughters.'

'On we fly on wings of thunder, never more to sheathe our swords,' Antokolsky had written, and in the aftermath of Bagration his words carried prophetic power. 'We felt we were flying on the wings of victory,' said Soviet private Veniamin Fyodorov of the 77th Guards Infantry Regiment. 'And everyone in our units, from ordinary soldiers to commanders, experienced this feeling – it was one of overwhelming triumph.' 'The Belorussian Operation was a classic,' Major Makhmud Gareev added appreciatively. By 10 July all German troops in the Minsk encirclement had been destroyed or had surrendered. In two weeks of fighting seven German corps had been annihilated and seventeen divisions wiped out; 409,000 German soldiers had been killed or taken prisoner. Army Group Centre had ceased to exist.

Letters from those Wehrmacht soldiers who managed to evade the Russians conveyed a mood of depression and shock: 'We are in constant action – there is hardly any rest,' complained Private Heinz Köncke on 15 July. 'We are sickened by it all – and waiting for an end to this war. I cannot say much about what has been happening here – but it is very different from the stories relayed in the newspapers!' 'Perhaps a light will finally come on when the higher-ups realize the Russians are almost at our border,' Private Fürlinger wrote a day later. 'It is only a matter of time . . .' 'Oh, if only this mess would end!' Private Karl Bitz added on 23 July. 'The only thing that matters to me is to extricate myself, unharmed, from this cursed war.'

On 17 July German prisoners were paraded through the streets of Moscow. Leading the procession were nineteen generals, in uniform and medals; behind them came a group of over a thousand officers. There followed 57,000 ordinary soldiers, unshaven, ragged, many without boots. In the rear were water cannon, to wash all traces of the Fascist invaders from Moscow's streets.

Within weeks, Soviet troops had pushed through Belorussia and entered Poland. The Nazi death camp at Majdanek near Lublin was discovered by the Red Army on 23 July 1944. Troops of the Soviet Second Tank Army reached it first. The SS had marched away most of its inmates, but had lacked time to destroy its infrastructure. It was the first functioning death camp captured intact by the

Red Army. In others, the Nazis had had time to destroy most of the evidence, but here the Red Army advance was too swift. Majdanek stunned its liberators. Political commissar Vasily Yeremenko, who was with the Second Tank Army, said: 'When we saw what it contained, we felt dangerously close to going insane.'

Soviet soldiers could scarcely comprehend what they were witnessing. 'We found warehouses full of belongings taken from the prisoners,' said newly promoted Captain Anatoly Mereshko, 'and piles of corpses. We had read about the existence of such camps, but to actually see one was completely different.' Mereshko's Eighth Guards Army had reached the camp a few hours after the Second Tank Army. The troops saw how the killing had been done with clinical efficiency. It was the crematorium which had the greatest impact. Red Army soldiers filed past it in utter silence. 'The ovens were still warm,' Mereshko said bluntly.

The scale of it all was hard to take in. 'There was a whole warehouse full of shoes,' Mereshko continued, 'hundreds of thousands of them, piled high to the ceiling, in all sorts of sizes. Many of them were children's. Our soldiers asked each other in bewilderment: "What has been going on here?"'

Konstantin Simonov was the first Soviet war correspondent to visit Majdanek. In a striking article in the army newspaper *Red Star* he warned its readers that his mind still refused the reality of what his eyes and ears took in, and that they were about to uncover something immense, terrifying and incomprehensible. For some Russian soldiers – still struggling with the atrocities they had witnessed in Belorussia – it was simply all too much. 'The Germans burnt my village near Mogilev, killing all its inhabitants,' said Red Army private Ivan Egorkin. 'My family may have ended up at this camp.' 'The Germans took my father, mother, wife and two children,' said another. 'They might have been killed at Majdanek.' Red Army nurse Anisya Zenkova – with the Soviet 160th Rifle Division – recalled the aftermath of the camp's liberation:

> We set up a hospital to treat the inmates from the camp. The things that had been perpetrated there . . . We tried to help them. Many had TB; others were suffering from deep psychological trauma. It was very hard to reach them, to re-establish a human connection. There was no longer the will to live. These patients would often predict their own death, although there was nothing physically wrong with them, simply announcing: 'I will die tomorrow'. And that is what invariably happened. We had six or seven such deaths every day.

Red Army troops from the First Belorussian Front reached Sobibor and Treblinka on 23 July 1944, the same day that Majdanek had been liberated. Both camps had been destroyed by the Nazis – the bodies burnt, the buildings blown to pieces, the land ploughed up. But at Treblinka Red Army soldiers found about forty survivors hiding in a nearby pine forest, and Jewish war correspondent Vasily Grossman was able to interview them.

Grossman was already working with fellow journalist Ilya Ehrenburg on *The Black Book*, a compilation of testimony about the mass murder of Jewish civilians in the Soviet Union by Nazi extermination squads, the Einsatzgruppen. The main question driving Grossman's research was how the Germans had managed to kill such a vast number of people. His conclusion: their goal had been achieved by deceit – victims had offered no resistance because they did not realize until it was too late exactly where they would be taken. On arrival they were intensely psychologically distressed and disoriented – for example, by the breaking up of family groups. Then they were subjected to terror. After completing the piece Grossman suffered a nervous breakdown.

As the fighting continued, simple acts of comradeship within the Red Army could instil hope and optimism as strongly as news of military success. On 7 August 1944 Medical Instructor Ariadna Dobrosmislova of the Soviet 308th Division was wounded. Another nurse risked her life to rescue her: 'One of our girls carried me from the battle-field,' Dobrosmislova related. 'Tonyusha pulled me for more than a kilometre and a half through a rye field, under enemy fire. How she managed this, all by herself, I do not know – but I shall never forget it. No hardship is terrifying when you see the goodness people are capable of at such times . . .'

Dobrosmislova remembered how – in the aftermath of this act of self-sacrifice – sheer relief turned horror into humour: 'Eventually we reached a large barn,' she continued,

> where I was laid down in the hay among 60 wounded men. Then they took us on to Mogilev by ambulance. We were very jolly along the way, because there were four lightly wounded Fritz with us, and the lads (also lightly wounded) pulled their legs so much that we almost died laughing. They were Joseph, Willy, Carl and Hans, but it was easier for us to call them all Fritz. We set one Fritz to giving us water, adjusting our pillows and so on, which he did with alacrity . . . And our boys engaged them in conversation, especially on political themes, so that the vehicle filled with laughter . . .

Even such a great success as Operation Bagration cost the Red Army substantial casualties. Soviet losses in the six weeks of the campaign totalled 176,000 out of the 2,330,000 involved in the fighting. For a brief period after D-Day the Western Allies experienced a similar intensity of casualties: 120,000 losses out of a total of 1,332,000 troops deployed in the first six weeks of the invasion of Normandy. But these figures decreased dramatically once British and American forces broke out from German containment and sped across France and Belgium in August 1944. On the eastern front there was no respite for Soviet forces.

Hitler's Reich was now under sustained military pressure from all sides. In the west, the German position was disintegrating. The Allied armies had broken out of Normandy at the end of July, staged further landings in southern France on 15 August and liberated Paris ten days later. In the east, the defeat of Army Group Centre allowed the Red Army not only to sweep into eastern Poland but to reach East Prussia and the Baltic. By August Soviet soldiers – moving along a 965-kilometre front – had pushed forward over 640 kilometres from their positions at the start of Operation Bagration. But now Panzer divisions brought up from the Ukraine began to slow the pace of the Russian advance, and Red Army units started to outrun their supplies. Soviet forces halted east of Warsaw, and stayed there while the Polish resistance mounted a desperate uprising in the city. Rokossovsky's First Belorussian Front was dangerously over-stretched, but it suited Stalin's ruthless political agenda to let the rivals to his pro-Soviet Polish government in Lublin founder. The Nazis crushed the Warsaw uprising with brutal force.

However, Germany's allies had begun to defect. Finland had opened negotiations with the Soviet Union, and a coup in Bucharest on 23 August quickly knocked Romania out of the war. Bulgaria – another ally of Hitler – received Soviet armies without a shot being fired. By mid-September the Red Army's Second and Third Ukrainian Fronts were poised to enter Hungary and Yugoslavia. To the north, some Red Army units of General Ivan Chernyakovsky's Third

Belorussian Front prepared to push into East Prussia. There, however, they were not strong enough to undertake a further advance against stiffening German resistance, reinforced by the troops of the Third Panzer Army. An attempt to breach the Wehrmacht's defences at Gumbinnen failed.

Red Army sniper Roza Shanina's 184th Rifle Division had been the first Soviet unit to enter East Prussia. Shanina had been awarded the Order of Glory for her sniping in Belorussia, where her tally had reached forty-six kills. She now commanded a platoon of female snipers. On one occasion a group of enemy soldiers attacked the trench where these women were stationed. Shanina recorded matter-of-factly: 'Some fell from our bullets; the remainder we finished off with bayonets, grenades and even shovels.'

Shanina was a skilful sniper and an energetic commander. On 17 October she wrote in her diary: 'I always want to be on the front line. It's hard to explain – it's as if some mysterious force draws me there . . . I want to fight!' She was soon in action again. Towards the end of the month she wrote: 'We lay concealed in the woods behind a railway embankment. The Germans began to crawl forward, only the tips of their helmets visible. We held our fire. They were 200 metres away, then 100 metres – we let them come on. And then they stood up. We finished them off at close range.' In battle Shanina was fearless. 'When I go into combat, I am not afraid of anything,' she said proudly.

To the south, Soviet troops of the Second Ukrainian Front had crossed the Carpathians and were fighting in Hungary. On 20 October Marshal Rodion Malinovsky's forces took the town of Debrecen. The troops were tired after several months of tough combat, and needed to be replenished and resupplied, but Stalin wanted to capture the Hungarian capital as soon as possible. The Soviet leader overruled

Malinovsky's concerns, and ordered him to advance on Budapest 'regardless of the cost in human lives'. On 25 October Red Army private Pavel Elkinson wrote in his diary:

> Today is a bad day – just like my mood. It's raining – and we are all wet. It's such a shame to die in a foreign land – and I feel so sorry for the guys who were killed near this city. They fought all the way from the Caucasus to Hungary – and after all that, to have to die here. What an awful shame! I want so badly to return home. I so badly want to live. Though I'm a bit drunk, I know what I'm writing. I just want to hurry, and move on, to Berlin, victory and closer to home.

Over 7 million Soviet soldiers were now deployed in a theatre of war that spanned the whole of eastern Europe. Red Army troops of the First Baltic Front were advancing towards Memel, the most northerly town of East Prussia and the foremost ice-free port in the eastern Baltic. On 1 November 1944 Soviet lieutenant Leonid Bobrov of the 102nd Rifle Division wrote home to his mother. He was proud of the way his soldiers had been fighting. 'We launched a rapid offensive,' he began, 'being in the main direction of the attack, and in the forefront of the action – although this time we were supported with tanks. We pursued the Germans back for over 60 miles . . . We learnt today that our division has been awarded the Order of Suvorov.' Bobrov recalled a particularly dangerous moment, when he and twenty of his comrades were involved in a night battle with a large enemy force. After six hours' fighting they outflanked the German position, making a river crossing on improvised rafts.

Two years earlier, in the autumn of 1942, Bobrov and other officers had undergone an intensive retraining programme. They were now using these skills to good effect.

Alongside the Order of Suvorov, the division had won the Order of the Red Banner and the Red Star. Bobrov paid tribute to his fellow combatants. 'I've been through hell with these seasoned fighters, and they have never let me down. But there are so few of them left . . .'

The Soviet troops of the First Baltic Front had amassed a substantial haul of booty. 'We captured many weapons, supply storehouses, even abandoned planes,' Bobrov continued. Then he added: 'None of this compared to our feelings when we liberated a POW camp. Some 2,000 of our soldiers were left inside it. You can't imagine how elated they were – they kissed and hugged our soldiers. We felt such joy. This moment compensated for all the hardship and difficulties we have suffered on our path.' Bobrov concluded: 'I never regarded myself as a malicious person. But now, when I shoot a German I feel not only satisfaction but outright delight. The further we advance, the more we find evidence of German atrocities – and the angrier we become.'

The Red Army troops of Marshal Leonid Govorov's Leningrad front had turned their attention to southern Estonia. Throughout the war young Leonid Krainov had written letters to the Leningrad front almost daily. His father, three uncles and an aunt – five members of his family – were all serving on it. In the summer of 1943 his mother had put up a map of Europe in his room: 'When we defeated the Germans at Kursk, and liberated Orel and Belgorod – and when they fired the first salute at Moscow – I stuck red flags along the front lines,' Leonid Krainov recalled. 'Following the radio reports, I moved these flags towards the west – further and further away from Moscow, and nearer to our borders. Every day I studied that map – first reading the names of our own towns, then of Polish and German ones. I dreamed of the day we would reach Berlin.'

Leonid told his father, Alexander Krainov, everyday details about his life: his work on the allotment, the contents of books he had read. The letters he received back in the late summer of 1944 were cheerful and optimistic. Troops of the Leningrad front had now advanced into the Baltic states. 'I hope very much', his father wrote in one letter, 'that we shall see each other again in the New Year.' In another he said: 'Soon, my dear son, we shall reach Berlin – and you will stick your last flag in the map. The world shall remember that the road to our great victory began in Moscow and Leningrad back in 1941.'

September 1944 was warm and sunny. 'There has been fierce fighting,' Leonid's father wrote, 'but we are moving forward again. I have been awarded a medal. Soon my son you will begin the fifth grade. I shall probably not recognize you when I return – you will have grown so much. You had only just entered the second grade when I left for the front.' This was the last Leonid heard from his father.

On 3 November, eleven-year-old Leonid received a letter from the front. It was from one of his father's fellow officers:

I have sad news for you. Your father, Alexander Dimitrievich Krainov, met his death bravely, defending our beautiful Motherland in battle near the Estonian town of Tartu. He was buried 40 kilometres from Tartu at the village of Purman. Your father was an able commander of his company and he led the attack. What can I say to comfort you? There are no words. You must only remember that there is no such thing as a war without casualties. Grow up, study, and be worthy of your father. Your sorrow will be great and I sympathize with you profoundly. Your father told me so many good things about you. I wish you and your mother health and happiness – and all the best in your life.

'I stopped receiving those little triangular envelopes, marked with my father's return postal address – Field Post 06511,' Leonid Krainov said. 'That address would be engraved on my memory for the rest of my life.'

Stalin was determined to install Soviet political power in the Baltic states and eastern Europe, regardless of the cost in Red Army soldiers' lives. Even Stalin, however, could not control everything. Colonel Dmitry Loza recalled how the 7 November 1944 edition of the front-line newspaper *Sovetskiy Voin – Soviet Fighting Man –* was eagerly awaited by the tank crews of V Armoured Corps, fighting in Hungary with the Second Ukrainian Front. The edition had been rushed through to carry the text of Stalin's speech on the anniversary of the Bolshevik revolution. The Soviet leader's title was boldly displayed, but through an oversight of both the proof-reader and editor the letter 'l' was omitted from the word *glavno-komanduyuschiy*, rendering 'Supreme High Commander' more colloquially as 'Shitter-in-Chief'. The editor was arrested by the NKVD and consigned to a penal battalion.

In the second week of November Soviet tanks had reached the outskirts of Budapest. The Germans were determined that Hungary would not go the way of Romania and Bulgaria. They installed a puppet government and made Budapest a key point in a ferocious defence of central Europe. Hitler brought up fresh Panzer forces and SS divisions. A Soviet attempt to capture the Hungarian capital on 11 November foundered on drenched and boggy terrain and determined resistance. 'There has been heavy fighting,' Red Army soldier Pavel Elkinson recorded on 11 November. 'Every day is difficult for us. The enemy does not give up even a scrap of land without a fight. We are losing some of our best people. A few days ago our intelligence officer was killed. I could not help but think of fate. Only a minute earlier I had been standing next to him. I moved on – and a shell exploded right by him.'

In August 1944 Elkinson had written proudly that he had taken part in the liberation of Bessarabia and now stood on the frontiers of the Soviet Union. Like most Red Army soldiers, he had never been abroad, and a new world seemed to be opening out for him. But strong enemy resistance around Budapest began to affect his morale, and that of others. 'We did not see why Russian lives should be sacrificed for German firing points on Hungarian land,' said Lieutenant Ivan Smagin, a platoon commander in the Soviet 68th Rifle Division. 'It was openly discussed among us. Our battalion commander tried not to send us into attack unless it was absolutely necessary.'

The Red Army had halted on the border of East Prussia, and would not advance again until a major new offensive was prepared in the New Year. But the Soviet Second Ukrainian Front was still moving to encircle Budapest. On 25 November Pavel Elkinson wrote:

> Heavy fighting has erupted again. When will this all end? The damned Fritz refuses to retreat. Planes bomb us all day long, without a break . . . Towards the end of the day enemy tanks paid us a visit. The weather was foggy, and they got within 350 metres of our position before we noticed them. We forced them back with difficulty. Another man was killed today – and two more wounded. What cost to one's nerves to live through such sights day after day, for three years – without a break? One thought keeps circling round my head: when will it be my turn?

On 27 November Sergeant Roza Shanina of the Soviet 184th Rifle Division noted that two of her fellow snipers had been captured by the Germans. In her heart she felt it unlikely that they were still alive. Yet when she encountered German civilians there was no thought of vengeance. 'I saw my first German Frau,' she wrote. 'Did I take revenge for the girls in my unit? No. However much I hate the Nazis, I will never kill one of them in cold blood.' And as Shanina realized this, for the first time she saw a future for herself, after the war had ended. If she did not go back to university, she would work in an orphanage, caring for the children there.

Her feelings of clemency were far from typical in the Red Army. 'I am alive and well,' Soviet artillery officer Ilya Meyerovich wrote home at the end of November 1944.

> We are experiencing a lull in the fighting – punctuated by the occasional skirmish – and I don't have much worthwhile news. Like all the guys here, I am waiting for a dramatic breakthrough in the war – it's long past time. We have been fighting so hard for the last three years – and I desperately want to be finished with the damned Krauts once and for all – they have caused us such unbelievable suffering. The topic of the day for all of us is what we'll do with the bastards once we cross the German border. Each of us sees before his eyes horrible pictures of destruction and conflagration, and the bodies of old people and children that we saw in the Ukraine and especially in Belorussia. We are truly livid, and that bodes nothing good for the Germans – revenge will be merciless.

On 13 December Roza Shanina recorded in her diary: 'Yesterday I got wounded in the shoulder. Bizarrely, only the night before I had a dream – and in it, I was also wounded in the shoulder. As I settled into my sniper's hideout I remembered the dream, and a few minutes later recoiled in shock. A German sniper's bullet had caught me in exactly the same place.'

As Shanina sought to improve her sniper's tally, Wehrmacht soldiers uneasily patrolled their front-line positions along the River Vistula. 'For the first time in many months I am gripped by fear when I conduct my night-time patrols,' German officer Hans Jürgen Hartmann wrote in his diary on 22 December.

> I see ghosts – I hear cracking sounds and soft cries, and am startled if a flare unexpectedly hisses into the sky . . . My nerves are shot. No reinforcements arrive to supplement our small force. I am filled with dread at the sight of the shadowy ruins, and the endless empty trenches that we creep along, machine guns and pistols at the ready. There is a light covering of snow on the ground and dark clouds hang over a monotonous landscape. On my right there is a T-34 without a turret quietly rusting away in a ditch. Occasionally a shot rings out across the deathly-quiet valley. The world seems to have sunk into hibernation, but appearances can be deceptive. We cannot let up our guard – even for one minute.

Hartmann rightly complained of lack of reinforcement. German military reserves had been swallowed up by Hitler's Ardennes offensive in the west. In eastern Europe, the Soviet Second Ukrainian Front had fully encircled Budapest on 27 December 1944, but a vicious siege would drag on into the New Year. The First Ukrainian and First, Second and Third Belorussian Fronts were now preparing for a major new offensive across the Vistula river into the remainder of German-held Poland and for a campaign in East Prussia. At the beginning of 1945 Roza Shanina – now recovered from her shoulder wound – was given permission to return to the front line. Shanina was delighted – she knew a fresh offensive was in the offing. She had had to lobby hard for her place in it.

The Third Belorussian Front of General Ivan Chernyakovsky was about to strike deep into East Prussia. But the
commander of the 184th Division, knowing that the offensive would be a bloody one, forbade Shanina's return. She
appealed to the military council of the Fifth Army. They also
refused her permission. Finally, she went to see the commander of the Fifth Army, Marshal Nikolai Krylov – the
former chief of staff of the Sixty-Second Army at Stalingrad.
There had been a burgeoning Red Army sniper movement
at Stalingrad, and Krylov had also encouraged sniper units
during the sieges of Odessa and Sevastopol. But his most
famous female sniper, Lyudmila Pavchenko, who had amassed
a total of 309 kills in both these sieges, had been withdrawn
from active combat once she was wounded. Krylov allowed
Shanina's return only with the greatest reluctance.

On the evening of 2 January 1945 Red Army lieutenant
Vladimir Gelfand went out to look at the Vistula river. His
301st Rifle Division – part of Marshal Zhukov's First
Belorussian Front – was camped alongside it. Gelfand knew
that a big attack was imminent, and that its first main objective would be the Polish capital. 'Crossing the Vistula,' he
wrote, 'is the springboard for our last major offensive. I have
had the honour to fight for great cities in this war: Stalingrad,
Kharkov, Odessa – and the next will be Warsaw. The battles
that lie ahead will be fierce, perhaps the fiercest we have yet
encountered. We will meet fanatical resistance from some
enemy soldiers, and once more death will walk within our
ranks. We are sure to have substantial losses.'

Gelfand continued: 'It is late evening. The fire crackles.
There is a strong wind – and smoke blows into my eyes. The
cold is all-consuming and I feel a terrible fatigue. It has been
six months since my last, brief period of leave. It is frightening to think of the battles ahead.' And then his attention was

drawn upwards, towards the night sky. 'For a moment a bright star can be seen – it is strikingly beautiful. Then it disappears amid the clouds.' Gelfand's tone abruptly changed: 'I cannot wait for our great advance, when we surge forward with an unstoppable momentum and smash and destroy the accursed enemy of our people.' He concluded: 'I am ready. If I do not make it through to the end of the war, I would like it known that I gave my Motherland the best years of my life, that I gave it my youth and health. I want that sacrifice to be remembered.'

That January Soviet war journalist Pavel Antokolsky also reflected on the theme of sacrifice – the sacrifice of millions of the Soviet Union's Jews to Hitler's racial extermination programme. He interviewed Red Army lieutenant Alexander Pechersky in Moscow, and heard from him moving details of the uprising in the death camp at Sobibor. After the break-out, Himmler had ordered all traces of the camp to be destroyed. But in the poem 'Death Camp' Antokolsky mingled images of horror with those of hope:

> We are these stars, we are these flowers.
> The killers hurried to be done,
> Becoming blinded by the powers
> Of naked lives, bright as the sun.
> The killers used their cans of gas.
> Because in the new waving grass,
> Death in its beauty would soon pass
> Down the highway from this morass,
> In the evening dew and birdsong,
> In grey clouds over the world's grime,
> You see, we are not dead for long
> We have arisen for all time.

On 12 January 1945 the great Red Army assault began as the ten armies of Marshal Ivan Konev's First Ukrainian Front struck from its bridgehead across the River Vistula. The Russian heavy artillery was ranged almost wheel to wheel, with more than three hundred guns for each kilometre of the front. 'At 5.00 a.m. flares bathed the ground around us in reddish light and artillery salvoes began an incessant booming,' remembered Soviet war correspondent Boris Polevoy. Polevoy had never before experienced a bombardment of such intensity.

'In the distance a mighty roar could be heard,' wrote German officer Hans Jürgen Hartmann.

> It was the Russians' major offensive! In the west, we saw the clouds lit by countless flashing lights ... For weeks we had awaited this moment. Now it had begun, the artillery barrage continuing for half an hour, then an hour, without the slightest pause. All of us remained silent. How would things look in the main line of the attack? No one could be alive in the foremost trenches. Our hearts went out to our comrades in those distant fires of hell. The fear of suffering a similar fate tied my stomach up in knots and I could not eat anything. The primal fear of captivity, torture, dying, which I had long suppressed, suddenly struck me like never before, vast and terrifying.

Konev's attack had been launched from the Red Army's bridgehead at Sandomierz, more than 160 kilometres north-east of the Polish city of Krakow. On 13 January Soviet general Ivan Chernyakovsky launched his offensive on East Prussia. Marshal Georgi Zhukov's First Belorussian Front joined battle from its own bridgeheads of Magnuszew and Pulawy, some 110 and 190 kilometres south-east of Warsaw. Hitler's Reich was reeling under a series of hammer blows.

The assault on East Prussia was to be another bold Red Army pincer movement, executed by the Second and Third Belorussian Fronts. On 15 January 1945 Lieutenant

Leonid Bobrov and his 102nd Soviet Rifle Division were about to join the East Prussian offensive under the command of Marshal Rokossovsky – promoted in the aftermath of Operation Bagration and now leading the Second Belorussian Front. To encourage Bobrov's unit forward, it was designated a Guards division – and Bobrov was delighted: 'On New Year's Eve our commander read out an order to us. Our unit was awarded the title of Guards for special services in fighting the enemy. Now we are Guards – that sounds great! We have dreamed about this title for a long time. And after all we have been through, we have definitely deserved it.'

The division was billeted in the small town of Rybinsk. It had briefly been pulled back from the front line, and the lull allowed a celebration party to be thrown on an epic scale. It went on for days.

'We drank vodka to our hearts' content,' Bobrov went on, 'and now I have spent all my "socialist savings", and have nothing left in my pocket. But I don't regret it. We had a lot of fun – after three years of solid fighting. The local people will remember us well, especially the girls . . .' And it was to the girls that Bobrov returned. 'We had such a good time – with many memorable moments. There were plenty of pretty girls around and you can imagine what we were like. Some even got married, and almost every officer had a date. I almost got shot because of a girl. She and I had gone horse-back riding when half a magazine of "friendly fire" was directed at me. But it all ended well. We sorted everything out, and sat in a car and laughed about it. Of course, everyone was totally inebriated.'

Red Army drinking certainly ran out of control at times. But these soldiers were under enormous combat stress. And the best Soviet units – and there were many of them – quickly pulled themselves together. Drinking to excess was part of a larger-than-life existence – on a scale that is difficult to fully comprehend. As Bobrov readied himself for battle once more, he put the recent festivities to the back of his mind. 'We will soon be fighting again,' he wrote. 'It will be our last campaign – and it will be a decisive one. I don't want to talk much about it. We have had a good break, and should be ready for anything.' Bobrov could see evidence of the war's destruction all around him. 'Everything is in ruins – nothing much is left of the towns and villages the Germans have pulled back from. It is an utterly appalling sight – and it makes us hate the enemy with an even greater intensity. As we fight our last great battle against them, our maxim will be "Blood for blood!"'

Bobrov wondered whether he would survive it all. On 15 January 1943 he had written: 'I'll probably get killed in the last few weeks of the war.' On 15 January 1945, conscious that he had survived countless engagements unscathed, he struck a different note: 'Of course, there is no avoiding one's fate,' he said, 'but I will trust in my lucky star. And if I survive, I will soon be back at home with you, my family, and we will live a new and happy life.'

A day later, Soviet sniper Roza Shanina was in a pensive mood. A snowstorm had blown up around the 184th Rifle Division's front-line positions. There was a biting wind. Her new white camouflage cape had too much shine, and was giving away her hideouts. Now she took a break from the fighting: 'I am sitting and thinking about fame,' she wrote.

There is a newspaper article about me – calling me a renowned sniper – and my picture is on the front page of an army magazine. It's strange to think of people who know me looking at that picture. But what have I really done? I am simply fulfilling

my duty as a Soviet citizen, stepping forward to defend
the Motherland. Today, once more, I am willing to go into the
heart of the battle. I am not afraid. I am ready to die for my
country.

The Red Army offensive was making good progress. At
the beginning of the attack, its infantry units were advancing
at a rate of 32 kilometres a day, its tank forces between 48 and
80 kilometres. On 17 January Shanina wrote a letter to her
friend Petr Molchanov, the editor of the Soviet Fifth Army's
newspaper: 'Sorry for the long silence,' she began.

> It is been hard to write. My life has been a constant round of
> fighting. There have been some really fierce clashes – but
> miraculously, I have stayed alive and unharmed. I am in the
> forefront of the action. Please excuse me for disregarding your
> warning about this . . .
>
> Well, I have just got into the dugout. I am exhausted – there
> have been three combat missions today. The Germans are
> resisting strongly. A hail of bombs and shells rained down upon
> us – and they still have enough firepower to keep us at a
> distance . . .

Then Shanina added: 'I have a feeling I am going to get killed
soon. If anything happens to me, could you write and tell
my mother. You may be wondering why I expect to die. It
is because out of 78 people in my battalion, only six are still
left . . .'

In her diary Shanina had recorded the qualities she most
admired: modesty and courage. She said: 'I am only truly
happy when I am fighting for the well-being of others . . . If
I have to sacrifice my life for this ideal – I am ready to do it.'
Shanina's last diary entry was on 24 January: 'Two days of
terrible fighting,' she wrote. On one occasion, enemy fire
had been so intense that she had been forced to take shelter

behind a self-propelled gun. But Shanina concluded optimistically: 'Now we are moving forward again!' Shortly afterwards, she was badly wounded in an engagement near the East Prussian village of Ilmsdorf. She died on 28 January 1945.

8

Lisa's Smile

O N 27 JANUARY 1945 Auschwitz was liberated by the Red Army. Of all the Nazi extermination camps Auschwitz was the most terrible. Terrible because the greatest number of people were killed there – a number conservatively estimated at over one million – the vast majority Jews from all over Europe, and over 200,000 of them children. Terrible because new, faster methods of killing – using Zyklon B cyanide gas – were first tested within the camp. Terrible because of the chilling architecture of the complex, with its sinister ramp where the selection process split families on their arrival and sent those unfit to work immediately to their death. Terrible because of the massive scale of its crematoria and gas chambers – which dispatched thousands of victims a day – and of its warehouses, where the possessions of those doomed to die were matter-of-factly stored, then recycled within Hitler's Third Reich.

This profoundly important liberation is still marred by oft-repeated assumptions that are misleading or downright wrong. The Red Army did not walk into a camp already abandoned by the Germans. They had to fight for it. Soviet soldiers were not so brutalized by the war that they were unable to emotionally engage with what they found there. They were deeply moved, shocked and disturbed by what they witnessed – even today, many still have nightmares about it. And news of Auschwitz was not repressed or hidden. It was reported within days, although reporting the horror of Auschwitz threw up enormous challenges to Red Army war correspondents, and the reality of what they had found there was subsequently distorted by the Soviet regime.

Red Army soldiers were cogs in Stalin's brutal and ruthless political machine. During the course of the war that regime did indeed progressively downplay the impact of the Holocaust, and it is critical to understand clearly how and why this came about. By 1944 the Soviet state rarely referred to the killing of Jews, and regularly described the victims of the Holocaust within its own borders with the anodyne formula of 'peaceful Soviet citizens'. Stalin's motives were complex, in part anti-Semitic, and in part arising from political suspicion of any racial or religious group that might hold an autonomous identity within the Soviet Union. As a consequence of his policy, at the beginning of 1945 most Soviet troops were poorly informed about the mass killing of Jews and had scant understanding of the wider implications of the Holocaust. 'It took a long time for us to fully comprehend the horror of Auschwitz,' said Red Army lieutenant Ivan Martynushkin. His political masters had done little to enlighten him, yet this fact makes the story of the camp's liberation all the more remarkable.

That story begins on 17 January 1945, when five days into the major Soviet Vistula–Oder offensive, Stalin's High Command gave Marshal Ivan Konev's First Ukrainian Front two new orders. The first was to send his leading forces, spearheaded by Colonel General Pavel Rybalko's Third Tank Army, racing for the German city of Breslau on the River Oder. The second was to use his two infantry Armies – the Fifty-Ninth and Sixtieth – to open up a second line of advance, taking Krakow in southern Poland and heading for the Upper Silesian industrial region. In the planning for this operation Stalin had made clear to Konev the absolute importance of securing this area, ringing it on a map and exclaiming to his Marshal, 'Gold!'

The Soviet supremo was not normally prone to exuberance when meeting with his military commanders. But Stalin was preoccupied with capturing Upper Silesia's coal mines and steel-producing industries as fast as possible, and denying these resources to Hitler's regime. Konev was left in no doubt about the importance of this. The city of Katowice – with its coal mines and steel-producing factories – was the crucial target – and the Soviet leader wanted it secured as a matter of urgency. There was a strong military logic in pushing hard towards Upper Silesia and denying the Germans vital economic resources.

Stalin was also well aware of a profoundly moral issue – that 32 kilometres south-east of Katowice, near the small town of Oswiecim, lay the Nazi's principal death camp, named by the Germans Auschwitz. But whereas Stalin's High Command made absolutely clear the strategic significance of gaining Upper Silesia, they made no provision at all for the freeing of Hitler's most terrible extermination centre. No information whatsoever about the existence of this camp was passed on to the Red Army. Konev's forces would find out about it purely by chance.

Information on Auschwitz had been carefully compiled by Soviet intelligence from the summer of 1944, drawn from documents captured from the extermination camp at Majdanek – which the Red Army had liberated on 23 July of that year – and interviews with escaped prisoners. Initially these investigations were conducted by the Ukrainian NKVD, but given the importance of the material, proceedings were then taken to a higher level. By 6 September 1944 a special file on the camp was held in Moscow by Lieutenant General Pavel Sudoplatov, head of the NKVD's Special Tasks Section, and Colonel General Bogdan Kobulov, Commissar of State Security, was being regularly briefed on its contents.

The reports made chilling reading. They detailed the layout and routine of a main camp and a new, larger complex. They described the terrible selection process, the inhumane cruelty of the camp guards, the methods used to gas and burn their victims. They emphasized that hundreds of thousands of Jews from all over Europe were being sent to Auschwitz, and that the mass extermination of helpless old men, women and children was accelerating.

Because the accounts were so powerful, and deeply disturbing, they were checked against captured documents and other witness accounts. But on 29 September 1944 the information was deemed reliable enough to be passed on to the most senior members of Stalin's government. On that date Sergei Kruglov, the Soviet Commissar for Internal Affairs, wrote to the Deputy Foreign Minister, Andrei Vyshinsky, one of Stalin's closest henchmen, who had presided over the notorious show trials of the 1930s. Kruglov informed Vyshinsky that the German camp at Auschwitz was a place of mass killing, and that hundreds of thousands had already died there. He made clear that this information was based on a whole series of witness testimonies, and concluded: 'Further interrogation of former prisoners at Auschwitz is continuing, with the object of uncovering yet more brutal crimes committed by the Germans in this camp.'

Vyshinsky's response was immediate. He wrote a note to Nikolai Shvernik, chairman of the Supreme Soviet, asking: 'Would it be worth publishing information about this place at Auschwitz?' It is inconceivable that the Soviet leader was not informed of Auschwitz at this stage – if not earlier. By early October, Stalin and the leading members of his government would have been well aware of the existence of the camp. But the information was not made public, and when Stalin met with Marshal Konev in November 1944 to discuss the New Year offensive no mention was made of it.

It is not immediately clear why Stalin did not make more of the existence of Auschwitz for propaganda purposes. On 27 November 1944 the Soviet trial of the camp commanders of Majdanek had opened. Increasing numbers of Red Army soldiers had toured the camp, and Russian and foreign war correspondents had written numerous articles about it. The effect had been powerful, with soldiers strongly motivated to smash Hitler's regime. Here was an opportunity to build on that sense of outrage. Perhaps Stalin, always disengaged from the human dimension, felt that Majdanek was enough. He had never issued specific orders to liberate any concentration camp.

Whatever Stalin's reasons for not publicizing Soviet intelligence on Auschwitz, as the Vistula–Oder offensive of January 1945 got under way, Konev's First Ukrainian Front stumbled upon evidence of the Nazi extermination centre by chance. 'We bumped into the death camp,' said Lieutenant Vasily Gromadsky of the 100th Rifle Division wryly. 'We had no idea that it was there.' 'Taking Auschwitz was never part of our original military operation,' added Lieutenant Ivan Martynushkin, commander of a machine-gun company in the 322nd Rifle Division. 'After the capture of Krakow we were supposed to push on into Silesia. But the plan was changed, and our division was diverted south-west, over the Vistula river. Then our new objective was announced: the liberation of Auschwitz.'

Konev had captured the town of Krakow largely intact on

19 January. The following day he ordered the Fifty-Ninth and Sixtieth Armies to continue their advance westwards, north of the Vistula river, and to attack Upper Silesia. He then swung his Third Tank Army south to execute a pincer movement behind the defending German forces. In doing this, Konev was prioritizing Stalin's directive to quickly secure the region. On 23 January the Sixtieth Army reached Chrzanow, and after the failure of a frontal attack prepared to outflank the town. As it did so it uncovered one of Auschwitz's sub-camps, at Libiaz Station.

By 1945 Auschwitz consisted of a series of camps. The first and oldest was Auschwitz I, created in mid-1940 from old barracks in the suburbs of the Polish town of Oswiecim, and gradually expanded, until it could hold between 12,000 and 20,000 prisoners. The second part was Auschwitz II – or Auschwitz-Birkenau. The Nazis began building this in the autumn of 1941 in Brzezinka, a village 3 kilometres west of Oswiecim. It was the largest camp in the Auschwitz complex, and by the summer of 1944 it held more than 90,000 prisoners. Here the Germans built their largest installations of mass murder in occupied Europe – a series of massive gas chambers and crematoria – and exterminated the majority of Jews deported to the camp.

Auschwitz's sub-camps, however, were labour camps rather than extermination centres, although working conditions were harsh and cruel and the inmates were forcibly confined within them. Alongside the complexes at Auschwitz I – the main camp – and Auschwitz-Birkenau there also existed a third camp at Monowitz, sometimes known as Auschwitz III. Monowitz – 5 kilometres south-east of the main camp – was a grim industrial centre, consisting of a series of factories and workers' barracks built by the German industrial company IG Farben, which was attempting to produce synthetic rubber. Prisoners from Auschwitz were used as slave labour here, and in the summer of 1944 there were more than 11,000 of them. And Monowitz had no fewer than forty-seven sub-camps: smaller compounds scattered over a wider area. They were established in the vicinity of coal mines, steel works and other industrial plants in Upper Silesia.

One of these sub-camps was at Libiaz, where some 900 prisoners had been working in nearby coal mines. Before fleeing, the Germans had killed the workforce there, but a handful had survived by hiding in a section of the mines. One – a Jew named Lever – was a former prisoner of Auschwitz, who had been transferred to Libiaz. He told Red Army troops of the Sixtieth Army about the existence of the death camp.

Lever reported to his Soviet liberators that the camp complex held a vast number of Jews from all over Europe. He reported on the selection process, 'that everybody who couldn't work – including women, children, the elderly and sick – was exterminated at once', that the killing was done in special gas chambers and the bodies burnt in crematoria. Lever did not know how many had died, though he knew the number was huge, and he estimated the number of Jewish victims to be nearly half a million. His dramatic testimony shocked those who heard it, and was immediately brought to the attention of the head of the political section of the Sixtieth Army, General Grishaev. Grishaev then passed it to the Sixtieth Army's commander, Lieutenant General Pavel Kurochkin.

Forty-four-year-old Kurochkin was a highly regarded commander, who had distinguished himself in the Lvov-Sandomierz operation the previous summer. His bold attack on strong German positions was conducted with great personal bravery, for which he had received the Order of Suvorov, and later that autumn he was awarded the title of Hero of the Soviet Union for his skilful command of the Sixtieth Army. He had a good working relationship with Marshal Ivan Konev, whom he had previously served as Deputy Front Commander.

With dramatic information about the existence of Auschwitz in front of him, Kurochkin made a decision to liberate the death camp as quickly as possible. He had some leeway in his planning – for faced with the rapid advance of the Soviet Third Tank Army, the Germans had withdrawn some of their forces from his section of the front. Kurochkin now changed the direction of his advance, allowing troops from three of his best divisions – the 100th, 107th and 322nd – to cross the River Vistula and advance on Auschwitz. After informing Konev, and gaining the front commander's approval for his course of action, he issued new orders on the evening of 24 January. Auschwitz was to be secured as a matter of priority.

General Petr Zubov's 322nd Division immediately readied one of its best units – the 1085th 'Tarnopol' Rifle Regiment. Its commander, Colonel Anatoly Shapiro, was Jewish. But the army did not yet understand that Auschwitz was a death camp primarily for the extermination of Jews. It saw its mission in more general terms, to liberate a huge prison camp, holding inmates from all over Europe, where it was believed the Nazis were putting everyone to death. That prospect was ghastly enough to galvanize Soviet soldiers. 'We already knew a great deal about Nazi atrocities and the tragic plight of those in their concentration camps,' said Colonel Georgi Elisavetsky. 'We resolved to take possession of the area around Auschwitz with the utmost speed.'

At 5 p.m. on the evening of 25 January the 1085th

Regiment swung south-west, reaching the settlement of Jankowice before nightfall. It had now received its new battle orders, to liberate the main camp at Auschwitz. Hearing reports that the camp's remaining prisoners were being kept in appalling conditions, and that many were suffering terribly, an emergency medical supply train was assembled. During its advance to Jankowice the unit ran into a minefield; a doctor was killed and five nurses wounded. But everyone felt the terrible urgency of the situation. The regiment's combat journal noted simply: 'No one wanted to turn back.'

The Germans quickly became aware of the Soviet advance. The following morning the regiment encountered strong enemy opposition and even had to fend off a counter-attack. Red Army troops were struck by their opponent's dogged resistance. 'The Germans were in full retreat,' said Lieutenant Ivan Martynushkin, 'yet as we approached Auschwitz we had to fight for every settlement, every house.' The regiment's combat journal noted: 'The Germans are resisting fiercely, defending all access roads to Auschwitz – the death factory – where they hold huge numbers of prisoners . . .' The troops were unaware that the majority of these prisoners – over 56,000 of them – had already been marched away by the SS, more than a week earlier, on 17 January. Just under 8,000 remained in the camp complex – scattered in barracks in Auschwitz I and Auschwitz-Birkenau – most too sick to move.

For Shapiro's men, 26 January was a day of heavy fighting. At the end of it, the regimental combat journal recorded that some two hundred German officers and soldiers had been killed or wounded and nine heavy artillery pieces destroyed. Eight Red Army soldiers had been killed and twenty-three wounded. The defending forces had now been identified: the

948th Infantry Regiment from the Wehrmacht's 359th Infantry Division, the 21st SS Police Regiment and auxiliary units. Nevertheless, steady progress was made – settlements were cleared of the enemy and a combat HQ set up in a church in the village of Wlosienica.

That day more prisoners were liberated from Auschwitz's sub-camps. The 1085th Regiment's combat journal noted that they had freed over one thousand Russian slave labourers, 900 Poles, 200 Yugoslavs and some French, Greeks and Czechs. Soviet soldiers had also captured a train and 86 goods wagons full of prisoners' possessions from the main camp. Uncertain how many lives were at risk, but fearing the worst, Shapiro's men determined to attack Auschwitz I without delay. At 2 a.m. on the morning of 27 January Soviet reconnaissance patrols crossed the River Sola, a tributary of the Vistula, and at 3 a.m. guns and mortars were moved across in readiness for an assault.

While Shapiro's men moved on Auschwitz from the south, the Sixtieth Army's commander, Lieutenant General Kurochkin, was becoming concerned by the strength of German opposition around the camp. On the evening of 26 January Major Vasily Petrenko had been told to prepare troops from the 107th Rifle Division for another advance against Auschwitz, from the north. The camp was to be encircled in a pincer movement. The following morning – as Shapiro's regiment crossed the River Sola – another strike force was assembled from the 107th Division's 522nd Regiment. Some thirty tanks were deployed, with seven or eight infantrymen on each – armed to the teeth – commanded by Lieutenant Fyodor Zharchinsky – a specialist in fast-moving operations behind enemy lines.

Sergeant Ivan Zabolotny was a member of this force. 'Our intelligence reports had located a Nazi extermination camp,' he remembered. 'We heard that the prisoners there were being incinerated.' At first light Zabolotny and his comrades broke through enemy lines at Bierun, and sped forward. Their mission was to make a second attack on the camp, from the north, and deny its defenders further reinforcement.

To the south, fierce fighting continued. Early on 27 January the Germans subjected the advancing Red Army 1085th Regiment to a heavy artillery barrage. They had set up a strong defensive position outside the camp, fortifying a series of trenches and anti-tank ditches. But the Soviet force pushed on through enemy fire. At 11 a.m. the majority of the troops were across the Sola river and the order was given: 'Break into Auschwitz!' The Second Battalion was left to clear the settlement of Stare Stawy on the far bank. The First Battalion would storm the perimeter of the camp. The Third would move up behind it and occupy the barracks.

The die was cast. The 1085th Regiment's combat journal stated: 'The German leadership has turned Auschwitz into a death factory. Hundreds of thousands of prisoners of all nationalities have been held here. They are now trying to eradicate all evidence of their crime before they pull back. In preparing its assault, the entire regiment is eager to break into the camp and free their brothers and sisters from slavery.' The Soviet soldiers and officers did not yet understand that these were not just 'prisoners of all nationalities' assembled in a cruel concentration camp, but above all European Jews, gathered in an extermination centre.

As the 1085th Regiment – part of the Red Army's 322nd Division – prepared to attack Auschwitz's main camp, troops of the 100th Rifle Division, advancing in support, were fighting to occupy the nearby town of Oswiecim. Lieutenant Vasily Gromadsky's 472nd Infantry Regiment led the way. 'There were plenty of stone buildings,' Gromadsky recalled, 'and the Germans had filled them with machine gunners and snipers. They had turned the town into a fortress. We were amazed at their ferocious resistance. We fought for Oswiecim house by house, splattering the enemy with grenades. Our soldiers were asking: "Why are the Germans holding out so desperately?" We were using pre-war maps, and there was nothing beyond Oswiecim to defend. All we could see was forest.'

The 472nd Infantry Regiment, advancing to the east of the 1085th, was supposed to cover the flank of Shapiro's force as it attacked the main camp at Auschwitz. But Gromadsky's soldiers were about to make a discovery of their own. At 11.30 a.m. reconnaissance patrols pushed past Oswiecim. They came under immediate artillery fire. Inhabitants of the nearby village of Babice warned the soldiers that 'there was a place deep in the forest where the Nazis burned people'. A decision was made to advance in force – and artillery and tank support was called up. Shortly after midday the regiment began to move north, through the snow-laden trees. Enemy fire intensified, as they bombarded both the forest and the town behind it.

At Auschwitz I the Germans kept up a last-ditch resistance. By 2 p.m. a further 150 of their officers and soldiers had been killed or wounded, 4 anti-aircraft guns and 2 mortars captured. Another fourteen Red Army soldiers were killed and eighty-six wounded. Soviet artilleryman Genri Koptev knocked out the German self-propelled gun guarding the entrance to the compound – for which he was later awarded the Order of Glory. Then suddenly all combat ceased. There was an eerie silence. The Red Army troops gathered outside the main gateway. 'It had some kind of Nazi slogan on it,' Ivan Martynushkin recalled. The inscription read 'Arbeit Macht Frei' – 'Work Makes You Free'. The Soviet troops stopped and gazed at it. 'The cynical Nazi greeting above the gates of the camp will always stand out in my memory,' said Colonel Georgi Elisavetsky. 'My blood runs cold when I think of it, even now.' 'When we saw that macabre sign,' Sergeant Genri Koptev added, 'we had a feeling that something was hideously wrong.'

The gates were padlocked. Snow was falling, and there was a smell of burning in the air. Inside were rows of barracks – but not a person could be seen. Instinctively, the Red Army soldiers raised their machine guns and shot off the locks.

'I had seen a lot in this war,' said Anatoly Shapiro, commander of the 1085th Regiment.

> I had seen many innocent people killed. I had seen hanged people, I had seen burned people. But I was still unprepared for Auschwitz . . .
>
> As we entered we saw rows of barracks, one after another. I opened the door to one. The stench was overpowering. It was a women's barracks, and there were frozen pools of blood, and dead bodies lay on the floor. In between them lay those still alive, semi-naked, only wearing thin undergarments – in January! My soldiers recoiled in horror. One said: 'I can't stand this any longer. Let's get out of here. This is unbelievable!'

But Shapiro had been ordered to inspect the whole camp, so reluctant Red Army soldiers entered another building: 'We saw emaciated, brutally tortured people,' Lieutenant Ivan Martynushkin remembered, 'wrapped in rags, clutching at each other. Most were unable to stand on their feet, and lay on plank beds or sat propped up against the wall. It was a terrible picture – an absolute vision of hell.'

Soviet troops tried to communicate with words, gestures, even sign language. 'As in a fog, I heard my soldiers saying "You are free, comrades!"' Georgi Elisavetsky remembered. There was no response. 'We tried Russian, then Polish,

German, Ukrainian . . .' There was still silence. 'The wraith-like figures stared at us with dull incomprehension,' Genri Koptev recalled. Finally Elisavetsky, a Jewish officer, tried Yiddish. At last there was a reaction, but not the kind he was expecting. 'They seemed to think I was provoking them,' he said, 'and some tried to crawl away and hide.' Elisavetsky unbuttoned his greatcoat, showing his tunic and Red Army medals, and repeated again and again: 'Do not be afraid. I am a colonel of the Soviet Army and a Jew. We have come to liberate you.' At last, there was a flickering of recognition in some of the prisoners' eyes. Was it joy? The Soviet soldiers were unable to tell.

'They hardly resembled people any more,' Genri Koptev said. 'Their skin was so thin, you could see their veins through it and their eyes were sticking out because the tissue around it had sunk. When they stretched out their hands, you could see every bone, joint and sinew. We felt a spreading horror. No one had prepared us for this.' 'As we looked round at Auschwitz's inmates,' Ivan Martynushkin recalled, 'we could not distinguish men from women, young from old. Their eyes were huge, their skin almost translucent. The lack of human reaction left our soldiers increasingly confused and disoriented.'

'Hardly any of the prisoners could talk to us,' Shapiro added. 'They had so little energy – they just lay there, listless and apathetic. Then one began to speak, with agonizing slowness. He said that once a day they had gone out to get a little water. But there was no bread, no food whatsoever, and no heating. They were all dying from hunger and cold.'

Soviet soldiers ventured outside again. Ivan Martynushkin found a house that seemed to have belonged to a camp administrator. In one room, belongings were scattered about chaotically – evidence of a hurried flight; in another, the table had been neatly set for lunch. Moving along an alley-way between barracks, Sergeant Genri Koptev stumbled upon a series of mounds, some over two metres high. As he got closer, he saw they consisted of alternate layers of logs and corpses. Perhaps the fleeing guards had not had time to ignite them. But Koptev, increasingly disturbed, was no longer able to make much sense of his surroundings. He entered a ware-house and found it full of prosthetic limbs. Outside a waiting wagon was piled high with more dead bodies.

'We discovered mountains of artificial teeth, spectacles and human hair,' Colonel Anatoly Shapiro recalled,

> piles of prisoners' shoes and suitcases. But we had not yet seen the children's barracks. Inside it there were only two children left. We learnt that all the others had been gassed, or were in the 'hospital', where medical experiments were performed on them. When we entered they cried out in terror: 'We are not Jews!' They were in fact Jewish children, and mistaking us for German soldiers, evidently thought we were going to take them to the gas chambers.
>
> We stared at them aghast. We saw it in their faces – saw that they had been through utter hell. We asked ourselves, what are children doing here? We were caught up in a vast war, involv-ing innumerable armies and millions of men, fighting on fronts that spanned thousands of miles. We had seen so many terrible things as we marched across our Motherland, repelling the Fascist invader. But this was the harshest sight of all.

Sergeant Genri Koptev visited the shower room and crematorium to the west of the main camp. He was utterly overwhelmed, saying: 'I could not comprehend how a human mind could conceive of this.'

It was almost impossible to understand. On the after-noon of 27 January Sergeant Ivan Sorokopud and troops of the 507th Artillery Regiment were sent to help secure

Auschwitz I. Sorokopud and his men had heard plenty of rumours: 'Red Army Divisions on our right and left had already liberated some of Auschwitz's sub-camps,' he recalled. 'We were told that the main camp was even worse than Majdanek, and that the first of our soldiers who had entered it had been stunned by what they had seen. We tried to prepare ourselves for what we would encounter.'

As Sorokopud and his men approached the camp they were given a quick briefing by a young lieutenant. He warned of the danger of infectious diseases, particularly typhoid, and the risks of giving too much food to prisoners who were starving. He reassured the soldiers that special medical units were being sent from the Sixtieth Army to help care for the survivors. Sorokopud felt a sense of unease, and as he did so, a particular memory came to him.

'Once I had seen prisoners reduced to the lowest level of misery,' he recalled.

> They were Soviet POWs under German escort that once passed through the village where I lived, under Nazi occupation, from 1941 to early 1943 – before I joined the Red Army. My mother tried to give some bread to the unfortunates in the column. They threw themselves on it, and in their desperation trampled over each other, tearing pieces from each other's grasp. I held this image in my mind as we approached the camp. I expected to see something similar.

The unit's truck drove through the gates of the main camp and the soldiers clambered out. 'But what I saw next was beyond any imagining,' Sorokopud continued.

> In fact, the memory still shakes me today. It is hard to find words for the effect it had on me: a mixture of fear, disgust, revulsion and pity. A sense of helplessness and guilt at being able to do so little, shame at being so full of life myself and relief at

being ordered not to do anything further – knowing that I would soon leave this place.

After entering the camp, we saw a dozen 'skeletons'. They moved with considerable difficulty. Through holes in their ragged undergarments we could see their emaciated bodies. The expression 'only skin and bones' was not a figure of speech here but an exact reality. A putrid odour emanated from these 'undead'. They were filthy beyond description. Their eyes were huge, and seemed to devour the whole face. The pupils were abnormally dilated. They did not seem human but animal-like, almost indifferent to their surroundings. Were they mad?

They did not speak to us, and made no attempt to talk. They kept at a distance, their eyes darting around. One prisoner, unable to walk, was slowly crawling out of a barracks. Our men stared at him, rooted to the ground.

It was unbelievable. After half an hour, back at the truck, no one could form a coherent sentence – only splutter insults and curses against the Nazis. When I returned to my artillery position, I struggled to regain some kind of composure. All I said to my comrades was 'Show the German bastards no mercy – smash them to pulp!'

This is not the response of a man brutalized beyond all feeling – rather of someone recognizing a level of atrocity beyond anything previously experienced. Sorokopud's reaction is fully human – a struggle to comprehend, then visceral emotion.

As Red Army forces occupied Auschwitz I, Lieutenant Vasily Gromadsky's 472nd Infantry Regiment – part of the Soviet 100th Rifle Division – was advancing north-east of the main camp, through thick forest. German artillery fire was constant. Shortly after 3 p.m. the trees began to thin. Nothing was marked on their maps, but ahead of them the soldiers could see barbed-wire fences and watchtowers, and beyond them barracks. 'We had no idea what we were discovering,' Gromadsky said, 'and wondered if we had stumbled on some kind of secret military installation.' The troops had reached Auschwitz II – Auschwitz–Birkenau – the principal death camp of the Holocaust.

As the Red Army troops came into the open, the Germans unleashed a torrent of fire. 'It was as if we had stirred up a hornet's nest,' Lieutenant Vasily Gromadsky said. 'The enemy opened up on us with artillery, machine-gun and sniper fire.' Vicious fighting went on around the perimeter of the camp for about an hour. The regiment's commander, Colonel Semyon Besprozvanny, was killed trying to break into the compound, along with another sixty-six of his men. Then Soviet tanks appeared, and smashed a way through the barbed wire.

The battle at the gates of Auschwitz–Birkenau was particularly hard, recalled artilleryman Enver Alimbekov of the 472nd Infantry Regiment. 'We lost our commander, a number of officers, more than sixty men killed and hundreds wounded.' Yakov Vinnichenko added: 'The Germans deployed artillery and heavy machine guns outside the camp, and also shot at us from watchtowers and barracks. We took heavy casualties.' The tanks saved the day.

Tankman David Dushman remembered arriving at Auschwitz–Birkenau at speed. 'The Nazis were trying to destroy all evidence of this death camp,' he said. 'We raced there, hoping not all the prisoners had been exterminated.' Fighting was still going on as the Soviet tanks appeared. Dushman's was one of the first to breach the compound. 'We tore through the barbed wire, opening up the camp's defences,' he continued. 'When the Germans saw that, they fled.'

Soviet soldiers warily entered the camp. They were taken aback by its size – the number of barracks seemed endless. In the snow lay bodies of women, children, old people – all shot at point-blank range. The remaining prisoners were nowhere to be seen.

'The light was fading,' Enver Alimbekov recalled.

Flurries of snow flecked with sleet drove against our faces. It was hard to find a proper pathway. As we approached the barracks the air around us began to change – becoming heavy and putrid. Some of my soldiers opened a door – and we glimpsed rows of bunks. But some instinct drove me on, until I was completely alone. I found a large wooden hut that was grey and dilapidated. I went through an entranceway and into a long dark room. At first I thought it was some kind of storeroom, containing bundles of clothing. And then in the gloom I saw bodies, bodies of little children, everywhere. Some were dead; others half-alive – horrifyingly thin, scraps of garments hanging from their emaciated bodies. As I stood there, some of the little bundles began to move – waddling, crawling, and making strange babbling sounds. They came closer and closer. I froze. Small hands, filthy dirty – with no flesh on them at all, just bone – clung to my boots.

Meanwhile, Soviet soldiers were investigating some of the other barracks. 'We encountered a netherworld of shadows and ghosts,' said Yakov Vinnichenko. 'Emaciated prisoners, so weak they could barely move or speak.' 'God forbid that anyone will have to see this again!' exclaimed David Dushman. 'Skeletal corpses – trying to rise from bloodstained bunks. I felt I had walked into a living nightmare.'

Alimbekov found an older girl in the barracks. She was Polish – but spoke some Russian. 'What are all these little children doing here?' he asked. 'These are children of Warsaw, the uprising,' she replied. 'They were rounded up by the Nazis. I fought with the Polish underground.' She was scarcely in her teens. Alimbekov and the girl went outside.

Some inmates were emerging from their barracks, walking with difficulty or crawling. They were in an appalling state. The girl turned to Alimbekov and said: 'They say that twenty-seven different nationalities are in this camp. Sir, the whole world is here!'

To the north of Auschwitz-Birkenau, Lieutenant Fyodor Zharchinsky's strike force had reached the perimeter fence. They had amassed an impressive tally of captured German lorries as they sped through enemy lines, and had caught some of the camp guard attempting to flee. The tanks encircled the camp; the infantry dug themselves in. Then Sergeant Ivan Zabolotny and a few of his comrades went into Auschwitz II to investigate. The men encountered another children's barracks. 'We had never seen anything like it,' Zabolotny said. 'The children were in rags – their enormous heads perched on famished little bodies, the eyes protruding like small yellow onions. We could not bear to look at them – the sight was so terrible.'

Red Army lieutenant Yuri Ilinsky found a stack of children's corpses neatly piled by the side of a building. 'Dead children – under a thin layer of snow,' he remembered. 'And in the barracks were two- and three-year-old boys and girls – emaciated, desperately ill. Nothing in all our years of fighting had prepared us for this.' A few prisoners were able to move and speak, and they began to approach the Soviet soldiers. Some – from Belorussia and the Ukraine – spoke Russian. Lieutenant Vasily Gromadsky was distracted, worried that the SS might launch a counter-attack to try to regain the camp. At first, he could not take in what he was being told. 'They said that hundreds of thousands of people were killed here, from all over Europe. They offered to show me the warehouses where all their possessions were stored. Suddenly, my hair rose in horror.'

Operation Bagration unfurls: Red Army soldiers gaze at a captured German banner, Vitebsk, 26 June 1944

Captured German troops, Operation Bagration, July 1944

Massacre in Belorussia: Russian civilians indiscriminately shot by retreating
German forces on the outskirts of Borisov

The ghastly remains of Majdanek, near Lublin in Poland, the first death camp captured
intact by the Red Army, 23 July 1944

The ovens at Majdanek: Soviet soldiers found them still warm

The perimeter fence at Treblinka

Red Army lieutenant Pavel Elkinson

Elkinson's diary chronicled heavy fighting as the Red Army moved into Hungary, October 1944

'Lisa', sketched by Red Army private Zinovii Tolkatchev at Auschwitz, shortly after the camp's liberation on 27 January 1945

Mark Slavin, editor of the Soviet 8th Guards Army newspaper

Fighting for Poznan, early February 1945

Soviet troops in Königsberg, 9 April 1945

Lieutenant General Vasily Chuikov of the 8th Guards Army at his command post.
The heroic commander at Stalingrad was now closing in on Berlin

A Red Army mortar company fights its way through Berlin's
suburbs, 22 April 1945

A street in central Berlin after its occupation by the Red Army. Food wagons have been brought up to feed the civilian population

Red Army lieutenant Alexei Kovalev holds the Red flag aloft over the Reichstag. His identity was subsequently suppressed for nearly fifty years

Gromadsky asked about the children. The camp's inmates told him that the only way of estimating the number killed had been to count the pushchairs and prams brought into the storerooms, and then shipped out of the camp. Sometimes there were hundreds, sometimes thousands.

'Battle for Auschwitz,' Gromadsky wrote in his diary. 'Met with prisoners of this camp. Huge numbers of people were taken to this place, including children. Twelve train wagonloads of children's pushchairs were dispatched from here.'

A few prisoners led him to the dynamited ruins of one of the crematoria. The blood-red sun was sinking below the horizon. Other Soviet soldiers were gathering at the remains. Gromadsky looked around him. 'My men formed a half-circle,' he remembered. 'Some were sobbing; others stood absolutely silent, rigid with shock.'

On 27 January Major General Grishaev reported to the First Ukrainian Front:

> Our troops have liberated Auschwitz and Birkenau, the largest of the Nazi concentration camps. The remaining Germans have now fled. At the time of liberation there were up to 10,000 inmates left . . . The complex was surrounded by several rows of wire with a high-voltage current. It was fiercely defended by SS soldiers . . . When trainloads of Jews entered the camp, German soldiers would stand on both sides, beating people with whips. Each morning hundreds of inmates were herded into the gas chambers. The Germans enjoyed the suffering of these unfortunates, watching through specially made windows. The smoke and stench from the ovens spread for miles around. What a sinister picture!

The military operation had been completed. The commanders of the 100th and 322nd Rifle Divisions − Major Generals Fyodor Kasavin and Petr Zubov − were later awarded the Order of the Red Banner for the successful liberation of Auschwitz.

The following morning Soviet scout Leonti Brandt walked round the camp with his reconnaissance platoon: 'We saw mountains of women's hair,' he recalled, 'stored by colour and length. Piles of shoes were sorted by size. Everything was so carefully thought out – order so scrupulously observed. In the midst of it all were well-maintained houses, where the guards lived, with gardens, a sports ground and even a swim-ming pool. Stunned, we walked through the camp – not able to believe our eyes. This was Auschwitz.'

Major Vasily Petrenko – commander of the Soviet 107th Rifle Division – also visited Auschwitz-Birkenau that morn-ing. He learnt that as the Red Army had approached the camp, SS execution squads were still gassing some of the remaining prisoners – keeping one crematorium open to dis-pose of their bodies – and shooting others. The rapid arrival of Soviet troops had almost certainly saved these inmates. If Russian forces had appeared even a week later, Petrenko reflected, the Germans would have wiped out the last survivors and destroyed all traces of Auschwitz:

> I had witnessed a lot of terrible things as our army fought its way westward. I saw my comrades dying. I found evidence of Nazi atrocities in the territories we had liberated – dozens of people hanged by the Germans, women and children shot to death. But what I discovered in this camp was beyond anything I had ever experienced. I saw eighty-two children – from three to fourteen years old – racked by criminal medical experiments. I saw women and children who resembled skeletons, who could not even smile in a human manner. They had tears in their eyes, but they could not sob.

Vasily Petrenko saw that Soviet medical teams were already in action. He could not forget the condition of the children: 'Their bellies were swollen with hunger, their eyes dull and listless, their legs were like matchsticks. Their little bodies were bent and distorted. They were completely silent, unable to interact in any way – beyond showing us the numbers that had been tattooed on their arms.'

Petrenko recalled one statistic. Crews were sent to inspect the shattered crematorium chimneys. When they clambered inside them, they scraped off human fat deposits that were 45 centimetres thick.

Soviet soldiers found remnants of the Zyklon B gas used to murder the victims. They found gas masks used by the SS while killing people in the gas chambers, and specimens from medical experiments performed on prisoners. They also found electrical equipment, used to maintain the high voltage on the barbed-wire fences around the camp. Over six hundred dead bodies of prisoners were found on the camp grounds. When the clothes store in the warehouses was fully inventoried, 348,820 men's suits were recorded and 836,525 women's outfits. It was impossible to count the shoes – there were millions of them. Soviet soldiers uncovered huge piles of tallises, the shawl Jews wore for daily prayer. Human hair was packed and sorted into thousands of bundles – their combined weight was 7.8 tonnes.

Major Ivan Goncharov, a staff officer with the Sixtieth Army, found a six-year-old girl – Masha Schwartzmann – cowering in a hiding place behind plank beds in a barracks. When he carried her out she was completely hysterical. He took her to the first-aid station, and as she began to recover learnt more of her story. She was from Vinnitsa in the Ukraine. Her parents had perished in the ghetto there, her grandparents had both died in Auschwitz, leaving Masha the only surviving member of her family. Masha was allowed to stay at the Sixtieth Army's HQ for a while, and was then sent to an orphanage in the Soviet Union. Later, she went to high school, and then university, where she graduated in law.

On 28 January Colonel Vasily Davidov, commander of an artillery regiment, visited Auschwitz. He wrote to his wife: 'Everything was still on fire or exuding smoke. Wherever we looked we saw piles of bodies. Those who survived looked like living skeletons. Many could not be helped. A few who could still walk took us around the camp and told us what happened there. It is hard to put it into words . . .' Twenty-six-year-old Private Pyotr Nikitin said in a letter to relatives: 'I talked to a few of the prisoners. They told me about terrifying inhumane tortures . . . I have no words to relate to you what we have just witnessed.' And Private Vasily Letnikov added: 'Two-metre-high electric fences enclosed the camp. The Germans mined its approaches. Watchtowers – with guards armed with machine guns – were placed at fifty-metre intervals. Not far from the death barracks is the crematorium. Can you imagine how many people the Germans burned there? Next to its exploded ruins are bones, bones and piles of shoes several metres high. There are children's shoes in the pile. Total horror – impossible to describe.'

The sheer size of Auschwitz–Birkenau was disorienting. 'There were hundreds of barracks in this section of the camp,' Colonel Georgi Elisavetsky recalled. 'They were the visual embodiment of a monstrous Nazi plan of oppression and annihilation.' In an attempt to get the scale of it all across, cameraman Alexander Vorontsov – serving in a film unit with the First Ukrainian Front – took his first shots of the Auschwitz–Birkenau complex from a plane. He said: 'I don't think our army command had any idea of the extent of the crimes committed at this largest of all concentration camps. These memories will be with me for the rest of my life. It was the most shocking and horrible thing I filmed during the whole war.'

On 28 January the commander of the First Ukrainian Front, Marshal Ivan Konev, was close to Auschwitz. He chose not to visit it: 'The day after the liberation of that terrible camp, which has now become a symbol of Nazi barbarism, I found myself comparatively near it,' Konev recounted. 'I had already received the first reports of what that camp was actually like. It was not that I did not want to see that death camp with my own eyes; I simply made up my mind not to see it. The combat operations were in full swing, and to command them was such a strain that I could find neither the time nor justification for abandoning myself to my own emotions. During the war I did not belong to myself.'

Even this most ruthless commander recognized that the paralysing horror of Auschwitz could disable him when he most needed to be effective. And beneath this lay Konev's overriding fear of Stalin. Stalin had made no mention of Auschwitz to his commander, and he wanted the industrial region of Upper Silesia secured without delay. Konev did not wish to be seen deviating from that task – even for a matter of hours – in case he incurred the Soviet supremo's displeasure.

In Auschwitz, Colonel Anatoly Shapiro's men were now cleaning out the barracks, to prevent disease from spreading. Field kitchens had been set up in the camp, but enormous care had to be taken over how to feed the starving inmates. The new Soviet camp commandant, Colonel Georgi Elisavetsky, recalled the frenetic attempts to help the prisoners. 'We knew immediate action had to be taken to try and save the survivors,' he said, 'people who had been crippled physically and psychologically by the camp. It is impossible to describe how our doctors, nurses, officers and soldiers worked – without sleep or food – to try and help these unfortunates, how they fought for every life. Unfortunately, many were beyond help.' The military hospital – mobile unit no. 2962 – run by Dr Maria Zhilinskaya, nevertheless managed to save 2,819 inmates.

Soviet war correspondents were now arriving at the camp. Arkady Friedner, who edited the Ninth Army's newspaper, was there within hours. Throughout the war Friedner had reported on the front-line fighting and interviewed soldiers in the trenches. He saw at first hand the devastating effect of that war on the civilian population. Now he would be the first journalist to enter Auschwitz:

'Shortly after the camp had been liberated I was there,' Friedner said.

> I saw the wide open gates, the watchtowers – now empty – where machine gunners had once stood guard, the railway track that led into the heart of the camp. Barracks on all sides, a few people walking around: skeletons – barely able to shuffle their legs. Smoke was still rising from the ruins of one of the crematoria, and a thick fog hung over everything. What really struck me, at the entrance to this crematorium, were the corpses of people – stacked neatly like logs for burning. A thin layer of snow lay on top of them. Inside the barracks were objects: children's things, little boots, little shoes, little hats, toys – scattered all over the place. It seemed the Germans had been forced to leave in a great hurry, and they didn't have time to burn the corpses or to hide the starkness of their crimes.
>
> This was Auschwitz – where they killed and suffocated hundreds of thousands of people in the gas chambers. I was the first person to write about it. I did a whole spread for the army newspaper, with an interview with a liberated prisoner. It came out the following day – on 29 January. I was proud to have written it – about the real Auschwitz, the camp of death. I will

never forget it – I never saw anything so terrible throughout the entire war. It pierced me to the very soul.

Gathering information about Auschwitz was an agonizing process. On the day after liberation cameraman Alexander Vorontsov explored the camp. 'We spoke to some prisoners – but the conversations were short,' Vorontsov recalled. 'The survivors were hungry, exhausted and sick – and they found it very difficult to talk about conditions there.' Usher Margolis – correspondent with the Soviet Twenty-Eighth Army – entered Auschwitz the same day. 'We were given a brief to interview the prisoners,' Margolis recalled,

but it was hard to do that – they were in a terrible state. But one woman was able to show us around. We entered a brick warehouse, three floors high, and began looking through its rooms. In one we found storage boxes – about a metre wide and a metre and a half high – filled with gold teeth. In the next were boxes full of women's hair. And then we found a room full of finished goods – purses, lampshades, wallets . . . Our guide told us 'They are all produced from human skin'. That was the moment when I just stopped, rooted to the spot, unable to ask any more questions, unable to speak at all.

These first commentators struggled to separate fact from terrible rumour, but their connection with the suffering of Auschwitz is clear. General Grishaev – the head of the political section of the Sixtieth Army – was gaining a fuller sense of the horror. He wrote to the First Ukrainian Front on 28 January:

This concentration camp – actually a series of camps – has a few thousand prisoners left in it, gathered from all over Europe. Many others were forced out, on to the roads [before our troops' arrival]. All are pitifully weak. A few are able to cry, and thank the Red Army. Most lie in the barracks, on tiered rows of plank beds. Each camp is surrounded by barbed-wire fences, through which a high-voltage current runs. I have not yet met a Jew – inmates say they were all being exterminated.

Grishaev concluded: 'It is a picture terrible in its tragedy.' The tragedy was reflected in the condition of the remaining prisoners. On 29 January a local Polish doctor, Tadeusz Chowaniec, visited Auschwitz. 'A gloomy, overcast morning,' he began.

In Stare Stawy, not far from the camp, the corpses of Wehrmacht and Soviet soldiers lay side by side near some farm buildings . . . At the gate of the concentration camp two Soviet wagons passed us, loaded with corpses. It reminded me of a medieval illuminated manuscript depicting death . . . I visited Block 11. The corridor, despite the prevalent cold, was filled with the sweetish smell of decayed corpses. It was stifling. I looked at the Soviet medical staff working there. Some faces were horrified, some enraged – all emotional. My first encounter with the inmates, with their near-transparent faces and cloudy, indifferent eyes, was deeply depressing. Figures sluggishly stirred on the bunks, with abscessed thighs and toothless jaws. They spoke in whispers, with strange hoarse voices. The folds of old age furrowed the skin of people in their twenties. The white smocks of Soviet physicians – men and women – moved among these patients. Is it possible that life will be restored to these near-skeletons?

On 29 January more journalists reached the camp. Foremost among them were Boris Polevoy – who wrote for *Pravda* – and Sergei Krushinsky, the correspondent for *Komsomolskaya Pravda*. 'We arrived shortly after our troops,' Polevoy recollected, 'to see the vast death camp left by the Nazis.' These men were experienced reporters – but describing Auschwitz threw up a terrible challenge. 'Most of the prisoners are more or less mentally ill,' Krushinsky warned the First Ukrainian Front. 'The wildest rumours are floating around here . . .' On arriving at the camp, Soviet war correspondents were confronted with a mass of information – of varying degrees of credibility – which they had to quickly forge into a narrative, based on their own intuition and common sense. Yet Auschwitz was unlike anything else these men had ever seen.

Nonetheless, the importance of publicizing what had happened at Auschwitz was evident to everyone. On 29 January journalist Boris Polevoy reported to the First Ukrainian Front: 'The camp at Auschwitz is more dreadful than the one at Majdanek – it was built earlier and has lasted longer. And it was at Auschwitz that new methods of killing people were first invented and put to use.'

General Grishaev also wrote: 'There were days when as many as 25,000–30,000 people were killed here – primarily Jews from all over Europe. The Germans then blew up the crematoria and scattered the ashes of their victims in the fields. The pits containing the burnt corpses have been levelled.' Grishaev finished: 'A special commission has been set up to investigate the heinous villainies of the German fiends at Auschwitz. It surpasses all atrocities known to us.'

On 31 January 1945, Colonel Okhapin, political officer of the 322nd Rifle Division, whose troops had liberated the main camp, wrote in clear terms that: 'The real task of the Auschwitz death camp was the extermination of all the Jews in Europe. And this extermination plan – the mass killing of completely innocent Jewish civilians – was largely accomplished.'

Then, on the same day, the Soviet Information Bureau released the news of Auschwitz to the Russian people. 'Recently our troops liberated the town of Oswiecim,' the bulletin began.

In its vicinity the German Fascist scoundrels built their largest concentration camp – named Auschwitz . . . Swiftly advancing Red Army units rescued the last of its inmates. One former prisoner – Lukashev from the Voronezh region – told us: 'The number of inmates of the Auschwitz camp was always between 15,000–30,000 people. Children, the ill, those men and women unfit for labour, the Hitlerites killed by gas and the corpses were burned in special ovens . . . Inmates fit for labour were forced to work in mines.' Those weakened through hunger, beatings and hard labour were then exterminated by the Germans. In their four years at the camp these Fascist villains have tortured and killed masses of people.

Here, in the Soviet Information Bureau's report, there is no mention of the Jews.

On 1 February *Pravda* carried a short report on Auschwitz and an interview with a survivor of the camp. It was related how: 'The Hitlerites killed the children and the ill by means of gas, as well as the men and women who were unfit for work. They cremated the corpses in special furnaces.' *Pravda* reckoned the number of deaths at hundreds of thousands. Again no mention was made of the Jews.

A growing chasm was opening between what the Red Army liberators now knew, and what Stalin's regime chose to disclose. On the same day General Grishaev wrote his final report to the First Ukrainian Front: 'The main purpose of the Auschwitz camps was the mass extermination of the Jews,' he began.

They were brought here from all over Europe . . . There were days when 8–10 transports arrived in the camp. 5 to 10 per cent of these – deemed healthy and fit for hard work – would be spared, the rest – exterminated. The victims were gassed; then four crematoria, each with ten chambers: about thirty 'ovens', were used to incinerate the corpses. Each chamber could hold up to 600 bodies. But on some days the crematoria could not cope with the load – and the remainder were burned in pits measuring 40 by 40 metres . . . The Jews in the camp have been almost completely wiped out.

On 2 February the Soviet newspaper *Pravda* carried a piece on Auschwitz by war correspondent Boris Polevoy. He powerfully described Auschwitz as 'a giant factory of death':

> It was an enormous industrial plant, having its own special facilities, each of which had a carefully designated area of responsibility. In one, the processing of the arrivals took place – separating those who, before death, could be put to work for a while, while the elderly, the children and infirm were sentenced to immediate extermination. In another, a section containing those so exhausted and worn out as to be barely fit for physical labour; they were assigned the task of sorting the clothes of the exterminated, and of sorting their shoes, taking apart uppers, soles and linings. But it is fair to say that every prisoner entering the branches of this 'industrial plant' was to be killed eventually . . . I saw the survivors. The Red Army saved them, and pulled them from the jaws of this hell. The martyrs of Auschwitz – people so worn out that they swayed like leaves in the wind, people whose age it was impossible to determine . . .

Polevoy understood well what Stalin's regime wanted to hear and his article had of course gone through a censorship process. In its finished form, he paid tribute to the martyrs of Auschwitz without once mentioning the Jewish people. Alongside this grotesque omission, his piece also contained a series of misunderstandings about Auschwitz, the worse being its continued references to 'an electric conveyor belt, on which hundreds of people were simultaneously electro-cuted, their bodies then carried to the top of the furnace'. The conveyor belt was non-existent – and Polevoy did not properly understand the function of the gas chambers either, and he placed them in the wrong part of the camp. Within the Soviet Union, Polevoy had the greater reputation as a journalist, but his fellow war correspondent Sergei Krushinsky had been more careful in his assessing of survivor testimony, and as a result had a better understanding of how Auschwitz functioned. He made this clear in a report to the First Ukrainian Front shortly after Polevoy's errors were realized: 'A group of prisoners was driven into a chamber. The door was hermetically sealed, and gas was introduced – a kind of gas which is known as "Zyklon B". After eight minutes the chamber was ventilated and the cremation of the corpses commenced . . .'

It was decided to check thoroughly all the details on Auschwitz before issuing further press reports. In the first week of February the commission set up by the First Ukrainian Front got to work, examining evidence for the working of the camp, interviewing witnesses and performing autopsies.

As that process commenced, Soviet camp commandant Georgi Elisavetsky wrote to his wife on 4 February 1945. 'My dearest Nina,' he began,

> it is hard to find words for what I have gone through in the last few days. In the three and a half years I have been fighting in this war I have seen a lot of awful and nightmarish things, but what I have just witnessed at Auschwitz defies the imagination. Picture a prison complex, surrounded by smaller camps, built to hold between 60,000–80,000 people from all over the world. To see the state the remaining people are in – and to realize what has been going on around them – is enough to make you lose your mind. There are the remains of 4 cremation ovens, ovens that could burn thousands of people a day. At peak times the capacity of these was insufficient and people were burned in special cremation pits, often being thrown into the flames still alive.

These prisoners were brought in for so-called 'decontamin-ation'. They were undressed and forced into a basement right next to the ovens. It was equipped as a shower room. When the basement was full the doors were locked and gas was poured in. After some 10–15 minutes the corpses were brought to the crematoria. These monsters of cruelty even made some of the prisoners – also doomed to death – assist in the cremation. A father was forced to put his son in the oven, children to burn their parents. Then they would become the next victims.

The camp is still in a horrifying state – there are corpses everywhere. It is an effort to even describe it. You enter a bar-racks and find four hundred living corpses stacked in rows. These people have been lying there for days – nobody brought them any food or water. They expected to be put to death. We have set up a field hospital that has already admitted nearly 4,000 people. When we carry prisoners there, and they realize that we want to help them, some moan with joy. And when they see bread others literally howl, kiss our feet, and become quite delirious.

There is a children's barracks in the camp. When we entered I just could not stand it any more. I gasped for breath, and then choked with tears. Jewish children of different ages, and twins, were brought here for experiments like guinea pigs. I saw a 14-year-old boy, for whom – for some 'scientific' purpose – kerosene was syringed into his arm. Then they took out pieces of his body and sent them to a laboratory in Berlin, and replaced them with someone else's body organs. Now he is lying in a hospital bed covered in deep, rotting sores. There is nothing that we can do. There is a girl walking around the camp. She is young and beautiful – but completely insane. I wonder that the experience of being here didn't drive everyone mad.

We have liberated death camps before, but this one at Auschwitz can justly be called 'a camp for the extermination of an entire innocent people'. They say that millions of people may have been killed here.

I feel that I am fighting to stay sane. I haven't eaten for four days, I can't sleep. I have fallen ill. I cannot smile or laugh any more. If I wasn't in such a state I would write something to be published and read so everyone can realize what these fiends are really like. Our war correspondents are struggling to describe the horror that was committed here – the bleak picture they are painting would reduce anyone to tears.

Now our troops are moving deeper into the territory of these animals. My heart fills with joy when I see these scoundrels fleeing before us. They have left piles of provisions here – whole rooms are stacked with them – so evidently they did not expect our surprise attack.

'My darling,' Elisavetsky concluded, 'now that the Red Army has liberated this camp, I am eternally grateful that you – and all those dearest to me – have been spared what was inflicted here on so many innocent people.'

On 7 February the inmates of Auschwitz-Birkenau were slowly moved to the main camp. The transfer took two weeks. A Soviet doctor remembered: 'They moved with enormous difficulty – it seemed that every gesture, even the smallest, had to be thought out beforehand. Their indifferent, cold eyes did not contain even a trace of joy. These people believed in nothing and nobody. They did not even believe in themselves. Everything was devoid of value.'

Most Soviet soldiers had now left the camp, though others would continue to visit it. The Red Army liberators had to move on – there was a war still to win. But it was hard to put the memories of Auschwitz aside. Lieutenant Ivan Martynushkin expressed the inner conflict felt by some of these troops: 'I was a soldier – and I had a unit to command,' he said. 'I had to remain professional: I couldn't just succumb to feelings. I had just turned twenty-one when we reached Auschwitz – but I had fought for over three years. And I had seen so much suffering already – the suffering of our own people. I had seen towns destroyed, villages destroyed, women killed, children maimed. There was not a settlement that had not experienced horror, tragedy.' Then Martynushkin paused, and his voice dropped: 'But the hell of Auschwitz was impossible to forget. I was utterly overwhelmed by it all. I felt such compassion for those people. The memory of that death camp will be with me to the end of my days.'

Lieutenant Vasily Gromadsky said: 'I was in charge of a platoon – and we had to get back to the front line. My fighting comrades were being killed every day – I was seriously wounded myself at Ratibor at the end of March 1945. We were surrounded by death – and we had grown accustomed to it. But I will never be able to come to terms with Auschwitz. The Nazis killed so many innocent people – and deliberately murdered children. All my soldiers were profoundly shocked by it.'

Soviet cameraman Alexander Vorontsov said of Auschwitz: 'Time has no power over these memories. It will never erase the horror of what I saw and filmed there.'

Inevitably, soldiers felt a strong desire for vengeance. 'We believed that the Nazis had sullied humanity itself,' exclaimed Vasily Gromadsky. 'We vowed to finish the war as quickly as possible, and send them all to hell.' Pyotr Nikitin pledged: 'There is no punishment horrible enough for these degenerates . . . We will forget nothing, and we will never forgive.' Vladimir Brylev wrote to his mother: 'I have seen Auschwitz. I saw everything with my own eyes . . . This will not happen again . . . We, soldiers, will take care of it.'

The anger was deeply felt. Red Army sergeant Ivan Zabolotny said simply yet powerfully: 'We still handed the camp guards over to our HQ, as we had been ordered to do.' The temptation was to tear them limb from limb.

Soviet soldiers were haunted by the memory of the camps. They had imagined beforehand that a mass of prisoners would be lined up to greet them at the gates, some waving red flags, and such a scene was indeed reconstructed at Auschwitz several months after its liberation and filmed for propaganda purposes. But it was so far from the actual reality that even Stalin's cynical regime baulked at showing it. Alexander Vorontsov said: 'This mock-up did not remotely resemble the horror of 27 January 1945 – and it was never used.'

For the Soviet troops who fought their way into Auschwitz a joyous welcome would have at least allowed them to value their role as liberators. But the tragic condition of the remaining prisoners – their sickness, apathy and numbness – denied them even that. Instead, the liberators were thrown back on their own resources. Tadeusz Chowaniec remembered of Soviet medical staff at the camp: 'Some faces were horrified, some enraged – all emotional.' A terrifying vista had begun to open up before them. What Red Army officers and soldiers saw there was beyond traumatic – it lay on an unimaginable scale of human depravity. In the abyss of Auschwitz waited the very worst of which human beings are capable.

It was hard to look into that abyss for long. Soviet war journalist Vasily Grossman had tried to describe Treblinka, but the experience of writing about the camp had caused him to suffer a nervous breakdown. When he returned to the front he remained obsessed by its evil. 'Grossman was deeply shaken by the death camps,' recalled Mark Slavin, editor of the Eighth Guards Army newspaper, 'and this worsened after the liberation of Auschwitz. He would refer to it all the time in conversation, saying "The horror, the horror of these Fascist camps". We all knew that they were terrible, but he felt another dimension to their evil, a dimension that we could not fully grasp.'

Slavin remembered Grossman talking of a horrible vision. In it, he saw Raphael's *Sistine Madonna* – an uplifting image of love and beauty and an icon of European civilization – with the Madonna holding the Christ child on a cloud, surrounded by saints and cherubs. In his nightmare the *Madonna* was transported to a Nazi death camp. A Jewish mother now walked beneath it with her child towards the gas chambers. She was surrounded by camp guards and the smoke-cloud from the crematorium. In the heart of Europe, everything that was beautiful and dignified in humanity had been contaminated. It seemed to Grossman that this stain could never be expunged.

Private Zinovii Tolkatchev – a Soviet Jew and war artist with the First Ukrainian Front – had painted scenes from the Majdanek camp. He was now sketching what he found at Auschwitz. 'I did what I had to do,' he related. 'I couldn't refrain from doing it. My heart commanded, my conscience demanded, my hatred for Fascism reigned. That hatred guided my hands, urged me on – the brutal reality inflamed my imagination.' He drew the camp's watchtowers and wire fences, the trains and their wagons standing in Auschwitz-Birkenau, the piles of Zyklon B gas canisters. A German soldier, with the motto '*Gott Mit Uns*' – '*God is With Us*' – inscribed on his belt buckle, trampled on the bodies of his victims. On a number of sketches he scrawled 'We will never forget'. One sketch was of a camp survivor called Lisa.

'One morning I walked along Auschwitz's train tracks towards the storehouses,' Tolkatchev wrote in his accompanying notes.

> The snow had covered everything – the wind piling it up in high drifts. Next to the partly opened door of one storehouse were piles of clothes. Before I reached the second, I noticed two women hastily leaving. One of them ran forward towards me.

My gaze was drawn to a pair of children's shoes – dangling by their laces – which the woman was holding in her hand. They were two different shoes – one bigger than the other – and in two different colours.

The woman's companion caught up with her. 'Lisa, Lisa,' she cried, 'wait – don't hurry.'

Tolkatchev noted: 'The woman holding the shoes stopped, and turned towards her friend. Her face – racked by suffering – was fully revealed to me. I saw her hunger-ridden features, the lines and wrinkles, the exhausted glance in her one remaining eye. From the empty socket of the other flowed a mucus-filled tear.'

Tolkatchev asked the one-eyed woman why she was carrying two different shoes. 'As a memento,' she cried. 'I took them as a memento!' Again, a large tear ran down her face. Tolkatchev and the two women took shelter in the storehouse to protect themselves from the wind and snow. And in this storehouse, next to the shoes of tens of thousands of the dead, Tolkatchev heard Lisa's story as related by her friend: 'The SS grabbed her children from her arms. She struggled with them. One of them hit her with a sharp object in the face. She fainted. Her friends took care of her and saved her . . .' In her despair, Lisa had now taken two shoes, two different shoes – one brown and one blue – because they were similar to the shoes worn by her children.

Tolkatchev's attention was drawn to the storyteller, her large grey eyes, black eyebrows and eyelashes, her coarsely shaven grey hair. She was still a young woman, though her body was bent in a monstrous position and her arms dangled uselessly at her sides, as if on a corpse. And Lisa herself – she had once been strong, though not strong enough to have saved her children.

The story was tragic — and spoke for a thousand other stories. But as Tolkatchev listened and looked, he was powerfully struck by the facial expressions of the two women:

> They radiated an intense vitality. It was possible to imagine, almost still to see, the beauty they once possessed. 'Lisa, Lisa,' her friend repeated. As I looked out at the cold, foggy sky I began to experience an eerie transformation of time . . .
>
> Lisa, Lisa – Mona Lisa. Everything in that painted Renaissance scene grew clear, harmonious and wondrous: her face, the folds of her garment, the landscape behind her . . . The more I contemplated her image, the more the riddle of her smile grew. Her face expressed tranquility and reflection.

It is for this reason that so many commentators have suggested that this enigmatic woman was pregnant. 'So the great Leonardo da Vinci saw her and painted her,' Tolkatchev continued. 'Writers and poets wove Mona Lisa into their works. She smiled for ever, through all generations, the wondering smile of motherhood.'

The howl of the storm broke Tolkatchev's reverie. What had they done to Lisa here?

Slowly, the wind quietened down and the two women left the storeroom. Only Tolkatchev remained: 'The world was covered in a white blanket. A chilling silence prevailed — as if time had stood still, as if there was no past, as if there would be no future . . . only the two bent-over figures of the women, disappearing into the distance.'

9

'We Tried to be Different'

A T THE BEGINNING of 1945 more than two and a half
million Soviet soldiers were poised to invade Hitler's
Germany. On 12 January Stalin's great offensive broke the
Wehrmacht's defences along the River Vistula, and a tide
of Russian soldiers surged westwards. Red Army private
Gennady Shutz and his unit crossed the border with Germany
by the River Neisse, near Kustrin. He and his fellow soldiers
were driving at night and many of his comrades – exhausted
by the continuous, heavy fighting – were sleeping at the back
of the truck. Suddenly Shutz saw a plywood arch. It had
been put across the road by Soviet troops advancing ahead
of them, and a caption was inscribed in large black letters:
'Here it is – Criminal Germany!' Shutz's skin was covered in
goose bumps. He called out for the truck to stop, and woke
the other men. 'Look,' he said, 'at last – we are entering the
beast's lair.'

The Russians always derided Hitler's regime in bestial
terms. 'This was the language we used about the enemy's
heartland,' said Captain Anatoly Mereshko of the Soviet
Eighth Guards Army: 'Our propaganda people did not speak
of "Germany", or "Berlin". It was always "the lair of the
Fascist beast", "the lair from which the war had come". So
we didn't feel we had crossed into the territory of another
nation-state, but rather that we had cornered a cruel preda-

tory animal. Killing it in its lair would bring an end to the war.'

'The lair from which the war had come' – this was a phrase which spoke to every Red Army fighter. Mark Slavin – editor of the Eighth Guards Army front-line newspaper – said: 'We were told we had entered "Accursed Germany" – and accursed it was. The Germans had destroyed my home and killed most of my family. Many of my comrades had actually seen friends and neighbours strung up by the Germans, and found entire villages burnt to the ground by the invader. The war had become unyielding in its cruelty.'

It is hard to comprehend the scale of such suffering. By January 1945 the Soviet Union had lost more than 26 million soldiers and civilians to the war. The Germans had left over 1,700 Russian towns and 70,000 villages in ruins, destroyed over 6 million buildings, 84,000 schools, 43,000 libraries, 40,000 hospitals and 400 museums. Soviet soldiers had been killed at the front, executed or left to starve as prisoners; civilians shot, burned alive and gassed in the Third Reich's extermination camps. Now Soviet troops were entering German towns and villages.

Fresh provocation lay in store, as advancing Soviet forces began to liberate thousands of Red Army POWs from German concentration camps. These prisoners were in a terrible state. At a camp near Lamersdorf Soviet troops liberated 15,000 emaciated POWs, and one of these unfortunates, Petr Antonov, described to shocked soldiers a horrifying regimen of sixteen-hour work shifts, frequent beatings and utterly inadequate food rations. 'In a few months even the strongest among us turned into cripples,' he related. 'Our comrades were shot before our very eyes; people went mad with hunger, chewed on leather belts and shoes, ate the corpses of their fellows.' Antonov appealed to Red Army soldiers to 'seek revenge on the German-Fascist monsters'.

'We steeled ourselves to maintain our discipline and contain our wrath,' Mark Slavin continued. 'We knew that Hitler would defend his Reich to the very last soldier, and that some of the resistance would be fanatical. We realized that really hard fighting still lay ahead, and we could not surrender ourselves to our emotions. We had to somehow hold back our anger if we wanted to finish the war as quickly as possible.' But the distinction between active supporters of Hitler's Nazi state and German civilians was not clear to the majority of Soviet soldiers. And others had less desire to control their rage.

Red Army lieutenant Mikhail Semiriaga commented: 'Some of our officers were well educated, and knew the history of Germany. They didn't feel the German people were to blame for falling victim to Fascism. Rather, they felt the blame should be put on those who had a vested interest in the war: the Nazi Party itself, the SS, the German military and industrialists engaged in armaments manufacture. These were the forces that should be targeted.'

But Semiriaga continued:

By January 1945, those who believed in humane treatment for German civilians were a minority. The majority of our officers and soldiers were not well educated – many of our soldiers could scarcely read or write. They thought that all Germans were responsible for spreading Fascism. This point of view was held particularly strongly by those whose families had lived in the occupied territories and who had been terrorized by Fascism. And unfortunately, this point of view was also reflected in our wartime propaganda, urging people to take revenge by killing Germans. This could only have a bad effect as we entered German territory.

Many Soviet soldiers wanted some kind of revenge for the suffering that had been inflicted on their country. Semiriaga put it simply: 'They wanted to pay the Germans back for starting the war and all the pain and hurt that had been caused by it.' What form that hunger to avenge would take, no one really knew.

Lieutenant Vladimir Gelfand – a platoon commander in the Soviet 301st Rifle Division – crossed into Germany on 28 January 1945. Near-deserted villages were going up in flames around him. 'Germany is burning,' Gelfand wrote in his diary. 'And for some reason it is gratifying to watch this terrible sight. A death for a death; their blood for our blood – I do not feel sorry for these haters of mankind. We found three sleeping Germans – all young. Terrified, they raise trembling hands, crying out "*Hitler kaput*" . . .'

'They started this war,' he continued, 'so it is only right that we should now take their possessions. They live luxuriously after all – the wealth and elegance of their homes is quite staggering. And our superiors turn a blind eye to our robbery – saying that the Germans have been stealing from us for more than three years. I am well satisfied.' Gelfand stepped in, however, when one of his comrades smashed a bust of Schiller, and rescued a Goethe from a similar fate. 'Such geniuses cannot be equated with the present German barbarians,' Gelfand declared to his bemused soldiers.

Gelfand's division was a tough fighting unit, awarded the Order of Suvorov during the Vistula–Oder offensive, and regularly praised by Marshal Zhukov – the commander of the First Belorussian Front – in his dispatches. Gelfand's diary entries focus on the fierce battles with German troops, and the military push towards Berlin. 'Each step forward now has an historic significance,' he noted. Discipline could not be allowed to slacken in the process. The goal was to destroy the last enemy forces, capture Berlin and end the war – and Gelfand chronicled an increasingly determined German resistance. 'Once again, death walks side by side with us,' he wrote.

Gelfand's courage and resolve were shared by many other Soviet soldiers – it would have been impossible to bring down Hitler's regime without them. Yet other accounts convey a darker picture. As Soviet major Lev Kopelev crossed the border he gave the command to his soldiers: 'This is Germany! Everyone out and relieve themselves!' It seemed humorous to Kopelev and his men, after having established the frontier line on the map, to be standing in a row by a ditch, solemnizing their entry on to enemy soil. They clambered back on to their truck, moving along the snow-covered asphalt highway. The first Prussian villages they reached, Gross-Koslau and Klein-Koslau, were already on fire, and the driver kept to the middle of the road. A tall tree smouldered in front of a burning church. No one was in sight.

The small town of Neidenburg was also in flames. Advancing Red Army soldiers were burning everything in their path. On a side street, by a garden fence, lay a dead old woman. Around her, Soviet soldiers were moving from house to house, some of them carrying bundles or suitcases. One of them explained to Kopelev that the woman was a spy. 'They got her by a telephone booth. Why fool around?' Her dress was ripped, a telephone receiver lay between her thighs. In a nearby house a woman lay in a pool of blood. She had been stabbed repeatedly in the breasts and stomach. 'Another spy!' Kopelev was told.

'Our sacred vengeance,' Lev Kopelev recorded. A moment of truth had arrived. 'Our compatriots had been mistreated in the most brutal fashion,' he continued. 'We came from Moscow, from Leningrad, from Stalingrad, across scorched earth, through smoking piles of rubble. In every family there were victims of war and abduction . . . Above all, our soldiers hated the enemy – and now they would take their revenge.'

Soviet reconnaissance scout Mikhail Baitman said frankly:

Our unit made no distinction between enemy soldiers and civilians. One mile across the border we came across a corps commander – a general. One of our men said to him: 'What can we do with the Germans?' He replied: 'Anything – it will be just retribution for the terrible crimes they have committed.' And that is what we said and thought. We shot unarmed civilians – we threw grenades into basements where women and children were sheltering. And we did it calmly – in matter-of-fact fashion.

Proper treatment of civilians was to some extent a matter for individual conscience, but Soviet soldiers also needed firm guidance from their superiors. Before Red Army sergeant Yuri Koriakin crossed the border at Bromberg, the company's political officer gave the men a little talk. 'We are entering German territory. They have brought innumerable evils into our land, so we have come to punish them. I ask you not to make contact with the local population – and indiscriminate killing of civilians is inadmissible, and will be punished.' Then he suddenly changed tack: 'Well – concerning the question of women, you can treat the German women rather freely, just as long as it doesn't look organized. One or two men can go, do whatever they need to do, return, and that's it.'

'Do whatever they need to do,' repeated Koriakin.

That was exactly what he said. He didn't seem to know himself what code of behaviour we were supposed to follow. And our treatment of German women certainly was free – and vengeful. Our propaganda had after all made no real distinction between

Hitlerites and Germans. I knew of a ton of cases where German women were raped but not killed, as if rape was not itself a crime and this was some kind of mercy. The head of our supply company set up an entire harem. German women lived with him, he used them and then he passed them on to others. A couple of times, when entering houses, we found old people in them who had been murdered by our troops. Once I found a woman lying on a bed with a bayonet in her chest. What had happened to her? We left without asking.

Understandably, most of the German population was terrified of the Red Army. 'The local population fled from us,' said Lieutenant Vasily Ustyugov of the Soviet Third Shock Army's 150th Division, 'they were afraid of atrocities, and they were quite right to be, for as we entered Germany we were preoccupied with revenge, and there were a number of "criminal moments", when civilians were killed. Our soldiers were shooting, killing and burning everything in their path.'

This terror was cleverly manipulated by the Nazi regime. When Soviet soldiers murdered most of the inhabitants of the East Prussian village of Nemmersdorf in the late autumn of 1944 Joseph Goebbels publicized it widely, warning that it was a foretaste of things to come. He called it 'atrocity propaganda', and his secretary, Brunhilde Pomsel, recalled: 'The news we received in our offices of Red Army atrocities was always multiplied. If three women were raped we would make it ten. Everything was exaggerated – in order to strengthen the deterrent effect and the German people's will to hold out.'

Sometimes this search for a deterrent took the most surprising forms. Soviet lieutenant Boris Gorbachevsky, a company commander in the 220nd Rifle Division, never forgot his entry into the East Prussian town of Treuburg – the first German settlement in his division's path. There was an air of unreality about it all – all the finest buildings lay blown up and destroyed, the church, the theatre, the sports stadium, bank and waterworks – but the terrible damage in the town did not remotely correspond to the brief fight several hundred German troops had put up on Treuburg's outskirts. The town had not been bombed or even subjected to prolonged artillery bombardment. How had so much destruction occurred?

Gorbachevsky's bemusement increased as he saw signs at road junctions proclaiming, in advance of the Red Army's actual arrival: 'Pay close attention to what the Bolsheviks have done to the first town taken by them in East Prussia. This is how they will treat all the towns and villages of your beloved homeland, and all of us Germans. Defend your Great Reich from the Red Barbarians!'

Interrogation of captured German prisoners provided an astonishing explanation. As the Red Army approached, Goebbels had ordered the destruction of all major buildings and the expulsion of the townspeople. Film crews and journalists were then bussed in to survey the ruins and to record the imagined ravages of Soviet soldiers. No detail was neglected. The swans in the town park were shot, and it was then announced that the 'Asiatic hordes' had killed and eaten them.

Gorbachevsky had stumbled upon a giant theatre set. Goebbels had fashioned it from race prejudice and hatred, the Nazi fear of the Slavic *Untermenschen*, the subhuman hordes advancing from the east. A report from Soviet marshal Konev's First Ukrainian Front, drawn up on 28 January 1945, began: 'Fascist propaganda tries to scare away the populace with stories of atrocities allegedly committed by the Red Army. When they see that our soldiers do not commit acts of violence against civilians they return home. In the village of Illnau there were just two elderly inhabitants when our troops entered it on the morning of 23 January. By the evening of 24 January 200 people had reappeared.'

Soviet captain Anatoly Mereshko – reluctant to believe the worst of his own army – thought that Nazi propaganda was fanning German people's fear of retribution. 'We found suicides – women who had taken cyanide on hearing news of our approach,' he said, 'and administered it to their children. We were shaken when we witnessed this – it seemed the final proof of their terrible hatred towards us.'

But in East Prussia there was good reason for the exodus of most of the native population. It was the first German territory entered by the Red Army, and as Wehrmacht troops – massively outnumbered by the Soviet forces opposing them – pulled back towards the city of Königsberg, Nazi officials delayed authorizing a general evacuation. When that evacuation finally began, on 20 January 1945, in temperatures below −25 degrees Celsius, the refugees collided with advancing Russian forces. Soviet troops showed scant regard for the hundreds of thousands forced to flee their homes in atrocious winter weather, and some even treated them as a legitimate military target. After Königsberg was besieged, a long trail of civilians slowly moved west along the Frisches Haff lagoon, a 72-kilometre-long spit of land, only a few hundred metres wide. There were no soldiers among them – just old men, women and children, struggling to escape the war.

Soviet pilot Yuri Khukhrikov said without a trace of remorse: 'We flew in groups of six planes over the Frisches Haff, west of Königsberg. We really worked that strip. And we turned so many people into mincemeat – only God knows how many. Thousands upon thousands died. Tens of thousands of people were on that road – you just couldn't miss. Only the start and end of it had any kind of air defence – a few German flak guns. The rest was entirely in our hands.'

Units from the German Fourth Army were fighting hard to keep Soviet land forces from reaching this coastal strip. The deliberate bombing of civilians strongly motivated them to keep resisting. 'Witnessing these atrocities had a very powerful effect on us,', recalled Panzer Lieutenant Leopold Rothkirch. 'We grew extremely angry, and resolved to hold out for as long as possible, to help our people evade the Russians.'

Brutality was endemic. Red Army tank commander Sergei Shuiskii said: 'There was no time for pity. We were chasing hard after the Germans. Sometimes we ran over complete columns of refugees. I personally drove straight at a horse-drawn wagon full of civilians, tipping it into the ditch. I did not even stop to see if the women and children were alive or dead.'

In the German town of Treuburg, Lieutenant Boris Gorbachevsky now saw this brutality at first hand. As he and his Soviet comrades moved down the main street no one was to be seen. The silence was punctuated only by the barking of stray dogs. Then, unexpectedly, an old man emerged from a partially ruined building. He held some sort of booklet in his hand, and with joyful exclamations he rushed out to meet the head of the column. The man was a German communist, the booklet proof of his Party membership – and in the Nazi state even to keep such a document risked imprisonment or death.

The old man's joy was short lived. One of the Russian soldiers, unable to speak German and with no interest in finding out what was going on, stepped out of the column and smashed the man's head with his rifle butt. Bleeding heavily, he fell to the cobblestone pavement. As he lay there, other soldiers left the line to taunt and kick him. Then they stabbed him repeatedly with their bayonets. Even his death did not satisfy them. More gathered round to spit on his corpse. Then a political officer stopped by the mutilated body. He lifted up the blood-soaked booklet – proof of membership of the Communist Party of Germany – and carefully wiped its cover and hid it in his map case, as if collecting a memento. Not a word of reprimand passed his lips.

Gorbachevsky caught up with the soldier who had smashed the man's skull in. 'Why did you do it?' he asked. 'He was not a soldier – there was no way he could have harmed us. An old man, a communist, he may have spent time in prison for his allegiance to the German Communist Party. He kept that Party card at the risk of his life.' The soldier replied gruffly: 'To me, Comrade Lieutenant, they are all the same – just scum. I won't find any peace until I kill a hundred of them.'

Gorbachevsky had witnessed his first civilian death in Germany. There would be many, many more, for the rage of these soldiers could not be contained. He recalled how troops, 'rabid with fury, burst into badly damaged homes and shattered or destroyed everything they could find . . . mirrors, dishes, porcelain, glass goblets, all went flying. Germans had lived here! They took axes to armchairs, sofas, tables and stools, even baby carriages. This was the way the first wave of hatred boiled to the surface. No one – not a single commander or political officer – tried to stay the soldiers' senseless destruction, understanding that to do so would be utterly meaningless: their frenzy was uncontrollable.'

In the aftermath of the war, the Soviet regime played down the extent of this frenzy – it did not want to besmirch the honour of the Red Army. More recently, some in the

West have portrayed the advancing Russians as an army of mass rapists, most of its troops ill disciplined and out of control. But even those Soviet officers and soldiers most critical of these atrocities never believed that they were conducted by a majority of Red Army soldiers. Major Lev Kopelev estimated that between 10 and 15 per cent of the army was involved. Its actions were absolutely horrific, and it was a substantial minority. Yet it was a minority nonetheless.

Kopelev speculated that many of the killings and rapes were orchestrated by a criminal underclass within the Red Army, prisoners serving in the punishment battalions or teenagers who had suffered under German occupation and had become habituated to violence. The frenzy arose from many factors, but at its root was the huge number of Soviet civilians killed by the Germans. Its impact can be seen in a letter written by Soviet private Vladimir Tsoglin from a recently liberated village in Belorussia in the summer of 1944: 'I found out, and want everyone to find out, what the Germans really are,' he exclaimed. 'They are not people, they are worse than beasts. Can people actually burn other people in houses, after pouring gasoline on them? I don't know what I'll find as I move further into territories that have been occupied by the Germans, but what I have seen so far is enough to warrant destroying them like rabid dogs.'

These Red Army soldiers had become utterly brutalized by the war. 'We were not avenging angels,' said reconnaissance scout Mikhail Baitman, 'fighting for some holy cause. The war had turned us into beasts. The Germans showed us how to behave like animals, and for three years they "schooled us well", killing and raping all across our country. Now we were following suit. I was a Jew, and I had learnt all about their barbaric cruelty. I felt not a shred of pity – only hatred, a desire to kill every last one of them.'

'Senseless burning, senseless murder,' wrote Captain Mikhail Koriakov. 'A tide of blind, pointless vengeance was being unleashed.' He witnessed a herd of cows being driven towards the rear of Red Army lines. It was important to gather these animals – supply lines had become overextended during the January advance and many units were short of food. But a Red Army lieutenant suddenly went up to one of them, unsheathed a knife, and struck the hapless creature a death-blow at the base of the skull. She immediately crumpled and fell – and the rest of the herd, bellowing madly, stampeded and ran away. The lieutenant wiped the blade on his boots, turned to Koriakov and said with quiet satisfaction: 'My father told me that the Germans had taken a cow from us – now we are even.'

Mikhail Koriakov then said:

> People were killed with no more compunction than that poor animal. The population of Kreuzburg had deserted the town. Only one deaf old man remained behind. The officers of the reserve regiment spent the entire time arguing whether they should burn the town and kill the old man. Later I learnt that the old man had been murdered. In another town I saw the body of a woman; she was lying across the bed, her legs spread – her skirt was round her shoulders and a bayonet was stuck in her stomach, pinning her to the wooden slats.

Koriakov was pushing into Upper Silesia in the wake of Colonel General Rybalko's Third Tank Army. Rybalko was a shrewd tactician and brave commander. In 1942 the Germans had captured and killed his daughter in the Ukraine. As his force prepared to advance into Germany that January, Rybalko had gathered his officers together and announced: 'The long-awaited hour, the hour of revenge, is at hand! We all have personal reasons for revenge: my daughter, your sisters, our mother Russia, the devastation of our land!' Rybalko did not condone rape, arson or looting, and orders were read prescribing the behaviour of troops on German territory. But as Koriakov quickly realized: 'Orders are pieces of paper, while the word "revenge" is a living thing, and can take any number of tempting forms.'

In Bunzlau, Koriakov rescued a girl being chased by four tank men from Rybalko's army. A sergeant – completely drunk – tried to warn him off. 'She has nothing to do with you,' he threatened. 'Our officers are expecting her.' Koriakov wondered how many men were waiting to share the poor girl – a platoon, a company or an entire tank battalion? In Liegnitz, Koriakov met a woman who claimed to have been gang-raped by over two hundred Red Army soldiers. He also found a twelve-year-old girl who had been multiply raped by soldiers, and was now dying. 'For three years the Germans inflicted a scorched-earth policy upon our country,' Koriakov wrote, 'waging war with unprecedented cruelty. Now Russians are setting Germany alight in return – and that cruelty has been matched.'

The cumulative effect of such experiences was explosive. 'There were cases when our soldiers ran amok,' said Captain Anatoly Mereshko of the Eighth Guards Army. 'These men had almost always lost their families during the war.' 'Many of my comrades had friends and relations in the occupied territories,' added Lieutenant Vasily Ustyugov of the Soviet 150th Rifle Division. 'And as our army advanced, these men often found out that everyone they knew had been shot dead. One man – upon learning that his parents had been murdered in Minsk – hanged himself that very night. War is war, but we were finding vast tracts of Belorussia completely laid to waste, with every village and settlement destroyed. The Germans burnt and killed for no good military reason – it was senseless, and we hated them for it.'

Soviet war photographer Yevgeny Khaldei remembered a Red Army soldier brought before a military tribunal, charged with raping a German woman. The man carried in his tunic a letter informing him of the fate of his family, who were from the Ukraine. It began: 'Vasya, the German Fascists shot your father, hanged your mother and then raped your sister in the garden before killing her . . .'

The arrival of Soviet soldiers on German soil was a powerful catalyst for these pent-up emotions. 'The hour of retribution had arrived,' Boris Gorbachevsky observed. After three years of terrible bloodshed on Russian soil, he could understand the hatred felt by the soldier who had smashed the man's skull in, and the hatred felt by those who had spat on his lifeless body. But he added: 'How many more Germans would they have to kill, humiliate and tear to pieces in order to soothe their grief, dull their anger and find some kind of inner peace?'

The prosperity of German towns and villages – with their houses solidly built out of brick and stone, their gardens full of neatly trimmed fruit trees – made them a tempting target for Red Army soldiers who had never owned a clock or watch, and for whom a working toilet was still a marvel of technology. Men from poor Russian villages, acclimatized to the spartan conditions of front-line military life, now found themselves surrounded by unimaginable wealth. From the outset, Soviet authorities had tried to control looting – limiting each man to a one-kilo pack of goods that he could send home to his family. But many soldiers took far more than that. 'Our soldiers wanted so many things,' said Fyodor Khropatiy, an officer in the Soviet Twenty-Seventh Army. 'Clothes, watches and jewellery – some took whatever they could. In much of our country living conditions were terrible. But they were also furious that such a wealthy country had invaded us in the first place. "With all these riches – what did they want from us?" soldiers said. I saw men opening fire on furniture – machine-gunning wardrobes, sideboards and mirrors. They were totally enraged.'

Germany – a relatively affluent country – had invaded the Soviet Union, a much poorer one, and Soviet soldiers' anger was understandable. But it was running dangerously out of control. Mark Slavin witnessed a comrade smashing a crowbar against a line of captured enemy vehicles. He disabled one after another – it was as if he was possessed. Slavin tried to restrain him: 'They are ours now – we can use them!' But the man could not stop: 'They are German!' he bellowed. Slavin was left highly disturbed by this scene – the man was out of his mind with fury.

Men changed when they crossed into German territory. Soviet Major Lev Kopelev wrote:

> Was it really necessary and inevitable that some of our troops turned into savages . . . the rape and robbery – did it have to be like that? In the newspapers, on the radio, was the call for 'Holy revenge'. But what kind of avengers were we, and against whom did we take revenge? Why did so many of our soldiers turn out to be mean bandits, who gang-raped women and girls – on the streets, in the snow, in house entrances – who killed unarmed civilians, and who destroyed, spoiled, burnt down everything they could not carry away?

The Soviet system was brutal – and army life harsh. 'Think about it,' said Soviet officer Fyodor Khropatiy.

> A soldier is conscripted into the army, and fights for three years – in atrocious conditions – without any proper leave. The pressure on him is relentless. Then suddenly there is the opportunity

for release. There was little attempt in my unit to curb our troops' behaviour. It was no big deal if a soldier raped a woman, or even a girl. On the contrary, men boasted to each other how many women they had taken. It was almost considered 'heroic' or 'courageous' to have had a whole series of women. And if someone was murdered, well, 'it was war'.

Alcohol played its part. The German military deliberately left great stores of it in front of advancing Red Army troops, thereby doing no favours to their own civilian population. 'It is impossible not to get drunk here,' a Soviet soldier wrote home from East Prussia in early February 1945. 'And what is happening around us is not easy to describe – if you drink, it is easier to deal with.'

The explosion of violence as the Red Army crossed into Germany – often fuelled by alcohol – was stirred up by Soviet propaganda. 'Hate the enemy! Kill the enemy!' war journalist Ilya Ehrenburg had exhorted from the summer of 1942 onwards. This prolific fifty-four-year-old Jewish communist wrote regularly for *Pravda*, *Izvetsia* and the army newspaper *Red Star*, and his articles and leaflets reached millions of Soviet soldiers. And these soldiers loved him. 'Our Ilya', they called him. Ehrenburg was the Red Army's prophet of vengeance: 'The Germans are not human beings,' he wrote in 1942. 'From now on the word "German" is a most terrible oath . . . We shall kill. If you have not killed at least one German a day you have wasted that day . . . Kill the German – that is your grandmother's request. Kill the German – that is your child's prayer. Kill the German, your Motherland demands it. Do not miss, show no mercy, kill.'

In August 1944 Ehrenburg wrote in *Pravda*:

We want to move through Germany with sword in hand, to destroy their love for that sword for all time. We want to destroy them, so that they never again try to destroy us. With us are the shadows of those tortured to death. They rise from their graves, from burial pits, from mine shafts. There are old men and babies, Russians and Ukrainians, Belorussians and Jews, Poles and Lithuanians. They all wanted to live; they all loved the sun and flowers. Torn to shreds, they cry out: 'Remember us!'

The picture of an endless column of victims screaming for atonement and revenge was conjured with biblical eloquence. After the liberation of the extermination camp at Majdanek in Poland this dark theme was continually trumpeted in Ehrenburg's articles. In January 1945, with Soviet soldiers entering German territory on a broad front, he wrote: 'It is not only armies and divisions marching on Berlin. The grief of all innocents from mass graves, ditches and gorges is marching on Berlin . . . The trees of Vitebsk – where the Germans hanged their unfortunate victims – the boots and shoes of those men, women and children shot and gassed at Majdanek – they are all marching on Berlin.'

And as that offensive gathered momentum in the second half of January Ehrenburg announced: 'The reckoning has begun . . . the heart of every one of us is filled with pain. We are utterly determined to get even with the Germans for all time.'

Ehrenburg was deeply in touch with the suffering of his country – and also the tragedy of Soviet Jews. He was the principal compiler of *The Black Book*, a record of the fate of more than two million Jews in Russia and the Ukraine brutally murdered by the Einsatzgruppen, the special task forces that moved into the occupied territories in the wake of the German army. The tragedy had reached its nadir with the liberation of the extermination camps at Majdanek and Auschwitz.

Ehrenburg's heart was full of pain and rage – and this allowed him to connect powerfully with millions of his countrymen. But his highly charged writing risked breeding something darker than either he or his readers fully understood.

Ehrenburg's influence over Red Army soldiers was enormous, and his emotive language was echoed in appeals to troops by the Soviet military command. On the eve of the January Red Army offensive General Ivan Chernyakovsky, commander of the Third Belorussian Front – which would spearhead the assault on the German city of Königsberg – enjoined his soldiers: 'There will be no mercy! Show no mercy to anyone – just as no mercy was shown to us. We are burning with hatred and revenge.' The Order of the Day of Marshal Rokossovsky's Second Belorussian Front called for: 'a total reckoning with the Fascists, for all their cruelty and atrocities, for the grief and torment of our people, for the blood and tears of our fathers and mothers, wives and children, for the Soviet towns and villages destroyed and plundered by the enemy'.

The troops of Marshal Zhukov's First Belorussian Front were told:

> The time has come for the reckoning with the German-Fascist rabble. Our hatred is great and burning! We have not forgotten the torment and grief which the Hitlerite cannibals inflicted upon our people. We have not forgotten our burned-down towns and villages. We remember our wives and children who were tortured to death by the Germans. We will avenge those burned in the devil's furnaces, those suffocated in the gas chambers, those shot and tortured. We will justly avenge all of them.

The appeal continued in the unmistakable tones of Ehrenburg:

We advance into Germany, and behind us lie Stalingrad, the Ukraine and Belorussia. We advance through the ashes of our towns and villages, over the traces of blood of Soviet citizens who were tortured and mutilated by the Fascist beast. Woe to the land of the murderers! Nothing will stop us now! We have sworn on the graves of our dead friends, we have solemnly promised our children not to rest until the offenders have been dealt with. For the deaths, for the suffering of our Soviet people, the Fascist robbers shall pay with vast quantities of their own black blood.

The effect of all this was utterly hypnotic. 'From Stalingrad to our arrival on the German border we were advancing under the slogan "Kill a German!"' recalled Red Army private Gennady Shutz. 'I can still see Ehrenburg's articles in front of my eyes.' 'The repetition was like a sledgehammer,' said Lieutenant Vasily Ustyugov, 'kill, kill, kill . . . it really got to our soldiers.' Captain Mikhail Koriakov added: 'All through the war Ilya Ehrenburg never tired of repeating that the Old Testament precept of "an eye for an eye" was outmoded. The new precept was "two eyes for an eye" and "a pool of blood for a drop of blood". Dark, savage instincts were stirred up – instincts that culminated in a tide of destruction.'

A Wehrmacht intelligence report, drawn from Russian prisoners captured and interrogated by the German Ninth Army, stated: 'Some Bolsheviks are now shooting at anything living – apparently out of pure joy at the sight of bloodshed. As a result of heavy drinking and the tide of violence the anger of Red Army soldiers is turning into a kind of "murder psychosis".' 'Now it is best not to look into someone's face immediately after an attack,' said a nurse from the Soviet Sixty-Fifth Army. 'There's nothing human there – somehow the face is entirely alien. It is hard to find words for it. You think you are among mental cases – it is a dreadful sight.'

Koriakov believed that the Soviet military leadership had underestimated the power of Ehrenburg's Old Testament language. It was concerned to maintain the drive and motivation of Red Army soldiers fighting a long and bloody war, soldiers who had at long last liberated their country and were now entering the land of their enemy. It did not want that drive to falter. But it had no real sense of what it was about to unleash. 'For over three years the Soviet soldier had been pounded by only one word, "revenge",' Koriakov continued. 'Up and down the ranks this word was constantly repeated, in speeches, leaflets and newspapers.' 'Revenge is powerful and dangerous,' added Mark Slavin of the Eighth Guards Army, 'and it had now become all-consuming.'

Its impact can be seen in a selection of letters from a Soviet motorized division in late January 1945. One of the men wrote to his family from the River Oder, less than 80 kilometres from Berlin: 'I have once again sworn before my Motherland and the Party to avenge the death of my brother. Hundreds of Germans will have to atone for his life. Not one who falls into my hands will survive.' The comments of other troops from the same unit carry a similar tone. 'The German mother will curse the day on which she gave birth to a son!' a soldier from the western Ukraine pronounced. 'The German women will now experience the terror of war!' Another said: 'Now we can see German homes burning, families wandering around, dragging their brood of vipers along with them. Now they see their own downfall. They cry out *"Hitler kaput"* in an attempt to save their own lives – but for them there is no mercy.' In a letter to his parents in Smolensk one soldier wrote: 'Every day we advance through East Prussia. And we are taking revenge against the Germans for all the disgraceful acts which they have committed against us. We now have free rein to do what we want with these

German rogues.' Another exclaimed: 'Now we are striking the Germans without mercy. We will put the rest in a big cauldron. How happy my heart is when we drive through a burning German town.'

The language echoes Ehrenburg's – and it is lurid and disturbing. The Germans are no longer people, merely objects of the soldiers' righteous wrath. It reveals a dangerous, vindictive anger.

Such sentiments are shocking to us. They were also shocking to many Russian combatants. 'Houses were pillaged and set alight – everything that couldn't be carried away was broken, destroyed,' said Soviet private Efraim Genkin, seeing the wanton destruction around him. 'The Germans ran from us like the plague . . . all this was depressing and repellent.'

Lieutenant Nikolai Inozemetsev was left badly shaken by the plight of German civilians in East Prussia, and the cruelty of his compatriots. 'Lines of carts full of refugees,' he wrote, 'the gang-rape of women, abandoned villages . . . these were the "battle scenes" of an offensive conducted by an army of avengers.' Fellow Red Army soldier Grigorii Pomerants was marching through East Prussia when he saw the naked body of a young German girl cast on to a rubbish heap. 'Was it us who had done this?' Pomerants wondered. 'And if so, who?' He flinched and turned his head away – but the picture of the dead girl would not leave his mind. 'Suddenly an entire layer of hatred towards *any* German was stripped away from me,' he said.

Other Red Army letters make no vows of hatred, and are more moderate in tone. These soldiers retained their military discipline, well aware that the war still had to be won, and that German troops would fight more strongly now they were in their own homeland. 'Greetings from Germany!' a reconnaissance scout wrote to his sister on 30 January. 'I am alive and healthy.' He added pointedly: 'The enemy is on the retreat but is still resisting fiercely.' There were no declarations of vengeance; instead, it was noted: 'I have already gone through many German towns and villages, and nowhere have I seen the inhabitants face to face.'

The picture was confused, for while some Red Army troops lost all control, many others retained their discipline and showed considerable restraint. 'We never harassed German civilians,' recalled Soviet lieutenant Evgeni Bessonov, commander of a tank company. 'We did not rob them – and we did not rape women. I was very strict about this with my soldiers – and other officers were of the same opinion.'

When Bessonov's tank column overtook a group of fleeing German civilians no one was mistreated, and the soldiers explained that they should return to their homes. For Captain Anatoly Mereshko – advancing with the Eighth Guards Army – a humane response to local inhabitants was the watchword. 'We were fighting against the Wehrmacht and the SS,' Mereshko said, 'not unarmed women, children and old men.' For Mereshko, who had fought all the way from Stalingrad, the order for the proper treatment of civilians was sacrosanct.

Soviet artillery officer Isaak Kobylyanskiy remembered seeing a graphic poster in the vicinity of Königsberg warning German women to evacuate the area immediately, lest they become victims of Bolshevik monsters and sexual predators. But when his unit first encountered civilians in the nearby town of Sidling in late January 1945 he felt no anger towards the frightened women, only pity. 'The troops took seriously the order concerning the proper treatment of civilians,' Kobylyanskiy said, 'and there were no incidents of sexual misconduct within our division.'

Lieutenant General Vasily Chuikov – commander of the Soviet Eighth Guards Army – always remembered the story of a soldier who wanted to show his comrades his home village in the Ukraine. When Soviet troops liberated it the village was in ruins. When the soldier reached the remnants of his house he saw that his parents and grandparents had been strung up in the orchard garden in front of it. Chuikov was struck by the soldier's behaviour on German soil, for he never harmed any of its civilians in return. Chuikov commented: 'A real hero is one who can contain his wrath.'

There were many examples of such heroism. On 29 January Lieutenant Vasily Churkin and his comrades from the Soviet 80th Rifle Division reached the town of Hindenburg – and saw terror on the faces of its residents, 'as if they had been condemned to death'. As the troops moved through the town, some civilians stood motionless, absolutely rigid with fear. Churkin, his platoon commander and a small group of soldiers spent the night in the home of a wealthy German, who for some reason had been unable or unwilling to flee. One of the Soviet troops spoke reasonably good German: 'We were met by the superficially polite owner, a young interesting man in his thirties, and his still very young but full-figured, tall, sympathetic wife,' Churkin recalled.

> He was a powerful bureaucrat; she was probably a housewife. Their two young girls attended a classical high school. Their apartment, which was rather large, occupied the first and second floors and was comfortably furnished – with expensive rugs, attractive curtains and valuable furniture. The parquet floor, diligently polished, reflected like a mirror. Apparently the girls lived on the second floor. A standing piano and nice washstand stood against the wall. Five fellows in our platoon and I were to spend the night on the second floor. We arranged ourselves on the shiny parquet floor. I remember how the chunks of melting snow from our boots stood out on it, forming giant puddles.

Even now I feel somewhat awkward at the memory – as if ashamed.

Churkin's wife and sister had died during the siege of Leningrad; his two brothers and both his sons had perished at the front. His entire family had been wiped out. And yet, there were no rapes, no robberies – only a Soviet soldier feeling awkward about the pools of melting snow left in a pristine German home.

Lieutenant Zeilik Kleiman's unit occupied a German village where nearly all the residents – mostly women and children – had remained in their homes. Kleiman wrote on 3 February 1945: 'Generally our men are behaving in a cultured manner, although there was an incident where a girl of sixteen complained that one of our soldiers had hit her with a pistol.' Kleiman – who knew a little German – summoned the soldier and admonished him, then translated what he had said for the benefit of the local residents: 'If not today, then tomorrow we will be in battle again. We will fight the enemy – and we will beat him. But do not sully your hands harming a defenceless woman – we are not Fascists.'

Then Kleiman turned to the village's inhabitants. He told them that the soldier's entire family had been shot by the Germans, and spoke of incidents when Panzer tanks had run over Russian children and German troops had smashed a baby's head against a stove. The following morning the Soviet soldiers marched out in good order, and a week later Kleiman died in battle.

Soviet officer David Kaufman hated the Germans for the trail of death and destruction they had left in their wake. Walking through the remnants of the liberated town of Gomel, he wrote sadly in his diary: 'A place that was once beautiful.' He added: 'Remember these ruins – and avenge them!' But when Kaufman crossed the German border near the town of Birnbaum, the first civilians he met were two elderly musicians and their wives. One of the women was paralysed and was being carried in a cart. On a sledge behind her was an untidy heap – all that was left of their belongings. Kaufman, seeing their suffering, forgot his anger – and talked with them about music. When he could not find a German word both he and the musicians used snatches of melodies from Brahms and Tchaikovsky as a form of 'communication'. A sense of connection developed.

When the musicians left Kaufman noted: 'Germany's woe – a deserved woe – passed before my eyes.' But the hunger for revenge had slackened, and he continued: 'I swore to myself that I would never harm the women or the children of my enemy.'

Soviet war photographer Yevgeny Khaldei, advancing into Germany with Red Army troops, said:

> Every day of the war had torn my heart out. I saw soldiers and civilians killed before my very eyes. I saw endless destroyed towns and villages. I saw how the enemy had ravaged our land. As we crossed the border I was in a fury of hatred. The Fascists had killed my father and three sisters at Donetsk in the Ukraine. And I learnt that they didn't shoot or hang them, but threw them – still alive – down a mine shaft. How does one come to terms with something like that? But when I came across German civilians, and saw the terrible state they were in, my rage began to fade. To my surprise, I even felt sympathy for them. I began to comprehend that Germans could also be victims, that the war might be terrible for everyone.

Restraint was not easy. Private Roman Kravchenko of the Soviet 356th Rifle Division was called to interpret for his captain. Some of the soldiers had found an old German couple hiding under a bed in a farmhouse near the small town of Mellenthin. 'We are the only ones left,' the man said. 'All the others ran away. They said you would kill everyone – children, old people, women.' The Red Army captain struggled to contain his anger. 'So why have you stayed here, then?' 'We were born here – we wanted to stay here. It's the end.' 'End of what?' the captain asked. For the first time, the old man looked up. 'The end of everything – Germany, our nation, our children – everything.' 'Which children?' the annoyed captain interrupted. 'My two sons – they both fell in battle,' was the reply. There was a pause, and Kravchenko could feel the tension in the room. 'Where were they killed?' the captain asked. 'Demyansk and Stalingrad,' the German responded. The two men looked at each other, and then the Red Army captain retorted: 'Well, we didn't invite them there!' Abruptly, he turned to Kravchenko and told him to take the couple away and find somewhere safe for them to stay.

The two Germans rose to their feet, holding hands, and the old man looked appealingly at Kravchenko. 'What did the officer say? Are you going to shoot us?' The captain exploded. 'Shoot you! Shoot old people! We are not Hitler's army.'

'We are not Hitler's army'. The situation in Germany at the beginning of 1945 defies easy generalization, and stories of remarkable self-control by Soviet soldiers coexist alongside those of wanton destruction.

The Red Army began to struggle with its conscience. Having seen the horror inflicted on its country by the Germans, it was now witnessing the horror meted out by its own soldiers. This was not an army impervious to human feeling – and an agonized debate broke out within its own ranks. Understanding the source of the soldiers' rage was one thing; condoning their actions quite another.

'I don't feel bad that the Germans are suffering,' Private Nikolai Safonov said at the end of January 1945. 'We can never forget what they did to us . . . But these cases of rape are shameful. They lower the dignity of each Russian individually – and the army as a whole.' In the East Prussian town of Allenstein, Soviet major Lev Kopelev found a mother and her thirteen-year-old daughter who had been multiply raped by Red Army soldiers. He took them to the safety of an army collection point. When the officer on duty learnt what had happened he was outraged, and cursed the perpetrators, 'those bastards and bandits'.

Others began to question what was happening around them. On 22 January Soviet private Efraim Genkin witnessed the destruction of the town of Gumbinnen. At first he was exultant: 'A crucified German city!' he began. 'It answers for the torment of thousands of our Russian brethren, turned into ashes by the Germans in 1941.'

'A crucified German city!' is a remarkable phrase for a Red Army private to use. It shows the powerful effect of Ilya Ehrenburg's biblical language on ordinary Soviet soldiers. But when Genkin saw the orgy of looting that followed, his tone abruptly changed:

In a matter of hours, wonderfully furnished apartments, the richest homes, were destroyed – and now look like a dump, where torn pictures are mixed up with the contents of broken jars of jam . . . This picture provokes repulsion and horror in me . . . It's vile to look at people digging into someone else's goods, greedily grabbing everything they can get their hands on . . . It's vile, disgusting and base! This is just like the Germans in the Ukraine.

For Genkin, the real horror was that the Red Army was beginning to turn into its enemy – Soviet troops now resembling 'a horde of Huns'. This was the crux of it. 'The killings, the orgy of destruction,' said Mark Slavin, 'were pushing our army to the edge of a precipice. We were losing our moral values, and losing our very dignity as human beings. Everything was in jeopardy.' Soviet troops were now faced with a stark choice: whether to rise above the monstrous excesses of their foe, or continue to deal out exactly the same in retribution.

On 24 January Soviet lieutenant Yuri Uspenskii also wrote in his diary about the burning of the East Prussian town of Gumbinnen. Initially, he had no qualms about the scale of the destruction: 'This is revenge for all the Germans have done to us,' he exclaimed. 'Now their cities are destroyed and their population is learning the meaning of the word "war".' Three days later – near Wehlau – he noted: 'Our men have treated East Prussia no worse than the Germans treated Smolensk. We hate Germany and the Germans so much.'

But that day Uspenskii too had his doubts about what his army was doing. He recorded an atrocity, and his justification of it. Beneath the harsh rhetoric, there was a trace of unease: 'In one house we saw a murdered woman with her two children. In the streets too we often see murdered civilians. And the Germans deserve these atrocities, which they themselves began. You only have to think of Majdanek and the theory of the *Ubermensch* to understand why our soldiers leave East Prussia in such a state.' The clinical killing of the extermination camps – fed by the Nazis' callous race doctrines – was fresh in Uspenskii's mind. But he could not easily forget the murder of a defenceless woman and her two children. 'To be sure, it is incredibly cruel to kill children,' he continued, before adding, 'but the Germans' cold-bloodedness in Majdanek was one hundred times worse.'

On 2 February in the village of Kraussen, on the outskirts of Königsberg, Uspenskii saw a column of German civilians in a desperate state, trying to flee from the city. The column – mostly consisting of women, children and old men – was being strafed by Russian planes. Again, his first reaction was a burst of defiant rhetoric: 'Now Germany must taste the tears which it once inflicted on the Russian people,' he exclaimed. 'Terrible atrocities are committed on this earth. And Hitler is the one who provoked them. And the Germans glorified these horrors – a cruel punishment is only just.'

One of the survivors was a ninety-two-year-old man. Looking at him, Uspenskii ceased all calls for vengeance, and the tone of his diary entry suddenly altered. 'This is terrible,' he recorded.

On 7 February Uspenskii reached a turning point. He witnessed a Soviet soldier attempting to rape a young German woman. She had a small child with her. The soldier hauled her across a road, in front of a column of Red Army tanks. No one intervened to help her. When she continued to resist he shot both her and the child. Badly shaken, Uspenskii wrote: 'Such deeds destroy the morale of our soldiers and seriously undermine the discipline and fighting strength of our army. I hate Hitler and Hitler's Germany with all my heart, but this hate in no way justifies such acts. We can take revenge, but not like this.'

In early February 1945 shaken Red Army officers began to seriously re-evaluate what was happening. 'What we had endured in the war could never justify rapes and killings,' declared Soviet officer Fyodor Khropatiy. 'These incidents were appalling – and our entire military discipline was now at stake,' said Lieutenant Vasily Ustyugov. 'A substantial minority of our soldiers were running riot, acting like a bunch of criminals. And these criminal activities – raping, looting, murdering – were spreading. Order had to be restored quickly and effectively. We could not defeat Hitler with a disorganized, out-of-control army.' Soviet officer David Kaufman added: 'An army of resistance and self-defence was imperceptibly becoming an army of ferocious vengeance. And as it did so, our great victories were turning into a moral defeat.'

Nazi leaflets found by Soviet troops now made great play of the atrocities in East Prussia. 'The Bolsheviks show mercy to no one,' one read. 'They take a frenzied delight in killing and torturing defenceless old men, women and children.' And it was evident that Red Army atrocities were motivating German troops to fight harder and with more determination. A report compiled by the intelligence section of the Soviet Fifth Guards Army found that many of the enemy – horrified by the stories they were hearing – were redoubling their efforts to halt the Russian onslaught. 'Hold out at all costs,' one Wehrmacht platoon leader told his men, 'or we all perish. Remember what the Bolsheviks did in East Prussia.' A captured German private – Ewald Schullenberg – related to his Soviet interrogators: 'Our company commander gathered us round him and said: "Friends, it is no longer about individual lives – it is the whole of Germany that is at stake. And we soldiers have to prove that we are real Germans. Imagine what will happen to your families when the Russians come – they will kill every last one of them."'

Soviet disciplinary measures were tightened up drastically. On 22 January Marshal Rokossovsky's Third Belorussian Front declared that 'robbery, plunder, arson and large-scale drinking binges serve only the enemy, who is looking to destroy and undermine the discipline of the troops'. Officers of all ranks were instructed 'to eradicate all activities shameful to the Red Army with the force of a red-hot iron', and it was demanded that 'exemplary order and iron discipline be imposed upon all units and formations in the shortest possible time'.

On 27 January Marshal Konev's First Ukrainian Front followed suit. 'The military councils and unit commanders must act far more forcefully in restoring order in the occupied territories . . . Every soldier is to be informed that any material left behind by the Germans is state property . . .' Soldiers who damaged respect for the Red Army through any act of indiscipline were 'to be punished severely and particularly dangerous scoundrels arrested and sent to punishment battalions'.

Red Army lieutenant Alexander Gordeyev remembered the impact of Konev's order: 'When the Germans were retreating in the Ukraine they were burning and destroying everything. And as we entered Germany each of us thought: "Now it's our time – we will show them!" But our commander's decree shook us out of that state of mind. We realized we should not harm civilians – and that is how we started to behave.'

In the Soviet Army newspaper *Red Star*, an editorial of 9 February 1945 announced a striking change of approach: '"An eye for an eye, a tooth for a tooth" is an old saying,' it began, 'but it must not be taken too literally. If the Germans marauded, and publicly raped our women, it does not mean we have to do the same. This has never been and never shall be. Our soldiers will not allow anything like this to happen – not because of pity for the enemy, but out of a sense of their own personal dignity . . . They understand that our anger is not irrational, our revenge is not blind.'

The records of Colonel Maljarov, the military prosecutor of the Soviet Forty-Eighth Army, show these new measures were strictly enforced. In a circular to all military police in

the army, he ordered that any 'unusual incidents' be immediately passed over to him for investigation. These included
damage to property and cases where soldiers used weapons
against the German populace, particularly woman and old
men. Maljarov demanded the severest punishments for those
who breached army discipline, and ordered divisional prose-
cutors and investigating judges 'to visit villages in person at
any time of day or night and arrest these louts'. Maljarov reit-
erated: 'In the Red Army, any action that harms the civilian
population is totally unacceptable, and using weapons against
women and old men is a criminal act – and those who are
found guilty will be severely punished.' One or two show
trials were to be held immediately to get the message across.

Lieutenant Vasily Ustyugov of the Third Soviet Shock
Army recalled that in his unit stricter discipline was
imposed quickly and effectively: 'tough new measures were
introduced – and our soldiers were firmly brought to order'.
But the bigger picture was more complex.

Other Soviet soldiers were bewildered by the sudden
change in direction. 'We received fresh orders,' recalled
Private Gennady Shutz, 'that now said we were a liberating
army, liberating the German people from Fascism – and that
we must treat their civilians as we would our own. But try
explaining this to ordinary Russian soldiers, who had relatives hanged or shot, and homes destroyed, telling them that
they must now put all this on one side. It was nigh impossible! Our troops were indignant, saying: "Why am I supposed to forget what the Germans have done to my land and
family?" It was a very painful transition.'

Ilya Ehrenburg himself now decided to clarify his position,
explaining in an article, 'Knights of Justice', that it had never
been his intention that Soviet soldiers should kill children or
rape women. Some Soviet soldiers viewed this declaration

with incomprehension or cynical disdain. Private Vladimir Tsoglin wrote from East Prussia on 14 February 1945: 'And if you now say to a fellow soldier, "Listen, comrade, you don't have to kill those Germans . . .", he would look up, eyebrows raised, and say "Are you no longer a Russian? They stole my wife and daughter from me." And he'd shoot. And he'd be right.'

Even supporters of Ehrenburg's clarified viewpoint struggled to surrender fully their right to revenge. One Soviet officer – Vasily Rogov – wrote to Ehrenburg from 'accursed Germany', agreeing that killing of civilians was not the answer: 'We should not do that,' Rogov affirmed, 'since we are better than they are and were raised in the Soviet spirit.' But then he continued: 'But how to make them feel and understand what we, our wives, children and old people lived through and are living through. I understand that the expression "an eye for an eye" does not need to be taken literally . . . But we should abase them in some way, put them on their knees in such a way that remaining among the living is worse than being under the earth. It seems to me that this would be very just.'

The head of the political department of the First Belorussian Front, Lieutenant General Sergei Galadzhev, noted: 'It must be said frankly that there are people in the Front's units who cannot resign themselves to changes in attitudes to the Germans. They are above all those whose families had suffered seriously from the Germans' atrocities, and who still entertain feelings of personal revenge.' And a report from the Front's military prosecutor, while observing 'a change in the attitude of Red Army personnel to German civilians', and that 'cases of shooting, theft and rape had decreased considerably', acknowledged that such cases still regularly occurred.

A real campaign had been initiated to turn from the path

of vengeance. It was flawed, and never fully successful. But the effort was being made nonetheless. Lieutenant Andrei Eshpai of the Soviet 146th Infantry Division said: 'We had seen the devastation unleashed by the enemy, and knew of atrocities committed by our own soldiers. We began to reach out to German civilians, to feed them from our field kitchens, to offer them protection. We tried to be different.'

Private Zoya Lukyanenko was one of hundreds of thousands of women fighting with the Red Army. She said: 'I felt such sorrow for our people in Belorussia. The Germans were shooting and killing everybody – burning villages. I wanted revenge. But when I entered Germany, and saw the state the children were in – alone and starving in devastated towns and cities – that feeling changed. My heart went out to those defenceless children.'

The story of the Red Army in Germany is a mosaic of such personal experiences. Its soldiers carried an overwhelming burden of rage and grief, and some expressed these emotions in the most terrible and destructive fashion. But many others renounced the right to vengeance, and pulled away from the brink. This was by no means universal, but in such terrible circumstances it was remarkable that it took place at all. Amid the agony of this war, Soviet soldiers abandoned the brittle self-justification of revenge, and searched for something else – something that would not harm the innocent, something that might take away a near-unbearable pain.

Soviet private Georgi Kudryashenko was stationed near the city of Königsberg. 'A gang of little children came to our door,' he remembered. 'One of the women in our unit gave them some bread. I turned to her angrily, saying "How can you help the children of our enemy?" But she replied: "I am a mother too – how could I refuse them?"'

Some Soviet troops had no compassion at all for a defeated

enemy. 'The hearts of our men have turned to stone,' Private Vladimir Tsoglin wrote from East Prussia. But for Georgi Kudryashenko, when his comrade reached out to German children, he found to his surprise that his anger began to lessen.

'How could I refuse them?' Thousands of German children were now homeless and starving in East Prussia. Kudryashenko had always loathed the enemy. At first he was indignant, then nonplussed. And then his heart began to open.

'I stood there, deeply moved,' he said. 'Throughout the war, I had carried such a weight – it had hardened within me. And now, for the first time, it began to go – the hatred, the bitterness, everything.'

10

Fortress Cities

'THERE WAS A MOOD of exhilaration,' recalled Mark Slavin, editor of the Soviet Eighth Guards Army newspaper, 'as we rolled across Poland. Intelligence reports warned us that Germans were to the left of us, to the right – but still we advanced. Our army commander, Lieutenant General Vasily Chuikov, told me: "We have learnt how to fight from our enemy. We are doing what they did to us in 1941 – moving fast, breaking through German rear positions, creating panic and crushing all opposition."' It was a Soviet Blitzkrieg.

As Red Army soldiers had prepared for the final assault on Hitler's Third Reich, they had struggled with their own deeply felt emotions: rage and hatred towards the enemy, and a burning desire for revenge. But they had felt the consequences of this rage: the breakdown of military discipline, atrocities against the German civilian population, looting and rape. As many recoiled from this and tried to find a different way to fight, one that did not descend into a vortex of darkness, a different question began to form in the minds of Soviet commanders, officers and soldiers. What was motivating the Germans to fight against them with such steely determination?

On 30 January 1945 Hitler made his last broadcast to the German nation. He told his people: 'However grave the crisis may be at the moment, through our own unshakeable will, our readiness for sacrifice and our own strengths, we will overcome everything. It will not be Central Asia that will win this war but Europe – led by this nation – which for 1,500 years has defended, and will continue to defend, Europe against the East.'

Hitler thus defined the last battle against the Red Army as a race war against the Slavic *Untermenschen*, and had given the Germans what he regarded as a sacred and historic mission, to protect Europe from the threat from the East. Red Army officers who read the translated text of this broadcast saw it as both delusional and highly dangerous. 'We found its content quite astonishing,' said Mark Slavin. 'And we wondered how many of the German people were still under their leader's dark spell.'

Phrases such as 'fanatical resistance' and 'absolute resistance' were now a watchword among Nazi officials. Men such as Erich Koch, the Gauleiter of East Prussia, made appeals to a historic destiny for the German people, even as that people was being obliterated by war. And they reinforced their decrees with draconian punishments for all those who deserted, retreated without permission or lacked the will for the struggle ahead.

And that struggle now took an increasingly fanatical shape. In the path of Soviet troops were Polish and German cities that Hitler had designated fortresses. Ulrich de Maizière, a staff officer in the operations section of German Army High Command, said: 'Hitler became possessed by the idea that you never surrendered any place voluntarily. He would suddenly designate a city as a fortress. All that actually meant was that the commander was obliged to hold the city to the last man. But if you think of a fortress in terms of well-prepared defences or supplies, there was nothing like that.'

De Maizière added:

Hitler was by this time a very sick man, with severe shaking
paralysis in one arm, a shuffling gait . . . But he had not lost his
'demonic charisma'. He was a man who had always excessively
identified with what he regarded as the destiny of the German
people, and was now living this out in the most destructive of
ways. He was convinced – and I heard him say it – that if
National Socialism failed, the German people would not survive. There would be an utter disintegration. So any measure
that postponed that end – however wasteful in human life – was
seen as justified.

To Soviet soldiers, such fanaticism was hard to fathom.
From a military point of view, it was unclear to them why
Hitler was relying on fortresses at all. Stalingrad had been
described as a fortress, and it had become a graveyard for the
German Sixth Army. In 1944 the Führer had designated a
series of Belorussian towns as fortresses, but his policy had
merely hastened the annihilation of German Army Group
Centre. Yet many of the enemy were still reluctant to
capitulate, even in the most hopeless of situations.

On 9 January 1943 surrender terms had been offered to the
surrounded German Sixth Army at Stalingrad. They had
been declined. A year later, a surrender offer had been made
to the German troops surrounded in the Korsun pocket in
the southern Ukraine. There was no response to that either.
In October 1944 Army Group North had been surrounded
by Soviet forces in the Courland Peninsula in Latvia. It continued resisting with dogged determination, with supplies
brought in by sea by the German Kriegsmarine, and had
repelled a series of assaults by the Soviet Second Baltic Front.

Wehrmacht officer Hans Jürgen Hartmann described a
remarkable pep talk by General Fritz-Hubert Gräser, the
commander of the Fourth Panzer Army, shortly before

the Soviet Vistula–Oder offensive of January 1945: 'He fired all of us up and filled us with fresh hope,' Hartmann said.

> He told us about huge increases in armaments production – never had so many tanks and aircraft been built, so much ammunition made, so many new guns sent to the front. The Red Army could throw what it liked at us. Panzers and reserve divisions were deployed in depth. New weapons were being produced, and resignation was spreading among the Russians and Americans in view of their huge losses. We enjoyed the advantage of shorter lines of communication, and this was increasingly having an effect. Our enemies were having endless supply problems. The time of setbacks was past – in short, who did not want to believe in ultimate victory?

It is quite astonishing to hear this military summary, but Hartmann concluded: 'It was truly intoxicating listening to him – the production figures alone were so incredible that it seems a turning point has actually been reached. I was inspired. If a German commander reveals such numbers to his officers, then those figures carry authority and there is reason for fresh hope. So let the Russians come then!'

Now the Russians were coming. As they moved across Poland and into Germany, the Red Army was faced by an array of different military formations, some of which did not seem to be regular army units at all. They were particularly bemused by the Volkssturm, the people's militia mobilized by Goebbels, and alarmed by the fanaticism that seemed to spawn it. In early February 1945 the political newsletter of the Soviet Fifth Guards Tank Army ran material for its soldiers on the Volkssturm's composition and also its underlying ideology. Red Army soldiers were told that it was a call to arms for all men between the ages of sixteen and sixty, who were encouraged to defend the Fatherland by any means possible. In their oath of loyalty to the Führer they swore to die in battle rather than surrender. They were also linked to the SS and to the Hitler Youth.

The Germans were mass-producing bazookas that were effective at close range against tanks, and required little training to use. Despite initial fears about this weaponry, Soviet intelligence soon assessed the broader military value of the Volkssturm as negligible. In the German capital, first efforts to mobilize the Volkssturm and to construct city defences were far from impressive.

On 4 February Horst Lange wrote: 'Makeshift fortifications are being thrown up around the city, hastily, haphazardly. These defences are worth next to nothing.' The following day Lange, who had been blinded in one eye during the Moscow offensive in 1941, was summoned to the Volkssturm. He was left distinctly unimpressed: 'For the first time I am back in military service again,' he noted in his diary.

> The jargon that is being used shows a distorted and tenuous grasp on reality – far removed from the actual progress of the war. Any layman can see from our battlefield positions on a situation map that there can be no more miracles. But propaganda and lies carry the day. We did training with bazookas and other weapons. Our instructors presented a sorry sight. The sergeants and non-commissioned officers were incapable of using a machine gun, and had no grasp of how it worked. But I was struck by some of the catch phrases. One began: 'When you are lying on the Potsdamer Platz, and five T-34s come rolling round the corner . . .'

On 6 February Lange recorded: 'Laughable makeshift barricades and tank traps are being scraped together by the Volkssturm. We use the junk and rubble of bombed houses. Around me, elderly men are carrying rusty guns on strings, barrel down. They seem proud of their pea-shooters. The first signs of the front-line fighting: filthy soldiers, draped in camouflage gear, wounded men, with blood-soaked bandages, dented, mud-splattered vehicles.' Lange concluded: 'A dull, damp, hazy sky hovers over our dying city.'

The military news was grim. On 9 February the US XXI Corps and French First Army finally reduced the Colmar pocket – the last outpost held by Germany west of the Rhine. Allied bombing raids were inflicting terrible damage on the German capital. The following day Horst Lange took a walk through Berlin. 'Indescribable scenes of destruction,' he began. 'Barricades up on the Potsdam Bridge, gaping craters everywhere and smashed, burned-out tram cars litter the streets.' A particular detail caught his eye: 'On the Kochstrasse – a fallen, plaster angel. It plunged from a cornice with the palm branch of peace in its hand and now lies bedded in the rubble.'

But regular army units were still fighting with discipline and the SS with an ideological and race hatred of its Russian foe. As Red Army soldiers entered Germany at the end of January 1945, and some Soviet troops committed terrible atrocities against the German civilian population, Hitler's regime began to build on people's fear of the Russians. On 10 February the Nazi newspaper *Völkischer Beobachter* proclaimed: 'Germany's fate now depends on the enemy biting on granite. He will flood back to the east in disarray once he has been convincingly taught that he can never conquer Germany . . . This year is a supreme test for our nation. Let iron necessity fill every soldier, every Volkssturm man and every woman and child. Whatever we must endure and sacrifice – be it life itself – we would lose anyway if we did not stand firm.'

At the Yalta Conference in the Crimea from 4 to 11 February 1945 the leaders of the United Kingdom, the

United States of America and the Soviet Union – President Franklin D. Roosevelt, Prime Minister Winston Churchill and General Secretary Joseph Stalin – agreed on securing the unconditional surrender of Nazi Germany, and that after the war Germany and Berlin would be divided into four occupied zones. But the Red Army had to get to Berlin first. Lange commented: 'And so approaches the final confrontation with the enemy we fear the most. And we send out German infantry to face Russian tanks.'

On 13 February 1945 the Hungarian capital Budapest unconditionally surrendered to General Rodion Malinovsky's Second Ukrainian Front after a bitter siege and desperate street fighting. The Red Army victory was marred by violence towards the civilian population, and rape. Within the Reich, German infantry – along with the few tanks that could be mustered – were still resisting strongly. Fierce fighting was going on in two fortress cities – Poznan and Breslau.

'We were racing across Poland,' Captain Anatoly Mereshko said, 'and we had been allocated a clear line of advance – a "corridor" – that we would push forward along, without straying into the path of other armies. But Chuikov had already developed a habit of disobeying these instructions.' Chuikov ordered the Eighth Guards Army to seize the Polish town of Lodz, although it was 6 kilometres inside the Sixty-Ninth Army's own corridor – taking advantage of the slowness of his neighbour's advance. 'Lodz was a success,' Mereshko continued. 'The Germans were caught completely by surprise and put up little effective resistance. We were welcomed into the town as liberators.'

Emboldened by this, Chuikov now resolved to seize the major Polish city of Poznan – although it was even further, some 11 or 12 kilometres, into the Sixty-Ninth Army's corridor, and he had no right to be there at all. Chuikov should have kept all his forces together and pushed on to the River Oder as fast as possible. But he believed he could capture Poznan in hours and present the First Belorussian Front with another fait accompli. This time things went badly wrong.

On the evening of 21 January Mereshko was summoned to Chuikov's HQ. He was told to pass the message on to divisional commanders that a quick night-time assault would be made on Poznan. 'Our reconnaissance had been poor,' Mereshko admitted. 'We thought there was only a small German garrison, and we failed to pick up the city's string of fortifications – which had been well camouflaged, and did not show up on aerial photographs. We blundered straight into a trap.'

Poznan lay on the main route from Warsaw to Berlin, and within it was an SS police force and a mass of highly motivated cadets from a German infantry training school. There were far more troops than Chuikov had bargained for, sheltering in a string of forts and an impressive citadel. Lieutenant General Chuikov now found himself fighting his way through a formidable series of obstacles: 'Each fort was ringed by a ditch 10 metres wide and 8 metres deep,' he recalled, 'and the upper works were sufficiently strong to provide reliable protection against heavy artillery fire.'

Here Hitler's 'fortress strategy' actually corresponded to some kind of reality. A quick assault turned into weeks of city fighting. To his credit, Chuikov, who had created storm groups two and a half years earlier, at Stalingrad, reorganized his forces, deployed storm groups and assault forces in Poznan, and found the right tactical methods to combat the Germans. On 18 February Red Army troops mounted a powerful attack on Poznan's citadel. Redoubts were neutralized by flame-throwers and explosives, and an assault bridge built across the protective flooded ditch. 'For our attack on the citadel itself we had to use armour-piercing shells,' recalled Major General Georgi Khetagurov, commander of the Soviet 242nd Rifle Division, 'as ordinary shells simply bounced off the walls. We concentrated our guns as if we were assembling a battering ram.' There were still problems. 'Even then, the citadel gates could not be blown up by our artillery,' Captain Anatoly Mereshko recalled, 'so we floated over barrels filled with explosives.' With a mixture of skill and improvisation Soviet troops finally fought their way into the citadel. Its garrison surrendered on 22 February – allowing Red Army Day on the 23rd to be a proper holiday for Chuikov's exhausted soldiers.

Stefan Doernberg remembered that after the surrender of Poznan General Chuikov wanted to question Major General Ernst Mattern, the German commander of the citadel. 'The interrogation was brief,' Doernberg recalled. 'Chuikov was in a hurry, and he passed him over to the Special Propaganda Unit, where I was told to question him more thoroughly.'

'Mattern looked at me rather quizzically,' Doernberg continued.

> I was after all just a very young officer, and he was a general. He asked me what my rank was, and why I spoke German so well. I replied that I knew German from my childhood, without going into any details. Then he gathered himself, a smile playing across his lips, and announced: 'Would you like to know the real reason for our surrender? You see, we could have defended the citadel a lot longer – but one of your artillery shells destroyed our main water pipe and I couldn't take my morning shower. That's why I ordered the garrison to surrender.' Needless to say, I chose not to pass this information to my superiors. But at least his sense of humour had survived Poznan intact.

The full record of the interrogation survives, and after this exchange of pleasantries Mattern was candid. 'Your last

assault broke our will to resist,' he continued. 'I was isolated in the citadel, radio and telephone communication
broke down and I had only 120 men left, many of whom
were wounded. A fire broke out, and we were unable to
extinguish it because of a lack of water. Our position was
hopeless.' When asked for his opinion about the war, he
added: 'After the Red Army crossed the River Vistula the
war was lost for us.' But Mattern and his troops had fought
well, and had held Poznan against Soviet forces for a full
month.

The Red Army was sufficiently concerned about the initial
failure at Poznan to hold a full inquiry into the operation. Its
findings pointed to poor reconnaissance, and an underestima-
tion of the enemy's strength and determination to resist. It
warned that Soviet soldiers were relaxing prematurely after
the tough fighting of the previous year. Chuikov was criticized for creating a situation where two different Soviet
forces – the Eighth Guards and Sixty-Ninth Armies – were
both fighting in the city without proper coordination and
cooperation. It found that on the first day of combat in
Poznan one battalion fielded only sixteen men instead of its
complement of 157 – the remainder were discovered drunk
at the homes of local Polish inhabitants. The artillery did not
cooperate properly with the infantry and did not know
where its targets were. And there was a distinct lack of
knowledge about how tanks and self-propelled guns should
be used in city fighting.

But the report also praised Chuikov for getting a grip on
the battle, improving army discipline and motivation and setting up assault teams – and recommended this as general army
practice. The impact of Chuikov's reorganization of his
forces at Poznan was soon felt all along the front. In February
1945, an order by the Soviet Thirty-Ninth Army in Samland

in East Prussia dealt with the use of storm groups in street fighting – in cooperation with artillery – stating:

> Artillery shall support the storm groups by directly shelling the enemy, when he has established himself in houses, ditches and ruined buildings. The guns will not take up position in streets or crossroads, nor on open ground, to prevent them being knocked out by German machine gunners or snipers. Instead, they will seek out protected emplacements and create fields of fire by smashing through walls. Ground floors will be destroyed by artillery fire to force the enemy to leave the cellars underneath.

The order continued: 'Storm groups should advance out of sight to the external walls of houses, and enter through windows, moving upwards through staircases and chimneys. The middle then upper floors must be occupied first, inconspicuously and silently, weapons at the ready. The group will muster again in the attic, and once the building has been cleared out, proceed to the next enemy strongpoint as quickly as possible.'

Storm groups were popular with Red Army soldiers because they were a more effective way of fighting in towns and cities, and led to far fewer casualties than frontal assaults against well-defended enemy positions. Soviet sergeant Umar Burkhanov – commander of a small anti-tank unit – said: 'Our soldiers were tired of being used as mere cannon-fodder. These new tactics worked well, and saved lives.' But the Nazis' ruthless determination to enforce Hitler's no-surrender strategy led to hard fighting nonetheless.

That February, Yevgeny Yevtushenko remembered attending a poetry reading by Pavel Antokolsky at Moscow University. The room was cold, but the audience sat spellbound as Antokolsky recited 'Son' in a booming yet sonorous voice. In the audience were Red Army servicemen, and the mothers and fathers of those fighting and dying at the front.

On 23 February – Red Army Day – the siege of Poznan had ended; that of Breslau in Upper Silesia had reached a bloody impasse. 'There is stubborn fighting for every house, usually every floor, every cellar every staircase,' wrote Soviet Sixth Army war correspondent Vasily Malinin. 'You have to use all your strength and cunning as a soldier.'

Breslau lay in ruins. One of its defenders, German paratrooper Rudi Christoph, recalled:

> We had practised the techniques of house-to-house fighting in a quiet sector of the front. But what greeted us when we were ordered into battle was appalling. Tottering ruins rose eerily towards the heavens. Entire blocks were shot up and burned out. Pylons, wires, street lamps and the remains of advertising hoardings lay scattered across the street, intermingled with piles of rubble. As we approached the front line we heard the rumble of artillery, and the rattle of machine guns. The roads were lit up by brightly burning houses. We were gripped by a terrible fear, as we saw the grim reality of street fighting against the Red Army.

This was a battle of attrition, and the Red Army was also wearying of it. 'The combat doesn't stop, even for one hour,' war correspondent Vasily Malinin complained in his diary. 'The fighting is hard and stubborn. The enemy does not want to surrender.' Red Army lieutenant Sergei Kravchenko was impressed by the tough professionalism of his soldiers. His force was leavened by veterans, some of whom had fought in the defence of Odessa in the autumn of 1941. In a brief lull in the fighting one of his men picked up an accordion and played a popular folk song. Kravchenko wondered how many of these men would still be alive at the end of the day. 'Death in combat is one of the harsh realities of war,' Kravchenko wrote, 'but it is especially painful when the end of that war is so close.'

The Red Army honed its own street-fighting techniques still further, and more training and instruction were carried out. The Soviet Sixth Army's news-sheet enjoined the troops: 'Danger threatens at every step. Toss a hand grenade around every corner, then advance. A burst of machine-gun fire, then advance again. The next room – hand grenade . . .'

A special leaflet was also issued to all those Red Army units preparing for an assault on the East Prussian city of Königsberg:

> Break into the house in twos – you and your grenade. The grenade first – you after it. The next grenade is already in your hand. In the house, be mindful of the number of rooms, and where the corridors are. In every dark corner – a grenade! Forward with all your might! A burst of machine-gun fire in the corner of every room. Another room – another grenade! Turn – another grenade! Rake the corridors with your machine guns. Have no fear – the initiative is in your hands. Storm even more furiously, even more brutally. More grenades, more bursts of fire at the heads of the enemy.

To improve their effect, infantry units in the storm detachments and storm groups were almost all supplied with automatic weapons, creating a concentration of firepower to which the Germans barely had an answer. In Army Group Vistula's section of the front, a German officer observed of Soviet tactics in Pomerania. 'At least 75 per cent of the Russians had automatic weapons and were very well equipped. The firepower of small Soviet units was always stronger than our own.' He concluded: 'It is striking that in every conversation with German soldiers they refer repeatedly to the greater number of tanks assigned to Red Army units and the superiority of their infantry firepower, which they see as playing a decisive role in battle.'

The Red Army had been wasteful with its soldiers' lives in the past, but was now – at this late stage of the war – making a genuine effort to lessen casualties. In Breslau, alongside hand grenades, the Soviet Sixth Army also hurled propaganda leaflets at the enemy:

> German soldiers – Hitler is your enemy! He began this war of plunder against the world, and has brought the hatred and wrath of all nations down upon Germany as a result of his crimes. Hitler is your enemy. In this criminal war against the freedom-loving peoples of the world, he has killed or crippled millions of Germans and he has made millions of German women widows, millions of children orphans. Hitler is your enemy. He has brought war to the heart of Germany, abandoned German towns and villages to destruction from the air and on land and is now laying your whole country to waste.

Such systematic attempts to combat the Führer's hypnotic grip on his people used the phrase 'Hitler is your enemy' almost as a mantra. Other, more spontaneous efforts were also made. By loudspeaker hailer and leaflets the German defenders of Breslau were promised fair treatment, decent food, delousing facilities and even sex: 'German soldiers come over to us,' one enterprising Red Army political officer broadcast. 'One hundred naked Caucasian women are waiting for you in a sky-blue bed.' Even Breslau's weary defenders smiled. 'It sounded,' wrote forward artillery observer Klaus Franke, 'an extremely attractive offer – in theory at least!' One of Franke's comrades grabbed a megaphone: 'You over there, keep your mouth shut! If you want some action come and join us – we'll kick your arse!'

These efforts to encourage Germans to desert – some

humorous, some carefully crafted – were based on a strong wish to avoid needless loss of life as the war drew to a close. On 24 February 1945 Soviet lieutenant Leonid Bobrov died in action near the East Prussian village of Bonstetten. It was snowing heavily. Bobrov and his men had been ordered to capture the village from the Germans. Bobrov did the rounds with his men, checking on the guns and ammunition. He passed round water from a flask and shared a piece of dry bread with his comrades. Artillery support opened up – the signal for the attack – and the Red Army troops stormed forward and seized the village. Then they pursued the defenders towards the forest.

But the Germans counter-attacked. Tanks and machine gunners emerged from the trees. The Soviet anti-tank weapons opened up, and soon the battlefield was wreathed in smoke. German gunners occupied a water tower and put the Red Army soldiers under sustained and accurate fire. Bobrov and his soldiers did not pull back. The fight went on the whole day. At the end of it, when reinforcements finally arrived, Bobrov had been killed and only nine of his company were left. The young lieutenant would never see the end of the war, precisely as he had once predicted. The village remained in Red Army hands.

On 2 March 1945 Soviet intelligence staff of the First Ukrainian Front warned: 'Despite the hopelessness of the position, signs of a collapse in the enemy's resistance cannot be easily discerned. German army units continue to fight very hard, and general discipline is good. The ordinary soldier is remarkably resilient, does not panic, but rather shows presence of mind in difficult situations.'

A pattern of defiant resistance was emerging. On 9 March the Soviet Fifth Guards Army presented a summary of prisoner interrogations. One captured Wehrmacht soldier had told his captors: 'Our company commander told us we must hold our positions to the last and never retreat. Anyone doing so will be shot. We have a powerful new secret weapon that Hitler will use in the spring to drive back the enemy.' The army's intelligence section set out the question: 'What is the reason for such dogged determination by German soldiers?' – then listed possible explanations: the culture of discipline and obedience in the German armed forces, or that hope still existed for a miraculous change in fortunes. Reasons for that hope might lie in wonder weapons, in a split between the Western Allies and the Soviet Union, or simply in divine providence.

Soviet intelligence was painfully aware that the looting, robbery and rape indulged in by some Russian units had presented Goebbels with a propaganda gift that he had exploited quickly and effectively, and that their army command still had not fully got a grip on the situation. Nevertheless, the Red Army adopted a carrot-and-stick approach. It strengthened its combat techniques and the power of its attacking forces – but also kept trying to encourage German soldiers to desert or surrender.

On the eastern bank of the River Oder, newly promoted Soviet lieutenant Mikhail Borisov was approaching his twenty-first birthday with some trepidation. Borisov's 58th Motorized Rifle Brigade was stationed south of Kustrin. On 22 March 1942 and on the same date the following year the young artillery officer had been wounded in combat. On 22 March 1944 a celebration had been held to defy Borisov's run of bad luck, with music and a group of singers from the Kiev Philharmonic. Festivities were interrupted by a German bombing raid. The shock waves knocked Borisov to the floor, leaving him concussed and buried in debris. On 22 March 1945 Borisov wondered whether he should ignore his birthday completely. But congratulations came in from nearby units, one artillery battery offering to put his position under friendly fire to keep up the tradition. So a modest table was laid and drinks put out. Suddenly a car drew up. It was the regimental commander, Colonel Shapovalov. Furious that no one was manning the lookout post on the roof of the building, he ordered Borisov up there. Five minutes later, the blast from an exploding German shell blew Borisov all the way down again. That evening his comrades gathered by his bedside – in a military hospital.

Celebrations and bonhomie helped alleviate the terrible pressure of the fighting. 'Concert brigades' were raised from theatres across the Soviet Union, and actors, singers and dancers would sometimes entertain the soldiers at the front. Occasionally a mobile cinema booth appeared, and units watched movies – the 'front-line film collections' – in which the chief character easily defeats a series of stupid and comical 'Fritzes'. But more frequently, front-line personnel went without such luxuries. 'There was little time for leisure activities,' said Red Army nurse Vera Kirichenko. 'No dancing or entertainment parties came to visit us. We had a small hospital – that was it.' Soviet signalman Meir Toker added: 'There were a couple of chess sets and several packs of playing cards in the platoon. But people didn't have many cultural demands on the front line. We didn't see books and didn't look for them. People lived one day at a time.'

Yet this run of birthday injuries, and his miraculous escape from the battlefield at Prokhorovka, convinced Borisov that in some strange way fate was watching over him – so many of his fellow soldiers had not survived. On the march through the Ukraine, Borisov had revisited a burial mound where members of his artillery unit had been buried a year earlier, during the retreat from the Germans. The atmosphere was sombre and quiet, and Borisov recalled it in a poem, 'On the Roads of War':

> A part of my soul is burned and bloodied.
> It cannot get used to the nightingale's song.
> I call out –
> Perhaps they will respond;
> Will my friends call back?
> But those friends who were dear to me
> Won't hear a word – nor read a line.
> Memory was frozen
> Along the steppe road;
> In the warm rain
> In the white blizzard
> In the dance of leaves
> And in the hours of recollection
> Lies the silence of the road.

'Memory was frozen,' Borisov wrote. In fighting in East Prussia from January through to the beginning of April 1945, 126,000 Soviet soldiers were lost. Another 80,000 were killed, captured or declared missing during the reduction of Budapest. Red Army losses in eastern Pomerania amounted to 53,000, during the Vistula–Oder operation in Poland around 43,000 and in Silesia 40,000. On the western front, British and US forces had advanced through northern Italy, France and the Low Countries and had reached the Rhine. In the most intense period of fighting, the German Ardennes offensive from 16 December 1944 to 25 January 1945, US casualties had been 19,000 killed and a further 23,000 captured or missing; the British had lost an additional 1,408 men.

Soviet forces were now carefully preparing for another major assault on a fortress city – at Königsberg in East Prussia. The German position was desperate. They were surrounded, cut off and subject to devastating artillery and air strikes.

Again a surrender offer was made. Soviet pilot Yuri Khukhrikov related: 'Their commandant was asked to give up the city. He was warned that we had three air fleets ready to bomb him – a mass of planes, and there would be no quarter shown. If they continued to fight, they had no chance of survival.'

The offer was rejected. Königsberg's garrison of regular troops and Volkssturm still held a narrow land corridor to German soldiers on the Samland peninsula to the west of the city, and the combined strength of these forces was nearly 130,000 men. They would face the assembled might of three Soviet armies, totalling more than a quarter of a million Red Army soldiers, with massive artillery and air support. The Russian preparations were carried out with little secrecy – military vehicles travelled to their positions with headlights blazing and radio messages were sent in the clear [uncoded]. The Germans did not have the resources to hinder their progress, and Soviet commanders understood the psychological value of letting their opponents see the steady build-up of men, equipment and ammunition.

The city was, however, well defended – and, like Poznan, could genuinely be called a fortress. Its nineteenth-century fortifications had been supplemented by anti-tank ditches, trenches and concrete bunkers. 'There were fifteen old forts with massive stone walls encircling Königsberg,' said Red Army lieutenant Isaak Kobylyanskiy. 'A deep, water-filled ditch surrounded each one of them.' Soviet commanders wanted to take Königsberg with fewer casualties than those suffered at Poznan and Breslau. Before launching their assault, the city's defences were subject to remorseless artillery and aerial bombardment.

'Sixty shells from my battery have turned a four-storey house – which the Germans had made into a powerful stronghold – into a pile of stones and rubble,' Lieutenant Nikolai Inozemtsev of the Soviet 16th Guards Artillery Group wrote happily in his diary on 4 April 1945. It was Inozemtsev's birthday – and the successful artillery strike seemed a good omen.

Inozemtsev recalled the thoroughness of Red Army preparations: 'For more than a month my artillery brigade had worked non-stop, making plans of German defences, observing their strongpoints and artillery posts.' General Athanasias Beloborodov, commander of the Soviet Forty-Third Army, described the composition of the Red Army assault forces: 'Three rifle companies – about 250 men – would be supported by ten tanks and self-propelled guns, 20 guns and about 60 mortars,' Beloborodov said. 'We saturated our units with artillery – and prepared strong supporting fire in readiness for our attack.'

On 6 April the Soviet assault on Königsberg began. 'At 9.00 a.m. our rocket launchers opened up,' recalled Soviet private Zoya Lukyanenko. 'They boomed – and the earth shook and burned. We were delighted – then the artillery joined in, and then the bombers. The bombardment went on for three hours, until midday. It was a truly awesome beginning.'

Then the tanks and infantry rolled forward. The Soviet Thirty-Ninth and Forty-Third Armies attacked from the north; the Eleventh Guards Army from the south. For Inozemtsev the occasion was tempered with sadness – his best friend Nikolai Safonov was killed at the beginning of the assault. A few days before the attack the two men had walked down to the Baltic Sea together and talked about childhood, adolescence and a life interrupted by war. Inozemtsev shared his future hopes and plans, and Safonov embraced him warmly: 'Make sure you stay alive!' he had joked. 'Three years front-line fighting,' Inozemtsev wrote, 'and my friend loses his life in one of our last combat operations.'

In the first day's fighting, advancing Red Army soldiers broke through the first defence line and surrounded the two strongest enemy forts. Counter-attacks by German forces on the Samland peninsula were beaten off. The following day, better weather conditions allowed Soviet planes to make precision bombing attacks on key targets.

On 7 April Inozemtsev noted:

Fighting has moved into the southern suburbs of the city. We have excellent air support – there are a massive number of planes overhead. The German defences are inexorably reduced. We are using artillery en masse, bringing down a colossal barrage of fire on specific targets for ten to fifteen minutes before we move in and attack them. We are also using a large number of flame-throwers – if a house has a garrison of one or more Germans they are simply smoked out, there is no need to fight for every floor or for possession of each staircase.

Inozemtsev added proudly: 'It is already clear to everyone that our assault on Königsberg will go down in history as a classic example of storming a big city.'

The battle was harder than Inozemtsev suggested, and mistakes were still made. There were incidents when Red Army artillery observers lost contact with their infantry and called down fire on their own men, and problems manhandling the guns through the rubble. 'It was hard to get our bearings as we approached the centre of Königsberg,' remembered Lieutenant Isaak Kobylyanskiy, an artillery officer in the Soviet Forty-Third Army. 'Our assault groups were regularly stopping to get more information on the enemy's positions and the general combat situation.'

But overall, the Russians were fighting well and they now

refined their assault procedures. Their artillery aimed for the attics and upper floors of enemy strongpoints, to kill or injure his observers and command staff. Engineering units were brought up to help the ground troops. 'The Soviet attack was very well organized,' conceded the German commander of Königsberg, General Otto Lasch, 'and by the second day's fighting we were struggling to hold our defences.'

On 8 April Red Army forces were pushing into the city centre. 'The enemy holds a shrinking strip of land and is under a devastating artillery bombardment,' Inozemtsev recorded. At noon troops of the Soviet Eleventh Guards and Forty-Third Armies linked up, splitting the defenders in two by isolating the city garrison from the troops on the Samland peninsula. The following day the German position quickly became hopeless. In the early afternoon Soviet marshals Alexander Vasilevsky and Konstantin Rokossovsky made another surrender offer to the defenders. It was refused, but a German break-out attempt was then obliterated by Russian air strikes. Shortly before midnight Königsberg's commander, General Lasch, opened negotiations with the Soviet forces.

Red Army casualties were greater than official figures ever acknowledged. The combat records for the Forty-Third Army show it suffered far more than the 1,100 losses publicly admitted. They reveal that in four days' fighting from 6 to 9 April 1945 9,230 soldiers were killed and 34,249 wounded. But the storming of Königsberg was a real achievement nonetheless. On 10 April the remnants of the defending garrison formally surrendered. 'Königsberg is ours!' exclaimed Inozemtsev.

Germany's East Prussian bastion had fallen. 'It is a sad sight,' Inozemtsev said. 'Miles of burnt-out, ruined buildings.' 'We have lost our largest fortress and outpost in the east,' General Lasch wrote. 'The fall of Königsberg will hasten the collapse of the Reich.' Hitler was furious that the fortress city had surrendered. He condemned General Lasch to death *in absentia*, and arrested his family.

The Red Army began gearing up for its final assault – on Berlin. It was also girding itself for a new assault on the loyalty of Hitler's Germany. Nikolai Inozemtsev was proud of his army's performance in Königsberg. But he said of the atrocities he had witnessed in East Prussia: 'Each rape debases our army and every soldier in it.'

Inozemtsev had seen a flurry of orders prohibiting arson, robbery and harm to German civilians. But he was struck by the power of Soviet war journalist Ilya Ehrenburg's 'revenge' articles, which had embedded themselves in the consciousness of ordinary Red Army soldiers. He wrote: 'It will require much energy from our commanders and officers to erase the effect of this.'

On 14 April 1945, two days before the Red Army launched its attack on the German capital, an article in *Pravda* appeared openly criticizing Ilya Ehrenburg, the prophet of revenge. It accused him of presenting an oversimplified view of the war, and of failing to distinguish between ardent supporters of the Nazi regime and ordinary German civilians. The article was written with Stalin's approval, and reflected a change of direction by the Soviet regime. The Russians had committed terrible atrocities in East Prussia, Silesia and Pomerania that had damaged their cause and strengthened the German will to resist. The Red Army would now make a real effort to treat German civilians and POWs with proper respect.

Hitler was preparing for a last stand, where his soldiers and people would be sacrificed on the funeral pyre of National Socialism.

11

Apocalypse Berlin

T HE BATTLE FOR Berlin began on the Seelow Heights, on the River Oder, on 16 April 1945. Here Hitler's regular troops made a last stand against the Red Army. The high ground on the west bank of the Oder was the last natural obstacle before the Russians reached Berlin. The Wehrmacht was attempting to shield the German capital – but it was desperately short of troops, ammunition and equipment, and the Russians had devastating air superiority. The Führer exhorted his troops to fight to the last man.

German commander General Gotthard Heinrici was a master of defensive warfare, with years of experience fighting on the eastern front. Although his resources were limited, he had fortified the Seelow Heights effectively, and the Red Army underestimated these defences. 'This terrible clash will always stay in my memory,' said Captain Anatoly Mereshko of the Soviet Eighth Guards Army. 'The Germans resisted with great determination, and we suffered considerable losses. The snow was melting, and the terrain was swampy and heavily waterlogged. Our plan was to hit the enemy hard – and overwhelm his defences beyond the Oder within a day. But it cost more than three days of fighting before we broke the Germans.'

Lieutenant General Vasily Chuikov, commander of the Eighth Guards Army, and Marshal Georgi Zhukov, commander of the First Belorussian Front, gathered at Chuikov's command post on the Reitwein Spur to watch the progress of the battle. Chuikov had sent Mereshko to meet Zhukov and take him to the HQ. 'I drove off,' Mereshko recalled,

> and soon encountered a line of trucks heading along the road. It was Zhukov and his staff – and the first thing I noticed was that they had their headlights on. I asked Zhukov to turn them off, because the area was periodically shelled by German long-range guns – on two occasions they had made V-2 rocket strikes along this very section of road. Zhukov was upbeat. 'Soon, we will blind the Fascists with our searchlights – and they will be completely finished with,' he declared. At that moment German artillery opened up, and two of Zhukov's staff cars were hit. The headlights were then switched off at speed.

Marshal Georgi Zhukov had a lot to think about. Stalin had entrusted him with the responsibility of smashing his way through to Berlin and ending the war. Yet preparations for the offensive were rushed. In March many of Zhukov's forces had been supporting Marshal Rokossovsky's Second Belorussian Front in Pomerania. It had been a colossal logistical operation to get them back in time, and bring in all the necessary artillery support. Stalin was once again toying with his commanders, for while offering Zhukov the prize of Berlin, he also dangled it in front of Marshal Ivan Konev, whose First Ukrainian Front was attacking the Germans along the Rivers Oder and Neisse, south of Zhukov's forces. Konev's original role in the planned attack – discussed by Stalin's High Command in early April 1945 – was simply to protect Zhukov's southern flank. But now the Soviet leader began to drop hints that if Zhukov moved too slowly Konev could wheel his forces towards the German capital and take the city himself.

There were also international complications. Although the Yalta Conference in February 1945 had been constructive, Stalin remained suspicious of his Western allies. He feared – and let Zhukov know this – that US troops might yet make a dash for Berlin. And finally, there was the simple yet over-whelmingly powerful desire of every Red Army soldier to end the war as quickly as possible and return home.

Marshal Zhukov was uneasy. Stefan Doernberg of the Soviet Eighth Guards Army's interrogation unit remem-bered discussing the testimony of one German officer, captured the day before the offensive was launched. The German had expressed complete faith in Hitler and his wonder weapons, which he still believed would win the war. 'It seemed insane to us,' Doernberg said, 'but it was a dangerous insanity, one that could cost many of our soldiers' lives.' Now Zhukov authorized a surrender offer to Heinrici's troops. They were warned of the force of the offensive, and the hopelessness of their position. Doernberg's first thought was that broadcasting it would remove any element of secrecy from the assault. But Zhukov replied: 'It will be worth it if we avoid a bloodbath here.'

Zhukov was aware that his reconnaissance of the enemy's position was inadequate, but he still hoped to overwhelm his foe. He gambled on a massive artillery strike to overawe Heinrici's soldiers. At 5.30 a.m. on 16 April 300 guns opened up on the Eighth Guards Army's section of the front. The bombardment was followed by a dramatic surprise, as 142 huge searchlights were switched on to dazzle an already shell-shocked enemy and light up the ground for the advancing Soviet troops.

'What could we do in that situation – absolutely nothing!' said German corporal Antonius Schneider. 'Soviet artillery fire was so intense it literally ploughed the earth in front of us, leaving my men covered in so much dirt that I could no longer recognize some of them. And when the searchlights were turned on, it was no longer possible to see where to aim our guns – it was as if the whole bank of the Oder had become a wall of fire.'

But the intensity of the artillery bombardment threw a huge spume of mud and dust into the air. The searchlights – powerful as they were – were unable to penetrate it. Mereshko said: 'The dust cloud that had arisen above the German lines reflected the beams back at us, dazzling our own soldiers.'

The bombardment did not pulverize the Germans as Zhukov had hoped. Instead, his infantry attacks ran into stubborn resistance. At 9 a.m. Mereshko was urgently summoned to the top of the spur. Zhukov and Chuikov were at the highest observation point, 40 metres above the Oder flood plain, looking out at the developing battle. Zhukov had a host of orders to deliver. The telephone cable was down, and for reasons of security radio transmission could not be used, so Mereshko was to deliver the instructions personally to Soviet corps and divisional commanders. 'Zhukov was angry,' Mereshko said, 'and used clipped, hard-toned phrases, each one accompanied by a threat. I was to find the XXIX Infantry Corps commander, and tell him to organize the storming of the Seelow Heights by 3.00 p.m., or he would be demoted and lose his Hero of the Soviet Union award. Further threats were made against the commanders of the 47th and 82nd Guards Divisions.'

'The order was duly delivered,' Mereshko continued, 'but its recipients all made the same point. Our reconnaissance had belatedly discovered that the main German position was on the reverse side of the Seelow Heights, and this had not been suppressed by our artillery barrage. The enemy's defences were still intact. Without repeated, powerful air strikes, it would be impossible to take the Heights.'

The German commander of Army Group Vistula, General Heinrici, had arranged his troops with considerable skill, making an unorthodox but highly effective deployment and putting the bulk of his soldiers behind the summit of the Seelow Heights. As soon as Red Army troops reached the high ground the Germans would open up from concealed, camouflaged positions with heavy machine guns and bazookas. Behind them, an armoured train was moving to and fro, ready to hit any Soviet combat groups that attempted to scale the summit.

The Red Army's last great offensive had not begun well, and everyone was feeling the strain. Mereshko was unable to reach Zhukov by phone to request the air strikes – the telephone cables had still not been reconnected – and when he returned to Chuikov's HQ the marshal was no longer there. 'Zhukov had lost patience. He ordered that our tank armies be thrown in behind our advancing infantry,' Mereshko said ruefully. 'Then he abruptly left.'

The original combat plan was to withhold Soviet armour until the infantry had taken the Heights and then strike the retreating Germans in the flanks. Soviet captain Vladimir Kravchenko was a company commander in the Second Tank Army. 'Fighting at the Seelow Heights was incredibly hard,' Kravchenko recalled. 'The German defences were very strong – they had prepared a whole series of obstacles, including concealed ditches. Nobody expected this kind of resistance. When our tanks were committed early on the afternoon of 16 April we took serious losses.' There was not the space to use tanks at this stage of the offensive, as only two good roads across the Oder flood plain remained, and they were being fully used by the Russian infantry. As soon as Soviet tanks and artillery moved off these roads, they became bogged down in the swampy ground.

The battle on the Seelow Heights would last more than three days and cost the lives of more than 30,000 Soviet soldiers. Many more lives would still be lost before Berlin fell to the Red Army.

'I have never seen so many dead bodies as I did on the Seelow Heights,' said Lieutenant Stefan Doernberg of the Eighth Guards Army. 'Thousands upon thousands of Soviet soldiers were killed on that small area of land. The most terrible thing was that these people were fighting and dying knowing that the war would be over in another couple of weeks.'

On 19 April Zhukov's troops at last broke through the German lines. There was now little in place to halt the attack on Berlin, although the Führer was throwing everything he could into the breach – SS units, foreign volunteers, the Volkssturm and even the Hitler Youth.

A day later, Stalin ordered his commanders to improve their treatment of German POWs and civilians. The Soviet leader was aware that Red Army atrocities had strengthened the Wehrmacht's will to resist. And now his soldiers were approaching Germany's capital. 'On 21 April we reached Berlin's outskirts,' recalled Soviet lieutenant Vladimir Zhilkin.

> I was engaged in artillery reconnaissance, searching for enemy strongpoints, and concealed positions for the placement of our guns. In one of the streets, a wide avenue, we saw some people emerging from a basement. They didn't look like soldiers, and using our field glasses we realized that they were teenage boys. At the time we had no inkling of the existence of the Hitler Youth, let alone that they had been recruited by the Nazis to help defend the city. It was our first encounter

with them. They were assembling in front of us, each of them armed with a bazooka. They were dangerous weapons for kids to be carrying. Fourteen-year-olds, maybe younger, and they were marching on us. Our infantry was at a loss – what should we do?

We asked our commanding officers – but they had no idea either. They replied: 'It's up to you – you decide. Scare them – perhaps they will run away.' So we fired several shots above their heads. It had no effect at all. If anything they were approaching even faster, at a run. We fired into the ground in front of them. It had the same effect. And then they started firing at us. We unleashed a volley at point-blank range. Some were killed – others fled, into basements of surrounding houses. And that was how we beat off their so-called attack.

Soviet soldiers were genuinely shocked. 'There were even boys of twelve fighting against us,' said Captain Anatoly Mereshko. 'I saw them with my own eyes – and I saw the bodies of those we killed. We had to shoot them. They were armed with bazookas, and these were very powerful anti-tank weapons.'

Seventeen-year-old Helmut Altner was part of a Hitler Youth detachment. He and his friends had been forced from their homes and ordered to join SS and Volkssturm units. Altner said:

We first saw action in the north-eastern part of the city. Most of our detachment was killed by Soviet machine-gun fire because we had to attack across open ground. We endured two days and two nights of city fighting – and during that time our position changed hands four times. That finished off another group of us. Then the Russians started bombarding us with their rocket missiles. We had had enough – we just wanted to finish and go home. But instead, we were ordered to join another defence position beyond the canal. My platoon leader – who refused –

was strung up on the nearest tree by the SS. He was fifteen years old.

Altner added: 'It made me sick. I had seen more than enough death. Our young people knew only killing and murder. Burnt people, asphyxiated people from the hail of bombs had become part of the scene. But to have to watch teenagers being killed because they had sought a way out of this insanity was beyond my strength.'

The attack on Berlin was led by troops of Marshal Zhukov's First Belorussian Front, although units from Marshal Konev's First Ukrainian Front were also in the city. The total Red Army strength was around 1,500,000 soldiers. They were supported by the First and Second Polish Armies – 180,000 Polish troops fought alongside Soviet forces in the German capital. These soldiers had supported the Red Army in the great Vistula–Oder offensive in January 1945 and in the vicious street fighting in Poznan, and they would sustain substantial casualties in the battle for Berlin, with some 7,200 killed and another 3,800 missing in action. But Red Army losses would be more than ten times this figure.

Berlin's commander, General Hellmuth Weidling, was struggling to organize a coherent defence. 'The city was divided into eight outer and one inner sector,' Weidling recalled. Communication was poor, and no regular army units were in place. Volkssturm, police and anti-aircraft units amounted to about 90,000 men. More German soldiers, recalled from the western front, and SS units were now arriving in Berlin, however, and fighting with fierce determination. The rubble-strewn streets (the aftermath of the Allied air raids) were creating favourable conditions for the defenders. The Red Army found it difficult to move its tanks, which were committed to the battle en masse, and they became an easy target for the defenders' bazookas.

'As we entered Berlin our losses grew steadily,' said Anatoly Mereshko.

> Moving such a large number of tanks into the city meant high casualties among their crews. The roads were strewn with rubble, and the tanks lost their main advantage – their manoeuvrability. They formed long lines on one, two or three parallel streets, and slowly advanced down them. They were an easy target: they were fired at from the first, second and third floors of buildings – and even from the cellars.
>
> We were forced to change our plans. Firstly, tanks were not to move without infantry support. Secondly – and more importantly – our tanks were instructed to work together in groups of four or five. The first tank usually opened fire at cellars and first floors; the tank after it covered the second floor and higher up. There were three-, four-, even five-storey houses in the centre of Berlin. With the upper floors, the tank on the right shot at the left-hand side of the street, the tank on the left did the same on the right. This model of cooperation and coordination within a tank group allowed us to locate weapon emplacements in time – especially if enemy soldiers were armed with bazookas – and destroy them in the cellars, the lower floors or attics. Then our losses declined dramatically.

The Eighth Guards Army pushed its way forward. 'Fighting raged continuously around the clock,' Red Army private Vladimir Abyzov recorded. 'The artillery roared and thundered. The mortars barked and machine guns fired constantly. The whole city was in flames. Dense foul smoke curled over the roofs and hung heavily over the streets. It seeped into houses and basements – there was no air to breathe. Yet on we ran, across streets and yards, throwing our grenades into the empty eye-sockets of the windows.'

It was a hellish landscape. 'What do I remember of Berlin?' said Lieutenant Vasily Ustyugov of the Soviet 150th Division. 'It was dark and gloomy – there was no functioning electricity, no water and always the smell of burning. The street fighting was tough. The combat situation was always changing and the enemy was all around us, with machine-gun units, snipers and bazooka carriers.' Conditions were chaotic. 'There were no clear front lines,' Abyzov continued, 'nor carefully worked-out combat missions. If we were on the first floor of a house, that was our front line. Theoretically the ground floor would be our rear position. But within five or ten minutes all would be confusion again. The Germans would appear on the ground floor; the second floor would be engulfed by a sea of fire. The infantry manual is not much use in such conditions.'

And yet, Red Army skill and improvisation were mastering these conditions. 'We are moving towards the centre of Berlin,' Soviet colonel Pyotr Sebelev wrote on 25 April. 'There is constant gunfire – fire and smoke is everywhere. Our soldiers creep through courtyards and run from building to building. The Germans were shooting at our tanks from windows and doors, but we have adopted a clever tactic. Our tanks move away from the centre of the street and advance along its sides, alternating their fire – some shooting on the right side, some on the left. The enemy is running from us.'

Other Germans stood and fought to the bitter end. 'Every fight we had in the city was tough,' said Soviet reconnaissance scout Mikhail Shinder. 'The Nazis came across as fanatics – contemptuous of death. One of the Hitler Youth had severed his leg. It was bleeding profusely, but he still continued to shoot at us.' Shinder remembered the bitter battle for the HQ of the Berlin Police Department. 'It was a very strong building,' he said, 'and it was defended ferociously. Two battalions of our storm troops were trying to take it for two days, but our dead were lying in heaps on the square next to the wrecks of burnt-out T-34s.'

Shinder's platoon fought its way round the building and broke into a side entrance. 'We began moving up the main staircase,' he recalled, 'tossing grenades into each room, followed by bursts of machine-gun fire.' By the time the Red Army soldiers had reached the first floor the Germans had counter-attacked, armed with machine guns, grenades and bazookas. Everything was on fire. Shinder's storm group finally took the building. His 36-man platoon had been reduced to 9.

Soviet assault groups were fighting round the clock. 'Days and nights of street fighting,' said Red Army machine gunner Matthew Gershman.

> There was shooting from every window, from every basement – and the roar of artillery fire all around us. On the streets we faced barricades, falling masonry, bazooka fire and the ever-present threat of snipers. Days merged into each other. One evening we captured a theatre and found a working piano. I went over to play it, sat down on the stool and immediately fell asleep! The men were delighted, and as we pushed into the heart of Berlin I received a barrage of requests for more music recitals.

Mikhail Shinder's Soviet 150th Division was now advancing towards the Reichstag. Many of its soldiers were fighting with courage and resourcefulness in atrocious conditions. A minority were not. Shinder found a comrade who had stolen a mass of rings and watches from German civilians sheltering in an underground station: 'I walked up to him,' Shinder remembered, 'snatched his pouch – where he had collected his "trophies" – and returned them to their owners.'

Shinder recalled a company commander, a decent man, whose behaviour had totally changed on German soil. Army disciplinary orders had no effect on him. 'He got drunk after one clash in Berlin,' Shinder said, 'raped a German woman and then shot her and the rest of her family.' The man was arrested and put before a military tribunal. He was sentenced to death, although this was later commuted to seven years in the prison camps. The 150th Division had 196 cases before the military prosecutor in Berlin where drunken soldiers had shot and killed one of their own comrades.

These incidents were not typical of most Soviet troops – but they represented the actions of a dangerously out-of-control minority. As Red Army commanders refined their fighting tactics, they sought to improve army discipline and the behaviour of their soldiers. On 25 April Colonel General Nikolai Berzarin was appointed Soviet commandant of Berlin. Fierce fighting was still continuing in the centre of the city, but Marshal Zhukov wanted to help the civilian population. The supply warehouses were on the outskirts of Berlin and many of the city's inhabitants were without food and water. 'On the front line I fought the Germans,' remarked Berzarin, the former commander of the Fifth Shock Army; 'in the rear, I am feeding them!'

His appointment had an immediate impact. On 28 April Soviet lieutenant Vladimir Gelfand wrote in his diary: 'General Berzarin – the former commander of my army – has been appointed commandant of Berlin. He has already sent out an appeal to the civilian population, saying Soviet authorities want a return to a peaceful way of life. The city streets farthest from the fighting are filling with people again.

The Germans wear white armlets. They are losing their fear of us.'

Berzarin worked hard to create orderly conditions in those parts of Berlin held by the Red Army. Rubble was cleared, factories opened and food distribution organized. Local commandants were appointed to supervise soldiers' behaviour and regular military patrols were set up. 'My aim is to drastically curtail looting and illegal conduct,' Berzarin told the army newspaper *Red Star*. 'We must cut down plundering and end violence against the local population.'

'In the courtyards of houses soldiers from the support services are handing out food to the city's population, which is starving,' Soviet Colonel Pyotr Sebelev wrote. Captain Vladimir Gell – a political officer in the Soviet Forty-Seventh Army – remembered:

> As we set up food canteens for the Berliners, and as people gathered round them, on their faces I could see a smile, a shy subdued smile, a smile against the tears – but nevertheless, a smile of hope. I was struck by that. People were happy that the war was ending, that they were still alive. I said, 'We have come not in revenge, but to liberate you.' Some didn't believe us. But we told them: 'No, we won't shoot anyone, we won't banish anyone to Siberia – we want peace.'

It is now known that a number of Red Army soldiers behaved far from peaceably. A Berliner's diary for 29 April recorded the fears of seventeen-year-old Liselotte G: 'Some hundred suicides are said to have occurred today … I wonder if Frau L is still pure, or whether they have violated her too.' The following day her fears had turned into grim reality. She wrote: 'The Russians are here. They are completely drunk. Rapes at night. Not me – but Mother. Some people 15–20 times.' This was the horror that the Red Army never fully eliminated from its ranks – a horror which besmirched its victory.

But many Soviet troops conducted themselves with honour. When Hitler flooded Berlin's underground system to impede the Red Army's advance, he fully realized that thousands of civilians sheltering there would be drowned. Lieutenant Andrei Eshpai of the Soviet 146th Rifle Division – a fluent German speaker – led a combat unit whose sole purpose was to rescue Berlin's inhabitants. 'Our orders were simple,' Eshpai said, 'to evacuate as many civilians as possible. But we had to do it with the SS infiltrating their ranks, and shooting at our backs.'

By 30 April 1945, 78,000 Red Army soldiers had been lost in the battle for Berlin. Russian troops were now closing in on the centre of the city. Captain Anatoly Mereshko's Eighth Guards Army had struck across the Landwehr Canal and into the Tiergarten; other Soviet forces had crossed the Moltke Bridge and were fanning out into the surrounding streets. The Ministry of the Interior building and Gestapo HQ were now under attack. German soldiers resisted desperately. 'We were amazed at the way the enemy kept fighting,' Mereshko said. 'It showed us the power of Goebbels's propaganda that a last stand should be made in Berlin. The overall position was hopeless – the city was cut off and our numerical superiority was overwhelming. However, the Germans did not give up, and SS units in particular would never surrender to us.'

But the Red Army was hungry for final victory over Hitler's regime. Marshal Zhukov exhorted his troops: 'Fellow soldiers, officers and commanders of the First Belorussian Front, let's mop up the last remaining strongholds of the enemy. We will finish off the Fascist beast in his lair with one last swift kick, and bring to a conclusion our complete triumph over Nazi Germany.' 'The street fighting continued without let-up,' said Lieutenant Vasily Ustyugov of the Soviet 150th Rifle Division. 'We were pushing the enemy hard, all the time. We were determined to stop him forming up a last defence line.'

Soviet lieutenant Mikhail Borisov had recovered from his injuries at Kustrin and had transferred to a new unit, the 14th Artillery Brigade. Borisov and his fellows were in the thick of the city fighting. 'We were hugely motivated to smash the last Nazi strongpoints,' he said. 'Our troops were in a state of frenzy. We hauled up our guns, and fired at German fortified buildings at point-blank range. We just wanted to finish them off.'

Every Soviet soldier knew that the end of the war was near. 'We felt a mixture of incredible hope, excitement and fear,' remembered Red Army lieutenant Andrei Eshpai. 'The saddest thing was to see comrades who had survived the whole war die in those last days of fighting.'

On 30 April advance detachments from the Soviet 150th Division took up positions around the Reichstag. The political significance of the building during Hitler's Third Reich had been minimal but it carried enormous symbolic power. When Marshal Zhukov appealed to Red Army soldiers to smash the enemy on the Seelow Heights, he then called for them to break into Berlin and plant a red flag on the Reichstag. The raising of that flag would symbolize the end of the war.

Soviet lieutenant Vasily Ustyugov had hauled his gun into position opposite the Reichstag. 'A dark grey building rose up before me, pockmarked with shellfire,' Ustyugov recalled. 'It was a lunar landscape. In the nearby park, not a single tree had survived. All were charred stumps.' Private Mikhail Minin remembered: 'We were in such a hurry to take the Reichstag. Our divisional commander General Shatilov

made a speech: "We will raise the flag of victory over . . .
Paris," he proclaimed. A political officer said loudly: "Berlin!"
The general swore at him: "It doesn't matter! Berlin or Paris,
wherever we are ordered, the banner will be there." All
the troops applauded him, as if to say: if it's war, it's war – we
are ready.'

This was an extraordinary lapse by Shatilov. 'We wondered if he had been drinking,' Minin said. 'Then came a call
for volunteers to storm the building. At the HQs and command posts the political officers explained to us that any red
banner, any red cloth, hoisted over the Reichstag would be
counted as the flag of victory. And any man who helped
put it there would be awarded the title of Hero of the
Soviet Union. We realized that these decorations could cost
us our lives.'

A succession of daytime attacks on the building failed. 'We
were losing people so fast,' Lieutenant Vasily Ustyugov
recalled. 'The Germans were raking the approaches with
strong artillery fire.' At 2.40 p.m. a storm group broke into
the Reichstag and a red flag was seen fluttering from a
window. It was announced that the Reichstag had been captured. The flag disappeared, and the storm group was expelled
from the building. As the prestige date of 1 May loomed,
attempts to capture the Reichstag – or at least plant a flag on
its summit – became ever more frenzied. A small assault
group was formed up on the night of 30 April. They were
five soldiers who had fought together for three years, led by
Vasily Markov, Alexei Bobrov and Mikhail Minin.

'There was shooting in the corridors,' Minin recalled.

We kept climbing, firing into the air to keep the enemy out of
the way and looking for an entry on to the roof of the building.
We smashed down a locked door and clambered outside the

Reichstag. And there we saw the statue Germania – we called it the 'Goddess of Victory' – and we rushed over to it. Everyone agreed that it was the best spot to raise the flag – the statue rose high above the parapet and was easily visible. I found a hole in the crown and inserted the metal pole in it. Then we stretched our flag along the pole and secured it.

I was absolutely delighted that I was participating in this – that I, a simple private, had been assigned this job. I felt sheer joy – it was a kind of euphoria. This terrible war, where the German military machine had inflicted such cruelty on our people, was being brought to a close.

On 1 May the news of Hitler's suicide (which took place on the afternoon of 30 April) reached Soviet commanders. It was relayed by German general Hans Krebs, who began the surrender negotiations with the Red Army. Soviet lieutenant Andrei Eshpai was told to escort Krebs to Chuikov's HQ. The men exchanged a few pleasantries and then Krebs paused. 'What incredible weaponry you have assembled here,' he said sadly. Eshpai sensed that etiquette required a compliment in return. 'Your bazookas are causing us a lot of trouble,' he responded. Krebs looked at him, and thought about the course the war had taken: 'This is not Moscow,' he said eventually, 'it is Berlin.'

Krebs arrived in Chuikov's HQ with some ceremony, escorted by a single German infantryman with a white flag attached to his bayonet. The soldier stood to attention, and the Russians burst out laughing. 'We asked Krebs if he was frightened of us, and wanted protection,' Captain Anatoly Mereshko said. The negotiations came to nothing. At the end of 1 May, the Reichstag was fully secured by Soviet troops, and Goebbels's suicide followed that of his Führer. The next day, at noon, General Hellmuth Weidling surrendered Berlin unconditionally.

The signing took place at Chuikov's HQ, with the defenders of Stalingrad now receiving the submission of Berlin. Staff officer Stefan Doernberg typed up the documents. 'I was struck by a phrase Weidling had used – "The Führer has left us" – as if he were some mystical being,' Doernberg remarked. 'It showed a dark hold over the German people.' That hold had now been broken.

Private Alexander Tsygankov and his comrades from the Soviet 181st Rifle Division had fought all the way from Stalingrad to the German capital. In the Ukraine and Belorussia they witnessed scenes of apocalyptic devastation, and they had visited Auschwitz within days of its liberation. As they watched vanquished German forces being led away, Tsygankov recorded: '"Work makes you free" the Nazis declared at the gates of their concentration camp. Now, as we rejoice in our victory, they will have a long stay in captivity to rebuild what they destroyed.'

In celebration, a group of Red Army soldiers attempted a most unusual ritual. The Soviet 308th Division had a camel as its mascot. And that camel – whose nickname was *Kuznechik* – 'Grasshopper' – was an irritable and unruly beast. War correspondents loved him. They awarded him medals for valour when he dodged shell blasts, and gave him an appreciative write-up when he spat at a German POW, 'in a most patriotic fashion'. 'Grasshopper' had made the long journey from Stalingrad to Berlin. From Poznan he had also been an ammunition carrier. Some Red Army soldiers, less enamoured of his charms, were hoping he might accidentally blow himself up. But 'Grasshopper' reached the heart of Hitler's Reich unscathed.

Sensing a photo opportunity, soldiers of the 308th Division tried to cajole 'Grasshopper' through the Brandenburg Gate. Journalists and photographers gathered round. 'Grasshopper' refused to budge. His comrades decided to push him through the Gate. 'Grasshopper' would not be moved. Reinforcements were called in. The reluctant camel was shoved partway through, and then he reared up and spat over the assembled group. A Red Army officer turned to one of the journalists: 'That's your story – the noble "Grasshopper", veteran of Stalingrad and countless other engagements, spits at the Brandenburg Gate, such is his contempt for Fascism.' The journalist liked the idea, but transported 'Grasshopper' to the Reichstag instead – feeling it made an even more appropriate target for the camel's wrath.

'Grasshopper' may not actually have been there, but that afternoon thousands of Red Army soldiers crowded round the walls of the Reichstag, celebrating the moment by writing graffiti – their name, and where they came from. It formed a simple but moving ritual, the marking of a long and terrible journey.

One of these soldiers was Mikhail Borisov. 'I wrote my name,' said Borisov, 'and added "this kid from Siberia got all the way to Berlin". I thought that would be the end of it and the war would be over for me. I was wrong. The war has stayed with me for the rest of my life.'

Borisov, and many veterans like him, experienced the pain and pride of victory. He had survived, but he knew the cost for the 27 million who did not. One of these was a young Red Army lieutenant named Vladimir Antokolsky, and at the end of the war his father Pavel wrote:

> There is no escape from this black grief – as though you were alive and were knocking at my door with urgent, burning hands, and try as I might I can't open the door to you. And all your life, for all these years, you desperately want to return and speak, live, love, and grow into all that you are destined for. There is no end to this, no escape, and whether another ten or

one hundred years pass, everything remains as it was: you, young, full of strength and hope, full of the right to life, love and happiness, snatched away by a rapacious gun, in the depths of a trench, your head fallen to your knees. Nothing has ended – neither life, nor death, nor love, nor injury, nor grief. For you – there is no end.

Epilogue

O N 2 MAY 1945 Soviet photographer Yevgeny Khaldei took a photograph of a Red Army officer holding a red flag atop the Reichstag. A panorama unfolds of stricken, ruined Berlin and the war that has come to the German capital. There are smashed buildings, billowing smoke, army vehicles and soldiers everywhere. The red flag, with its star, hammer and sickle, billows as the officer secures the pole to the Reichstag parapet. Two other soldiers stand on the parapet's edge, gazing out over the city. And the officer himself is supported by one of his fellows as he raises the flag. The composition is dynamic and powerful. An individual holds the flag aloft, but it is a collective achievement. The image is famous throughout the world. It symbolizes the end of the Second World War in the West, and the defeat of Nazi Germany. It captures an extraordinary moment of triumph.

The photographer and film-maker Yevgeny Khaldei was twenty-eight years old when he took the picture. From the war's outset, he had followed the fortunes of the Soviet Union's armed forces, its army, navy and air force, as a reporter for the Soviet news agency TASS. To facilitate his work, TASS secured an honorary rank for Khaldei – that of navy lieutenant – and arranged his travel documents and destinations. He had a remarkable degree of freedom: Khaldei would arrive at an army headquarters, get coupons for food and decide what to do next. He often travelled with a film crew. He was able to show a kaleidoscope of emotions and themes: heroism, grief and endurance.

Khaldei saw at first hand the terrible cost of the war on the eastern front, and the price it exacted on soldiers and civilians. He wrote of Red Army attempts to take Kerch on the Crimean peninsula:

> There was a landing at Kerch in November 1943, but the fighting went on through December, January, February and March. Only in April 1944 did we take the city. For six months we were in a 'meat grinder'. An offensive was prepared to take a particular hill, and I spent the night before it in the trenches with the soldiers. In the morning the cook arrived with a large bowl of porridge but nobody wanted to eat. Everyone was thinking: 'What's going to happen in half an hour, during the offensive? Am I going to live, will I see my wife, my children, my parents?' I didn't take any pictures, I just couldn't. Then the offensive took place. They didn't take the hill, and the dead were left on the ground. In the trench where I was staying, less than half the men returned.

Khaldei understood this suffering. He was from Stalino in the Donbass region of the Ukraine. He was Jewish, and he found out that his family had been murdered by the Nazis and their bodies hurled down a mine shaft. As he travelled westwards with liberating Red Army soldiers he took pictures of Nazi atrocities against the Soviet civilian population, and of the murder of Jews. State censors approved of the former, but were uneasy about the latter. A photograph of POWs shot by the Nazis in Rostov was published immediately; one of Jews killed in a synagogue was never published at all.

As a photographer, Khaldei captured factory workers pulling down a swastika at Kerch, a pile of German helmets at

Sevastopol. As the Red Army marched into Europe, Khaldei documented the taking of Bucharest and Belgrade, Budapest and Vienna. At Berlin he arrived with a flag made out of a red tablecloth: 'And then the Reichstag – I got out on to the roof with some soldiers and looked for a good angle. I found my spot, and told the soldier "Climb up there". And he said, "OK, if somebody holds me by the feet."' The result is justly famous.

But the real identity of the man raising the banner has only recently been revealed. It was not – as claimed for fifty years by Soviet propagandists – a Georgian, Meliton Kantaria, a choice made solely to please Stalin, who came from Georgia himself. The man's real name was Alexei Kovalev. He was from Kiev in the Ukraine, and his remarkable story can now be told.

Soviet lieutenant Kovalev was chosen for the honour of Khaldei's photograph because he was one of the first soldiers to reach the Reichstag. Kovalev was admired within the army as the brave leader of a reconnaissance platoon. In the early afternoon of 30 April he fought his way into the building and placed a small red flag on one of the first-floor windows. The Soviet attack was later repulsed. It was not until the late evening that Mikhail Minin hoisted a red flag on the Reichstag's rooftop. History has not been kind to either Kovalev or Minin. Both were passed over so that Stalin could be flattered by crediting a Georgian soldier with the achievement.

On the morning of 2 May Marshal Georgi Zhukov visited the Reichstag. He met with Kovalev, and asked about his exploits in storming the building. Kovalev told him about a frenzied charge, rushing up the staircase to the first floor, machine-gunning two Nazis hiding behind a mattress. Kovalev remembered shards of material flying through the air, dripping bright red with blood. He attached a red flag to a first-floor window. Zhukov was delighted, and presented Kovalev with his personal map of Berlin as a memento. When Khaldei arrived to take his picture, Zhukov insisted that Kovalev be shown raising the banner. Kovalev was the Red Army's choice for the honour. Soviet censors – uncomfortable about looting in the German capital – airbrushed out the two watches on the wrist of Kovalev's helper. They also changed Kovalev's identity, and he was told to keep quiet about it. Now we can pay tribute to his courage.

Kovalev's red flag over the Reichstag symbolizes an achievement that we in the West are happy to honour – the fighting exploits of our Soviet ally, who ripped the guts out of the German war machine. We are far less happy with the cruelty, ruthlessness and sheer indifference of the Soviet system. We are right to be critical of the brutality of some of its soldiers, the looting, killing and rapes. They tarnished the Red Army's triumph. But that criticism has to be tempered with understanding. We did not have to endure what the Soviet Union endured. We did not suffer what they suffered. And we did not witness the atrocities their soldiers witnessed. Until we realize this, the wounds of this terrible war will never fully heal.

It took ruthlessness and an extraordinary degree of sacrifice to defeat the German army, an army that Red Army veterans acknowledge in private was the best fighting machine in the world. At the start of the battle of Kursk, on 5 July 1943, no Allied soldier had yet set foot on mainland Europe. And even after D-Day, more than three-quarters of Germany's armed strength was concentrated in the east. There was no Geneva Convention on the eastern front, where the biggest, bloodiest and most important land battles took place.

Kovalev was a brave man and a tough soldier, always in the

forefront of the action. 'I have killed more people than I have hairs on my head,' he said. It was a matter-of-fact statement. But what followed was not.

Kovalev's voice began to choke. 'As a reconnaissance scout, I was always ahead of our army, and I needed to gather intelligence. I would use local people – I would take them and question them about the whereabouts of the Germans. They were Russian people, good people, and they wanted to help me. They told me all they knew.' Kovalev struggled to carry on. It was hard to say this, particularly to a Westerner. But Kovalev looked me straight in the eye and continued:

> Imagine this. I seize a young Russian woman, washing clothes by the river, a kid, playing in a village, or an old man sitting outside his house. I question them. They help me all they can. And then, the 'iron rule of our army': I have to kill my sources, without exception. I cannot take the risk that the Germans will take them, interrogate them and find out our troops are near by. I cannot endanger our army for the sake of an individual life.

Kovalev made a sudden gesture with his hand. There were tears in his eyes. 'I cut their throats with a knife. I murdered hundreds of my own people, decent, kind, honest people. I murdered them – so that we could defeat Nazi Germany. This is the price I paid. I have to live with it every day of my life.'

An extraordinary victory – founded on unimaginable suffering. And a red flag flies over the Reichstag.

Notes

Eyewitness accounts, memoirs and diaries are usually cited on their first appearance in the text.

Introduction

The comments of Hotenkov and Studenikov are taken from my piece 'The Will to Win', *BBC History Magazine* (May, 2005). Two major surveys on the war and the Red Army are provided by Bellamy, *Absolute War*, and Merridale, *Ivan's War*. Also valuable is the interactive presentation 'Soldiers of the Great War' – interspersed with veteran testimony – on www.pobediteli.ru.

Chapter 1: A Year of Living Dangerously

All material on Antokolsky is from the family archive, courtesy of Andrei Toom. Goncharov's testimony is from Artem Drabkin's 'I Remember' site on www.russianbattlefield.com; Semenyak's and Khonyak's comments are found in the 'Soldiers of the Great War' project on www. pobediteli.ru. Ponomerenko's report to Stalin is from Merridale, *Ivan's War*. I owe the Heinz Postenrieder quote (from his diary held in the Pforzheim Stadtarchiv) to Professor Jeffrey Kleiman. Alexander Bodnar was interviewed by me, and I also used transcripts from Russia Today's 'War Witness'. Hosenfeld's diary entries are from *Briefen und Tagebüchen*. Leonid Bobrov's letters are from the RIA Novosti 'Our Victory' project. Red Army casualty figures here and throughout are from Mawdsley,

Thunder in the East. These losses do not include those wounded in combat, some of whom subsequently returned to their units. The full story of the terrible battle for Moscow is told in my book *The Retreat: Hitler's First Defeat*.

Chapter 2: Fire on the Volga

For a balanced discussion of Stalin's 'Not a Step Back!' order, see Geoffrey Roberts, *Victory at Stalingrad*. Comments of Burkovski, Dallakian, Mereshko, Orlov, Schönbeck and Tsygankov are from interviews with me. I am grateful to Maria Faustova of the Sixty-Second Army (Eighth Guards Army) Veterans' Association for facilitating these meetings. The accounts of Beregevoy, Bogdanova, Kryzhanovsky, Kuryshov and Streltasova are from Russia Today's 'War Witness' Archive. Nikolai Sokolov's diary is at www.russianbattlefield.com. For the fighting at Rzhev: Gorbachevsky, *Through the Maelstrom*, Pabst, *Outermost Frontier* and Beshanov, *The Year of 1942*. Alekseyev's and Orlyankin's diary extracts are from the Volgograd Panorama Museum Archive. Skripko's remarks about the bombing raid are from his memoir *On Targets Near and Far*, Yeremenko's are in his *Stalingrad*. Richthofen's diary extracts are from Bundesarchiv, Freiburg, N671/4; Grossman's comments are found in *A Writer at War*.

Chapter 3: The Tide Turns

I have tried to avoid replicating quotations from my earlier works, *Stalingrad: How the Red Army Triumphed* and *Leningrad: State of Siege*. Much background information is drawn from Alexei Isaev, *The War We Did Not Know*, and Beshanov, *The Year of 1942*. For Vasily Churkin: *Diary of an Artilleryman*; Leningrad supply officer Goldberg and sniper Petrova: Bely, *Life At War*; Selenkov's diary is in the Volgograd Panorama Museum Archive; Kaberov's and Segal's letters are from the Blavatnik Archive. Additional documentary material is drawn from the Sixty-Second Army War Diary and 138th Rifle Division Combat Journal: Russian Defence Archive, Podolsk. The definitive account of fighting in the city and its approaches is now David Glantz and Jonathan

House, *To the Gates of Stalingrad* and *Armageddon in Stalingrad*, and for Lyudnikov's Island, Jason Mark, *Island of Fire*.

Chapter 4: Psychological Attack

Rudashevski's account is in *Diary of the Vilna Ghetto*, Laskier's in *Rutka's Notebook* and Kravchenko's in *Victims, Victors*. Vasipov's experiences are from Bely, *Life at War*, Benesh's and Zhiburt's in Omsk Museum, *Letters from the Front*. Antipenko's observations are from his memoir *On the Main Line*. An important reappraisal of Kursk in general and Prokhorovka in particular is found in two major works of Valeriy Zamulin, *Prokhorovka: The Unknown Battle* and *Kursk Declassified*. Material on Borisov is from interviews with me and his collection of war poetry *Image of the Motherland*. Accounts of Bryukhov, Bulatov, Chernyshev, Ivanov and Malikin are from interviews with me. I am grateful to Mikhail Bulatov of the Kursk Veterans' Association for facilitating these meetings. Zoya Babich, a local guide at Ponyri, has kindly allowed me access to Puzikov's account. Rokossovsky's letter is in the Korennaya Historical Museum, Kursk. Komsky's diary is from the Blavatnik Archive; see also Oleg Budnitskii, 'Jews in the War: Soldiers' Diaries', *Lech* 5 (2010).

Chapter 5: The Dam

The planning of the attack on Zaprozhye is described in Chuikov, *Guardsmen*, and Russiyanov, *Anniversary of Battle*. Iskrov's battle report is in Wilbeck, *Tiger Tank Battalions*. For Dobrosmislova: *Letters from the Front*; Abdulin: *Red Road from Stalingrad*; Temkin: *My Just War*. Recollections of Peshkova and Kuznetsov are from 'I Remember', Zhuravlev from the Voice of Russia archive. Accounts of Lutsenko, Osadchinsky, Zarubina are from interviews with me, additional transcripts kindly provided by Lena Yakovleva. Fein's story is from Russia Today's 'War Witness' archive. For Gelfand: *Tagebuch*; Bocharova, Kogan, Yagel: Blavatnik Archive; Boulgakov and Golbraikh: Drabkin *Red Army at War*.

Chapter 6: Killing Fields

Testimonies of partisans and the local Belorussian population are drawn from Alexievich, *War's Unwomanly Face*, and Adamovich, *Out of the Fire*. Konstantinova's account is from Cottam, *Defending Leningrad*, Yuri Sarkisov's letter was kindly made available by Caroline Walton, and Treshovski's testimony is in Rees, *War of the Century*. Material on German anti-partisan operations is largely from Gerlach, *Kalkulierte Morde*. For Ozarichi, on the German side: Rass, *Deutsche Soldaten an der Ostfront*; Perau, *Priester im Heere Hitlers*. The Soviet Sixty-Fifth Army's report of 21 March 1944 is on the Belorussian State Archive website: www.archives.gov.by. The text of the commission of inquiry is from Batov, *Campaigns and Battles*, the medical response is described in Gulyakin, *There Will Be Life*.

Chapter 7: A Lucky Star

General context is provided by Walter Dunn, *Soviet Blitzkrieg*. For Red Army preparations, and the assault on Parichi, see Litvin, *800 Days on the Eastern Front*. In April 1944, German Army Group South had been divided into Army Groups North and South Ukraine, and on 28 June 1944, Hitler appointed Field Marshal Walther Model Commander of both Army Groups Centre and North Ukraine. This measure came too late to avert a military disaster. Bobrov's letters are from the RIA Novosti 'Our Victory' project, accounts of Gareev, Mereshko and Zenkova from interviews with me. The interview transcript for Yeremenko was provided by Lena Yakovleva. The German reaction is from Perau, *Priester im Heere Hitlers*, and Hartmann, *Zwischen Nichts und Niemandsland*. Leonid Krainov, 'Field Post 06511', is from the Russian Veterans' journal *Forum* 36–38 (2005), Fyodorov's comments are in Rees, *War of the Century*. Ingor's account is in *Letters from the Front*; for Elkinson and Meyerovich: Blavatnik Archive. Stalin and 7 November is from Loza, *Fighting for the Soviet Motherland*. Roza Shanina's diary and letter excerpts are in Molchanov, *Thirst for Battle*. I am grateful to Professor Maxim Shrayer for permission to quote from his translation of Pavel Antokolsky's poem 'Death Camp'.

Chapter 8: Lisa's Smile

I am grateful here for the help of Professor Ilya Altman and archivist Leonid Terushkin of the Russian Holocaust Centre, Moscow. Background about the camp is drawn from Strzelecki, *Liberation of Auschwitz*. Testimonies of Gromadsky, Martynushkin, Slavin and Vinnichenko are from interviews with me. For Dushman and Friedner: Blavatnik Archive; Elisavetsky, Margolis et al.: Russian Holocaust Centre; Zabolotny: *Red Army Infantrymen*. Petrenko's recollections are in *Avant et Après Auschwitz*. Koptev's and Shapiro's interviews are from the archive of the United Jerusalem Foundation. The accounts of Sorokopud and Alimbekov are in Sophie Lambroschini and Basil Karlinsky, 'L'armée rouge entre dans Auschwitz', *Libération* (25 January 1995, that of Brandt from 'I Remember'.). The combat journal of the Soviet 1085th Rifle Regiment is from the Russian Defence Archive, Podolsk. Tolkatchev's account is from Yad Vashem's *Private Tolkatchev at the Gates of Hell*. Of particular value has been Anita Kondoyanidi, 'The liberating experience: war correspondents, Red Army soldiers and the Nazi extermination camps', *The Russian Review*, 69 (2010) and 'What the Soviets knew about Auschwitz – and when: the liberation reports', on www.rodoh.com.

Chapter 9: 'We Tried to be Different'

This chapter has benefited greatly from Oleg Budnitskii, 'The intelligentsia meets the enemy: educated Soviet officers in defeated Germany', *Kritika*, 10 (2009). Also helpful were David Glantz's interviews, kindly made available to me, filed under *Red Army Officers Speak! Interviews with Veterans of the Vistula-Oder Operation* (1997) and *Memories of War: Private Gennady Shutz* (2001). Additional material on Khaldei, Kopelev and Semiriaga is from the Liddell Hart Archive, King's College London, *The Cold War Interview Transcripts*, 28/1, 9 and 14. Documentary material is drawn mainly from Manfred Zeidler, *Kriegsende im Osten*, but also see Alexander Orlov, 'The price of victory, the cost of aggression', *History Today*, 55 (2005). Mereshko and Slavin's comments are from interviews with me. For Kopelev: *No Jail for Thought*; Baitman: 'I Remember'; Gorbachevsky: *Through the Maelstrom*; and Inozemtsev: *Frontline Diary*.

Chapter 10: Fortress Cities

The story of the attack on Poznan – relayed by Mereshko, confirmed by other Eighth Guards Army veterans and the inquiry by the First Belorussian Front – is very different from the version presented in Chuikov, *The End of the Third Reich*. Chuikov's blunder left his army split between Kustrin and Poznan – and prevented a rapid attack on Berlin in February 1945. Lieutenant General Galadzhev's report of 31 March 1945 on the battle for Poznan is on www.soviethammer.devhub.com. Testimonies of Borisov, Burkhanov, Mereshko and Slavin are from interviews with me. Khetagurov's comments are from Karalus, *Kernwerk 1945*. For the interview with Mattern: Doernberg, *Fronteinsatz* and *Russian Archives: Battle for Berlin*. Material on Breslau I owe to Richard Hargreaves and his forthcoming book on the siege. The accounts of Kirichenko and Toker are from *Red Army at War*. For Königsberg: Beloborodov, *In the Thick of Combat*, Kobylyanskiy, *From Stalingrad to Pillau*, and Inozemtsev, *Frontline Diary*.

Chapter 11: Apocalypse Berlin

For an excellent recent survey of the fighting at Seelow and in Berlin see: Hamilton, *Bloody Streets: the Soviet Assault on Berlin*. Zhukov's surrender offer – revealed for the first time by Doernberg – was dismissed by the Germans. Altner's comments are from *Berlin: Dance of Death*; Zhilkin's from Russia Today's 'War Witness' archive. Accounts of Borisov, Doernberg, Eshpai, Gell, Kravchenko, Mereshko, Ustyugov, are from interviews with me. I owe 'Grasshopper' and the Brandenburg Gate to Eighth Guards Army machine gunner Sergei Romanovtsev. I am grateful to Alexander Ivanov of the Russian Council of War Veterans for facilitating these meetings. For Schneider: Russia Today's 'War Witness' archive; Sebelev: Beevor, *Berlin*; Gershman and Schinder: 'I Remember'; Berzarin: RIA Novosti 'Our Victory' project; Gelfand: *Tagebuch*; Minin: TV programme 'The End in Berlin'. Abyzov's testimony is drawn from *The Final Assault*.

Epilogue

Nakhimovsky, *Khaldei*. I owe the interview with Alexei Kovalev and additional transcripts to Lena Yakovleva. Kovalev's companion in the photo was Sergeant Abdulhakim Ismailov. Both men had been awarded the Order of the Red Banner for penetrating behind German lines in Poland and capturing a Wehrmacht staff officer shortly before the Vistula–Oder offensive, and a day before their storm group broke into the Reichstag they had seized an enemy strongpoint in a surprise attack, killing thirty Germans and capturing another twenty-four.

Bibliography

German sources have been kept in their original form; the Russian ones have been translated. Articles and documentary references are individually cited in the Notes.

Mansur Abdulin, *Red Road from Stalingrad* (Barnsley, 2004)

Vladimir Abyzov, *The Final Assault* (Moscow, 1985)

Ales Adamovich, Yanka Bryl, Vladimir Kolesnik, *Out of the Fire* (Moscow, 1980)

Svetlana Alexievich, *The War's Unwomanly Face* (Moscow, 1985)

Helmut Altner, *Berlin: Dance of Death* (Staplehurst, 2002)

Nikolai Antipenko, *On the Main Line* (Moscow, 1967)

Albert Axell, *Russia's Heroes 1941–45* (London, 2001)

Pavel Batov, *In Campaigns and Battles* (Moscow, 1974)

Antony Beevor, *Berlin: The Downfall 1945* (London, 2002)

Antony Beevor and Luba Vinogradova, *Writer at War: Vasily Grossman with the Red Army 1941–1945* (London, 2005)

Chris Bellamy, *Absolute War: Soviet Russia in the Second World War* (London, 2007)

Athanasias Beloborodov, *In the Thick of Combat* (Moscow, 1978)

Arkady Bely, *Life at War* (St Petersburg, 2005)

Vladimir Beshanov, *The Year of 1942 – 'Training'* (Minsk, 2003)

Evgeni Bessonov, *Tank Rider: Into the Reich with the Red Army* (London, 2003)

Mikhail Borisov, *The Image of the Motherland* (Moscow, 2000)

Paul Carell, *Scorched Earth: The Russo-German War 1943–44* (Atglen, Pennsylvania, 1994)

Vasily Chuikov, *The Beginning of the Road* (London, 1963); *Stalingrad*

Guardsmen March West (Kiev, 1972); *The End of the Third Reich* (London, 1967)

Vasily Churkin, *Diary of an Artilleryman of the 80th Rifle Division* (St Petersburg, 2005)

Kazimiera Cottam (ed.), *Defending Leningrad: Women behind Enemy Lines* (Newburyport, MA, 1998)

Stefan Doernberg, *Fronteinsatz: Erinnerungen eines Rotarmisten* (Berlin, 2004)

Artem Drabkin, *The Red Army at War* (Barnsley, 2010)

Artem Drabkin and Isaak Kobylyanskiy, *Red Army Infantrymen Remember the Great Patriotic War* (Bloomington, IN, 2009)

Artem Drabkin and Oleg Sheremet, *T-34 in Action* (Barnsley, 2006)

David Dragunsky, *A Soldier's Life* (Moscow, 1977)

Christopher Duffy, *Red Storm on the Reich: The Soviet March on Germany, 1945* (New York, 1991)

Walter Dunn, *Soviet Blitzkrieg: The Battle for White Russia, 1944* (Mechanicsburg, PA, 2008)

John Erickson, *The Road to Berlin* (London, 1983)

Vladmir Gelfand, *Tagebuch 1941–46* (Baden–Baden, 2002)

Christian Gerlach, *Kalkulierte Morde. Die Deutsche Wirtschafts- und Vernichtungspolitik in Weissrussland 1941 bis 1944* (Hamburg, 1999)

David Glantz, *Soviet Military Deception in the Second World War* (Abingdon, 1989)

David Glantz and Jonathan House, *When Titans Clashed: How the Red Army Stopped Hitler* (Edinburgh, 2000); *To the Gates of Stalingrad* (Lawrence, KS, 2009); *Armageddon in Stalingrad* (Lawrence, KS, 2009)

Boris Gorbachevsky, *Through the Maelstrom: A Red Army Soldier's War on the Eastern Front, 1942–1945* (Lawrence, KS, 2008)

Nikolai Gorshkov, *By the Light of Half a Candle* (St Petersburg, 1993)

Mikhail Gulyakin, *There Will Be Life* (Moscow, 1989)

Stephan Hamilton, *Bloody Streets: The Soviet Assault on Berlin, April 1945* (Solihull, 2008)

Hans Jürgen Hartmann, *Zwischen Nichts und Niemandsland* (Dessau, 2006)

Max Hastings, *Armageddon: The Battle for Germany 1944–45* (London, 2004)

Nikolai Inozemtsev, *Frontline Diary* (Moscow, 2005)

Alexei Isaev, *The War We Did Not Know* (Moscow, 2005); *Berlin 1945* (Moscow, 2007)

Maciej Karalus, *Kernwerk 1945: Historia Zdobycia Cytadeli Poznańskiej* (Poznan, 2009)

Vladimir Karpov, *Russia at War, 1914–45* (London, 1987)

Isaak Kobylyanskiy, *From Stalingrad to Pillau: A Red Army Artillery Officer Remembers the Great Patriotic War* (Lawrence, KS, 2008)

Ivan Konev, *Year of Victory* (Moscow, 1969)

Lev Kopelev, *No Jail for Thought* (London, 1977)

Mikhail Koriakov, *I'll Never Go Back: A Red Army Officer Talks* (London, 1948)

Roman Kravchenko-Berezhnoy, *Victims, Victors* (Bedford, PA, 2007)

Horst Lange, *Tagebücher aus dem Zweiten Weltkrieg* (Mainz, 1979)

Rutka Laskier, *Rutka's Notebook* (Jerusalem, 2007)

Nikolai Litvin, *800 Days on the Eastern Front* (Lawrence, KS, 2007)

Dmitry Loza, *Fighting for the Soviet Motherland* (Lincoln, NE, 1998)

Ulrich de Maizière, *In Der Pflicht* (Bonn, 1989)

Erich von Manstein, *Lost Victories* (London, 1958)

Jason Mark, *Island of Fire* (Sydney, 2006)

Evan Mawdsley, *Thunder in the East. The Nazi–Soviet War 1941–1945* (London, 2005)

Catherine Merridale, *Ivan's War: The Red Army 1939–45* (London, 2005)

Petr Mikhin, *Guns against the Reich* (Barnsley, 2010)

Pyotr Molchanov, *A Thirst for Battle* (Moscow, 1976)

Alexander and Alice Nakhimovsky, *Witness to History: The Photographs of Yevgeny Khaldei* (New York, 1997)

Omsk State Museum, *'I Write for Perhaps the Last Time': Letters from the Front* (Omsk, 1994)

Richard Overy, *Russia's War* (London, 1998)

Helmut Pabst, *The Outermost Frontier* (London, 1957)

Josef Perau, *Priester im Heere Hitlers* (Essen, 1962)

Vasily Petrenko, *Avant et Après Auschwitz* (Paris, 2002)

Boris Polevoy, *From Belgorod to the Carpathians: A Soviet War Correspondent's Notebook* (London, 1945)

Christoph Rass, *'Menschenmaterial': Deutsche Soldaten an der Ostfront* (Gebunden, 2003)

Laurence Rees, *War of the Century: When Hitler Fought Stalin* (London, 1999)

311

BIBLIOGRAPHY

Geoffrey Roberts, *Victory at Stalingrad* (London, 2002)

Konstantin Rokossovsky, *A Soldier's Duty* (Moscow, 1988)

Yitskhok Rudashevski, *Diary of the Vilna Ghetto* (Ghetto Fighters' House, Western Galilee, 1973)

Russian Archives: Great Patriotic War (vol. 15): *Battle for Berlin* (Moscow, 1995)

Ivan Russiyanov, *On the Anniversary of Battle* (Moscow, 1982)

Elke Scherstjanoi, *Rotarmisten Schrieben aus Deutschland: Briefe von der Front 1945* (Munich, 2004)

Nikolai Skripko, *On Targets Near and Far* (Moscow, 1981)

Andrzej Strzelecki, *The Evacuation, Dismantling and Liberation of KL Auschwitz* (Oswiecim, 2001); *Voices of Memory: The Evacuation, Liquidation and Liberation of Auschwitz* (Oswiecim, 2008)

Gabriel Temkin, *My Just War: The Memoir of a Jewish Red Army Soldier in World War Two* (Novato, CA, 1998)

Tony Le Tissier, *Race for the Reichstag: The 1945 Battle for Berlin* (London, 1999); *Marshal Zhukov at the Oder* (Stroud, 2008)

Thomas Vogel (ed.), *'Wilhelm Hosenfeld: 'Ich Versuche Jeden Zu Retten' – Das Leben Eines Deutschen Offiziers in Briefen und Tagebüchen* (Munich, 2004)

Alexander Werth, *Russia at War 1941–1945* (New York, 1964)

Christopher Wilbeck, *Sledgehammers: Strengths and Flaws of Tiger Tank Battalions* (Aberjona, 2004)

Yad Vashem, *Private Tolkatchev at the Gates of Hell: Majdanek and Auschwitz Liberated – Testimony of an Artist* (Jerusalem, 2005)

Andrei Yeremenko, *Stalingrad* (Moscow, 1961)

Valeriy Zamulin, *Prokhorovka: The Unknown Battle* (Moscow, 2005); *Kursk Declassified* (Moscow, 2007)

Manfred Zeidler, *Kriegsende im Osten: Die Rote Armee und die Besetzung Deutschlands Ostlich von Oder und Neisse 1944–45* (Munich, 1996)

Georgi Zhukov, *Marshal Zhukov's Greatest Battles* (New York, 1969)

Yuri Zhukov, *Notes of a War Correspondent* (Moscow, 1975)

Earl Ziemke, *From Stalingrad to Berlin: The German Defeat in the East* (Honolulu, 1984)

Index